SCOTTISH WRITERS TALKING 3

Scottish Writers Talking 3

Interviews with
JANICE GALLOWAY
JOHN HERDMAN
ROBIN JENKINS
JOAN LINGARD
ALI SMITH

Edited by Isobel Murray

JOHN DONALD

First published in Great Britain in 2006 by
John Donald (Publishers), an imprint of Birlinn Ltd
West Newington House
10 Newington Road
Edinburgh
EH9 1QS

www.birlinn.co.uk

ISBN 10: 0 85976 646 2
ISBN 13: 978 0 85976 646 3

The publishers acknowledge subsidy from

Scottish
Arts Council

towards the publication of this volume

British Library Cataloguing-in-Publication Data
A catalogue record for this book is available on request from the British Library

Typeset by Speedspools, Edinburgh
Printed and bound in Great Britain by Bell & Bain Ltd., Glasgow

CONTENTS

Acknowledgements   vi

Introduction   vii

Janice Galloway   1
John Herdman   59
Robin Jenkins   101
Joan Lingard   147
Ali Smith   187

ILLUSTRATIONS

Janice Galloway (courtesy Calum Colvin)   2
John Herdman (courtesy John Herdman)   60
Robin Jenkins (courtesy *The Herald*)   102
Joan Lingard (courtesy Gunnie Moberg)   148
Ali Smith (courtesy Sarah Wood)   186

ACKNOWLEDGEMENTS

Thanks first and of course to my five victims, for all their patience and co-operation. And to Bob Tait. Historically, to the University of Aberdeen Development Trust, and more recently to the University Arts and Divinity Faculty Research Committee. As ever, to Jennifer Beavan and Christine Miller, and the staff of the University's Queen Mother Library, and to Myrtle Anderson-Smith and Iain Beavan in Special Collections.

Thanks for help of all sorts from Paul Bohan, David Borthwick, Mig and Frank Brangwin, Professor Ian Campbell, Dr Barbara Fennell, Professor Douglas Gifford, Professor Brian Harrison, Professor David Hewitt, Dr Jeannette King, Dr Clare Loughlin, Dr Alison Lumsden, Julie Mortimer, Dr Jane Potter, Professor Alan Spence, Nicola Thomson, Graham Trengove, Professor William Nicolaisen, Dr Dominic Watt, Maureen Wilkie, Thomas Wratten.

Isobel Murray

INTRODUCTION

INTERVIEWS CAN BE a fascinating source of new information about a writer whose work is admired or loved, puzzling or exasperating. But they are always secondary to what the writer has already written and published: new readers should certainly not start here! However, reading an in-depth interview can satisfy some not illegitimate curiosities; can fill in background, can provide a context for the work, depending on how the writer chooses to respond to the experience.

There is an important sense in which an interviewer does not know what to expect beforehand. She wants to ask some fairly obvious questions – for a start, perhaps, where did you come from? what was your childhood like? – but she also has to try to remain very responsive to what an author thinks is important, what an author feels like talking about. A pre-determined set of questions is likely to produce a planned and maybe predictable interview.

This is true, whether one is meeting an interviewee for the first time, as I was meeting Robin Jenkins or Joan Lingard; or whether one has known them for many years, as was my case here with John Herdman and Ali Smith. I think it is important to tell the reader what the initial relationship was, because that can change how one reads the conversation, but the interviewer has to remain open to surprise or deviation from all subjects at all times: one must be ready to pick up a cue. This is a unique circumstance, in which a writer is being encouraged to talk about her basic *raison d'etre*, by someone who has prepared carefully for the conversation, by reading or re-reading. And it is not an ordinary conversation of give and take: both parties know that they have a subject, a focus: that it is the writer's career, performance, plans, preoccupations that they will centre on, that the 'politics' of 'normal' conversation are suspended.

The hope is that the interviewer, and by extension the reader, will learn something new and interesting about the work, or what the writer was aiming to do, or the circumstances of composition, that can send them back to the original work with a new angle, or insight, or even puzzle.

Repeat: interviews can never substitute for works of art, or make them what they are not already: they have thus arguably a minor function, but a lucky interview can provide the tool for new readings. This was something of the hope with which these conversations began, many years ago now. Let me be personal for once, the last thing a good interviewer can afford to be.

I have been teaching at the University of Aberdeen for many years now. When the Aberdeen University Development Trust gave me a tape-recorder and expenses to begin recording Scottish writers in 1982, I told a reporter from the local paper who wondered how long it would take that the project would last 'for ever'. To anyone perversely attentive to the halting progress of this series of interviews, it must begin to seem that I was all too right. Bob Tait and I started recording with George Mackay Brown in Stromness, Orkney, in 1984, and my most recent recorded interview here was with Ali Smith in December 2002. Have I got twenty-years-worth of recordings to show for it? In a word, no. I continued to record after the first flush of grant, in a small way, nabbing Writers in Residence, for example, William McIlvanney, Bernard MacLaverty, Alan Spence. And Bob has continued to help when available.

Reasons for the falling off are multifarious. Research moneys soon dried up, and continue to be hard to find. Other projects demanded my attention, with different degrees of urgency. I had turned to teaching and research in Scottish literature partly because my previous work, on Oscar Wilde, seemed to have dried up: I had edited *Dorian Gray*, and the *Complete Shorter Fiction*, and Oxford University Press had no further plans. But then they launched a new series of fat volumes, and I landed the happy but extensive task of editing the Oxford Authors Oscar Wilde, published in 1989 (now in World's Classics as *The Major Works*). Oh, and while I was at it, would I also edit *The Soul of Man and Prison Writings* (1990), and then the *Complete Poetry* (1997)? All was done, and with enthusiasm, but it left a gap in my Scottish coverage.

Then my growing enthusiasm for twentieth-century Scottish writing led me to accept the onerous behind-the-scenes job of Assistant Editor of what would become *The Oxford Dictionary of National Biography* (Scottish writing, 1870-2000). I was bribed to accept by the then Editor, the late Colin Matthew, a fellow Scot, who offered me a lot of new space, and encouraged me to promote women writers – the old *DNB* had one female Gaelic songwriter only in my field, now unremembered. So I undertook that, 1996-2002, with great satisfaction. If interested, see my article, 'DNB to New DNB: Good News for Dead Scottish Writers, Especially Women'.(1)

Meanwhile, some of the writers already interviewed, if not transcribed, began to need my attention. I persuaded Naomi Mitchison to let me edit a volume of her short fiction, in very different modes, *Beyond This Limit: Selected Shorter Fiction of Naomi Mitchison* (1986). This was so that undergraduates would not be put off for ever by the epic length of her available novels. I wrote pieces on Mitchison, and we collaborated to edit *A Girl Must Live: Stories and Poems*, an anthology of her mainly un-collected work, in 1990. Robin Jenkins agreed that I should edit his *Guests of War* (1956) with a new Introduction (1988). I was asked to contribute to different periodicals about his work: I gave papers to conferences. I was asked for Introductions to Mackay Brown's *Magnus*, to Crichton Smith's *Consider the Lilies*. And so on. And lectures and seminars for under-graduates, far from my lowest priority!

The case of Jessie Kesson was a stunner. After the interview, I wrote three or four pieces about her work, which I find absolutely fascinating – and then out of the blue her daughter asked me to write a biography. She furnished me with the black polythene waste bags full of miscellaneous scraps of paper, scripts, letters, drafts, that Jessie called her 'office'. The biography, *Jessie Kesson: Writing Her Life*, was published by Canongate in 2000. And in that year I published *Somewhere Beyond*, an anthology of her unpublished or uncollected work. And in its wake, the country's many Kesson-admirers demanded several more papers. . . .

Then I returned to the interviews, late, but with undiminished enthusiasm. This volume contains conversations with five very different writers. Since I am in personal vein here for once, I have been struck by the variety of attitudes to university found here, which may disturb some of our basic assumptions. Robin Jenkins, first of his family to go to university and a brilliant student, was not impressed by his university teachers, and says so with unabated scorn. Joan Lingard might well have revelled in the whole university experience, whether she read English, or History, or French. Lingard is still applying herself willingly to learning, in this case Spanish, but she did not go to university, simply because it did not occur to anyone to suggest that she did. One wonders how many bright and promising teenagers *that* happened to. John Herdman, edu-cated toward the English system by an established Edinburgh family and the teaching at Merchiston Castle School, went to Cambridge with a scholarship, only to find when he was soaking in an alien culture, that he was at heart a Scottish nationalist. Janice Galloway had little chance of enjoying university, preoccupied as she was by other grief and loss. And Ali Smith flourished at university in Aberdeen and for the most part at Cambridge, but reacted against the changing times as a university teacher at Strathclyde, and left the profession. At a time of endless reorganisation, vast classes, endless paper-chases, perhaps this should make some of our masters pause.

To the undergraduates who will rightly ignore this introduction, and turn to the words of the author of their choice, I wish all the luck they will surely need.

Isobel Murray

(1) *Scottish Affairs*, no 29, Autumn 1999, pages 157-166.

JANICE GALLOWAY

ANYONE WHO BROWSES Janice Galloway's website is disarmingly taken into her circle of acquaintance. As well as the important technical details, the selected bibliography with details of publications, of translations, of dates and anthologies, there are frequent updates, and the browser finds some very personal essays, such as 'Objective Truth and the Grinding Machine', an account of the development of her reading experience, from 'Oor Wullie' and 'The Broons' to a gradual realisation that it was generally believed that women couldn't write – and her subsequent decision to start writing. Watch this website! [*http://www.galloway.1to1.org/index.html*]

I had admired Galloway's writing from the start, and used *The Trick Is To Keep Breathing* as a galvanising text for undergraduates. I had heard Galloway read, superbly, to our students, and met her briefly in that connection a few times, when we met again at the launch of a critical book on twentieth-century women writers, *Scottish Women's Fiction: 1920s to 1960s: Journeys into Being* [*Edited by Carol Anderson and Aileen Christianson, Phantassie, 2000*]. There and then I discovered that we shared an abiding admiration for the work of Jessie Kesson, and I promised her a copy of my soon-to-be-published biography [Jessie Kesson: Writing Her Life, *Edinburgh, 2000*]. Knowing she had had a couple of bad experiences with the press, and might therefore be chary, I asked her if she would consider doing a long interview with me, and we fixed it up, and in the event our interview righted at least one major journalistic misunderstanding (pp 8-9, 11).

Before that I tried to pick up on the wider Galloway. I managed to acquire a copy of *Pipelines*, the beautifully produced volume from the Fruitmarket Gallery that was the outcome of her major collaboration with sculptor Anne Bevan. And 'still the wonder grew', at the range of her talents and interests.

When I visited her on two mornings in Glasgow, it was fairly soon after the publication of *Clara*, so that novel and its subject, music, was naturally

at the front of our minds. But even so, the major new realisation that the interviews gave me was of the real and abiding importance of music in Galloway's life. In the interview (p 37) she mentions a piece she wrote for the Scottish Chamber Group. This is now available on the website. The text of a stage event commissioned for Mayfest 1995, it linked the musical performances with accounts of four women composers, and the consistent neglect or subordination they met during their lives, and a breath-taking, well-chosen anthology of comments from a' the airts about the impossibility of women being creative in any sphere. This was 'a text that would thread together the lives of four female composers for a concert featuring some of their work'. The composers were Janet Beat, Lili Boulanger, Fanny Mendelssohn Hensel, – and Clara Wieck Schumann. In 1996, Galloway supplied the words for the song cycle, 'Woman's Life and Love' which Sally Beamish composed. Originally Robert Schumann had supplied music for the German words of lyric poet Chamisso. In the event, the novel was structured round the eight parts of this song cycle. The novel that was at last to result from Galloway's involvement with Clara Schumann was to involve much research, and was six years in the making.

Meantime, Beamish and Galloway collaborated again, as our interview shows, on *Monster*, an opera about Mary Shelley, the author of *Frankenstein*. I was unable to attend the production, but was delighted with the cooperation of Scottish Opera: in response to my enquiry, I was sent not only a copy of the very informative programme, but also a copy of Galloway's libretto, which makes fascinating reading. (It is published by the Scottish Music Information Centre)

It was after the interview, in May 2003, that Galloway and pianist Graeme McNaught provided the highlight of Aberdeen University's WORD Festival, with a programme of words and music, Galloway reading from *Clara* and McNaught playing works by Clara and (mainly) Robert Schumann: a unique experience.

22 July 2002 at the Glasgow home of Janice Galloway. Present, Janice Galloway, Isobel Murray.

IM Janice is the first writer I have talked to who has an active website, and I therefore happily refer all interested to the helpful information and essays there. [*http://www.galloway.1to1.org/index.html. All readers are directed there, for reliable bibliographical fact, and intimate and revealing essays about her youth and aspects of her writing.*] But I'd like her to tell us briefly about the part of Scotland she comes from, the kind of place it is.

JG Saltcoats. At one time it was the place where Glasgow people used to go their holidays; it was a seaside town on the west coast of Scotland. It still is in literal terms a seaside town on the west coast of Scotland, but people used to do the Fair fortnight there. A Saltcoats childhood was very shorey; it was cold, when you went walking down the shorefront, I remember that vividly, and I do remember dire warnings to keep away from the Glasgow folk, because they were urban and slightly dangerous. And I remember Glasgow people sitting out in the rain, on the shore, because they only had their fortnight, and they were damned if they were going to waste it. I remember kids waiting outside pubs for the parents of an evening: there were three cinemas, and that was reasonable for then – I imagine still is for a small town. There were very few restaurants; there were fish and chip shops that people could go to – that kind of a place. The kind of small place that people with not a lot of wealth in the background could go for the only period of holiday they'd get in the year. And the rest of the time Saltcoats was a pretty well shut-up kind of place. It was well served by cafes, selling ice-cream or chips, because of the Glasgow tourist trade partly, and I guess that means there must have been a reasonable Italian immigrant population. And that's mostly what I remember about it – the beach, and half-light – we had orange sodium lights fairly early on. I remember Saltcoats in half-light: I remember it as a series of graveyards. I remember it as the War Memorial right at the corner where there is now a supermarket, where an old church used to be. The place we used to stay was on Hamilton Street, one of the main drags, and the first house I remember was a single room above a doctor's surgery where me and my mother and sister used to live. The place was too small, but there were three of us in it: Nora worked in a broker's office in Glasgow. But it was my mother who did the raising.

IM Okay, let's go to school. Jack's Road Primary. Is Saltcoats big enough to have several primaries?

JG Oh, yes! In common with every other place in Scotland and I think Northern Ireland, it was segregated schooling, and we were right bang next door to the Catholic School, and used to throw things over the wall at each other at playtime, in what I may say was a fairly jocular and friendly way, but we did use to hurl things at each other. And there were the dire questions on the way home: if stray gangs of boys, or indeed girls, stopped you on the way home, the first thing they'd ask was, are you a Catholic or a Proddy, and you always had to assess the faces very carefully before you answered. There was another primary in Kyle's Hill, where my mother was a school dinner-lady. It was not the school I went to. I think there must have been about three or even four so-called non-denominational primary schools, so there were probably about four Catholic schools too.

IM So you were a bright wee girl, and liked school, and therefore were popular, as you say on the website.

JG I was popular with teachers: I wouldn't say I had a lot of friends. I always had very few, very intimate friends: I don't have large groups of acquaintances.

IM Right. And before we leave the Catholic/Protestant thing, was that of any importance at home? Was religion important at home?

JG Not at all. To get the guilt off her back, my mother used occasionally to go with her Communion Card thing, and she would go with her contribution – she used to put two bob in a wee envelope – and she would take that. It was very important to her to give her contribution to the church. I think she had a profound social conscience about some things, and seemed to think this was very important. The church was doing good things with this money she was handing in, so it was important to hand it in. The closest I got to religion was that you wore a hat in church. Apart from that I couldn't tell you anything about church ritual.

IM Okay. Let's move on to Ardrossan Academy. How far away was that, for a start?

JG Not very. Ardrossan's the next town of three I think now called the Cunninghams; Stevenson, Saltcoats and Ardrossan. Saltcoats was the holiday town, Stevenson didn't have a great deal going for it at all, and Ardrossan was where the ferry came in from Arran. I didn't get a bus; I walked every day. I would say it's one and a half or two miles – which is reasonable, when you're young. I've always been fairly sturdy; and I used to get attendance prizes, so the weather didn't make any difference to that. Attendance prizes until I got to Fourth Year, Secondary Four, and then the discovery of boys made a profound impact on my capacity to turn up at school.

IM And on your hemlines.

JG   And my hemlines shot up to mid-thigh. (L) I got sent home on more than one occasion because my skirts were too short, and then when midi skirts came in got sent home on more than one occasion because my skirts were too long. It was that kind of school. They also complained about kipper ties: the boys got hell because the ties were too thin, or the ties were too thick, or the hair was too long – boys used to get sent home. They were *very* picky about uniforms, which made me very hacked off about it. I got cheesed off, I think, with school round about Secondary Four, because the daft wee rules started to impinge more on me personally. In Secondary One, Two and Three they hadn't really: I didn't mind people expecting me to wear certain things. When sex hove into the picture, I cared deeply about being told to wear certain things that made me feel dowdy, and that I thought were simply power-gaming, and to a certain extent they *were* simply power-gaming. And a lot happened, the way it does with people, the introduction of sex into your life, and the awareness that is there, and the fact that you might be a player in this game, changed my life drastically on a number of fronts, and one of them was academically. I started to wish to pass exams, not just because I could – I knew the trick of how to pass exams – but now it was a matter of spiting the school. (L) It was a matter of saying, even when I don't turn up to your rotten classes, and even when I wear the wrong things, and even when you're sending me home all the time, I can still pass your sodding exams. It was a kind of one in the eye thing. Being clever at school I tended to associate with rebelliousness, fortunately: some people do the other thing.

IM   (L) Well, it's more common, I think!

JG   They opt out of the school. But I found a devious way to keep studying, and yet feel the necessary degree of rebellion that you need at that age.

IM   And meanwhile at home, was Mother worried about your hemlines and your make-up and all that, or did she just let you get on with it?

JG   Not so much that, no. My mother seemed to have a profound understanding of the female sex drive, shall we say? (L) It's never occurred to me before, but she did: my mother was pregnant when she married; my sister was pregnant when she married; we seem to be a family that's quite driven in that direction. (L) My sister had umpteen children when she left her husband as well. Sex has always been a driving force in my family, and it was taken for granted that sometimes you ended up 'caught out' or 'in trouble': it was one of those things. It wasn't something people felt particularly easy talking about, but no judgments were made: it was one of those things that happened to lassies. It was your bad luck; there was no moral judgment that meant you were a bad person. So wearing make up, wearing short skirts, was just seen as learning the craft of being a female: there was no problem about that.

She did have a few problems with me being clever at school, because it meant I was given forms, and asked if I'd like to apply to university. I didn't really know what that meant very well; I hadn't got a good grasp of that. She was very proud that I was able to do this thing: I gained the impression that it was an important thing to do, or a thing that one could be proud of. But she didn't know much about it, and what it meant in very literal terms was that I wouldn't be bringing in a wage packet, and that I think gave her a big moral dilemma: whether she was going to insist that I left school, which as a widow would have been her right, at the age of fifteen, or whether I was going to be let to stay on. And it was a teacher called Ken Hetherington, a music teacher, who went to see her –

IM This is the Ken Hetherington to whom *Clara* [*2002*] is dedicated.

JG Another life-changing influence. It was he who went to see my mother, at Kyle's Hill School, when she was through the back, when she was serving out dinners; she was completely mortified – a teacher had seen her in her dinner-lady outfit. And I think because she was mortified said yes, she can stay on. So that was school dealt with. And then he went to see her again, because I was going to apply to music college. He went to see my mother and said, not music college, university. And to my great surprise it was my mother who said to me, you're going to university (L). It took a few years before I found out Ken had been supplying her with information for years: they both kept the secret very well.

IM So you weren't fooling everyone as well as you thought you were.

JG No one ever does: I'm absolutely sure of it (L).

IM Okay. Let's move to university. You say on the website that you didn't much like it. And you've said in many places (L), and I know this feeling, that there were no women writers, and especially no Scottish women writers. You get to the point, women can't write. Myself, I thought it was true, in my innocence as a student. I thought it was just one of those things that men were better at.

JG   Well, you also believe the evidence of your eyes. If there's no evidence under your eyes, what proof do you have that this is a feasibility?

IM   Did you make the few close friends at university?

JG   Yes. A very few close friends. This is a good place to say this. There's been some dreadful rubbish in the press about me. The press is an extraordinarily inaccurate vehicle, increasingly. When I first started writing and there was first this 'being interviewed' thing, it foxed me a bit. You learn a new job slowly, and I thought this was just part of the price of the ticket, you just had to do this thing. I got fairly accurate press to start with, and then all sorts of dreadful havers and crossed lines and things like that. One of the things I read, an extraordinarily badly written thing, about the Music Department there, having been dreadfully unkind to me, or something like that. That is not the case. One of the friends I made and still have was a music lecturer called Warwick Edwards, and the Music Department was actually very tolerant of the kind of needs that I had.

The English Department was so vast – everybody – Jack Tamson and his dug – wanted to study English (L). They put us in a science theatre where we got to watch the lectures over the telly, because we were the overspill. I did English because I was good at it at school – I didn't know what university was for. An awful lot of first genera-tioners don't. You do this thing, and you get a ticket at the end that says you're allowed to earn more money than you would have otherwise – that's how you understand it. You don't realise there's any importance in choosing stuff – you just pick things out the book because you fancy the sound of them, because they've got funny names, or, well I was good at that at the school and I know what that is. And I did English because of that – I was not driven, Isobel. I know some people want to be writers. I didn't know what I wanted to be; I hadn't a clue what I was going to end up doing.

But I knew I was doing this thing now, *terribly* excited at the prospect of doing more music. The only thing that came into my head was Musicology, because I knew if you stuck 'ology' at the end of something it made it academic. And I *loved* music. The Music Department disappointed me, but it was not the individuals there at all. I possibly used flattened terminology with journalists who then elaborated the whole story. It was the subject, and how tedious it could be if it was not one-to-one. Ken Hetherington had spoonfed and encouraged me, had tailored how he taught music so individually and personally to my needs, that the shock of not getting that was physical. And I felt dizzy and sick within about a month when I realised what I had lost. I think what was wrong with me at university was a form of grief. That and the fact that I seemed clueless must have irritated some of my lecturers, because I didn't really know what I was meant to be understanding here. They told me stuff and I sat an exam in it. Some people actually came up front. A music lecturer whose name I forget said that. I used to ask why – I used to ask these questions; it was a stupid thing to do (L). Do I go away and study this after you've finished talking to me, or should I go to the library, should I do this or that, and he said, No, you just write down everything I say and you turn it out in the exam at the end of the year, and you'll pass (L). He *may* have been being ironic with someone he saw as too green for words, but that was like a physical blow as well. Nobody actually cares what I do. I wanted somebody to care. I think that was it. I'd lost the person that did, that cared whether I passed the exams, and was interested.

IM   Although he was still caring.

JG   He was very ill. He had Parkinson's disease, and I couldn't go to Ken and say help, help, help, keep me afloat: he needed cared for himself by that time. So I felt very stranded, and the Music Department was just so vast, no one could give me individual attention there, of course they couldn't – hundreds and hundreds of students. So the sudden impersonality of the place landed on me like bricks, and I never really recuperated from that. I started Junior Honours – again, I found exams easy, I always have – that's just a knack, it's got nothing to do with cleverness or real genuine intelligence, press certain buttons and things fall into place. And so it was automatic again, you could do Junior Honours. I started Junior Honours, and that was when I had the big crisis about what the hell is this about; what the hell am I doing this for, and it was Warwick Edwards I chose to speak to about it.

IM   Well at least this clears the name of the Department.

JG   I hope so. I wrote personally to Warwick to say, this was just bad journalism. Hogwash does the rounds. And now it's all on microfiche, they each read each other's inaccuracies, add another layer on top, and you end up with it being actually unrecognisable to yourself. So, no, university was not unkind to me particularly. I think I was suffering from the loss of someone who was very dear to me, who was also very sick at the time.

IM   And also you had this thing about feeling you should be doing something socially useful.

JG   Yeah. I went to Warwick at the start of Junior Honours. I became more and more isolated. I had three good friends that I went to university with. I was travelling from home: again, a great many first time entrants to university do that, especially at Glasgow. I was travelling in from Saltcoats every day, partly because it was a cheaper way to do it. I got maximum grant, because the family had no money whatsoever: my mother had nothing to contribute. So that was good: I felt I wasn't a drain on the household in that way. But every so often she would say, you could be bringing a wage in, and I was acutely aware of the fact that I was not, and that she was unhappy about it. Every so often my sister, who was a very insecure individual in a number of ways, would say, you think you're better than us, going to the university. Which didn't help anything really. And I chose to do Baroque music, whereas everyone else in the Music Department was doing Romantic music. It's almost like I isolated myself more and more on purpose. But my interests were in that direction. And it was me and Warwick in a room, and one day Warwick was talking to me about the finer points of seventeeth-century harpsichord technique, and my mother had been giving me a verbal going-over that morning how it was bloody well useless, the university, and I wish you'd never gone, and the money. And my sister used to hit me: she'd given me a going-over the night before. And I started to cry, with Warwick sitting there. Of course Warwick went into a fair tizz, you know, having a strange teenage girl crying in front of you (L) can't be an easy experience. He was very gentle. He was very nice to me indeed. He calmed me down, and said something's wrong, I don't know what it is. I couldn't speak. He said go to the University Health Service. I also thought I was pregnant: you know the way teenage girls do, when you feel lousy, when your life's down, you can focus it on a phantom pregnancy scenario, and that way you can get someone else to share the anxiety. I wasn't pregnant. (L) I had myself talked into the fact that my life was finished. I went to the Medical Department there, and an awfully nice man chatted to me for about three days running, said, there's nothing wrong with you; you're fed up and you're run down; you're not very sure if you want to be here. Why don't you have a year out? It was a wonderful feeling of someone opening a door (L) and the sunshine just came in. It had never occurred to me that you could say, I want a year out, I need to get away. I need to work out what the hell I'm doing.

So I had a year out, and I was a kind of social worker. There was a new department called the Welfare Rights Department being set up and I was one of the guinea pigs for that. I still remember everybody who was there, a delightful team; and everyone was kind, and everyone was fun, and to have a work life, and to have friends at that level was a new thing for me. And people coming in and saying, my house is damp; what can I apply for, what can I get. It felt great to begin with, until you realised that the bulk of what you could offer was not very much at all, in terms of helping these people's lives. And a lot of that idealistic thing, late teenage/early twenties thing, but I thought, oh, social work doesn't necessarily save the world; I bet a whole lot of other things I think will, won't either. I might as well go back to university and finish the degree. So in an extremely jaded, disaffected, almost cynical frame of mind I went back and thought, if I'm going to have to have a degree, this is just it, this is what the world is like: you get your degree and do 'I'm all right, Jack.' I'm going to take the quickest one. I finished an Ordinary. Oh yes, the papers. A man called Philip Hobsbaum, a strange man, seems to have been under the impression that I did sit Honours and was a poor student. I don't think I was ever a poor student. I was unengaged.

IM (L) I find both parts of that profoundly believable!

JG Philip again has said to the press that I got a poor Third Class Honours degree. This is not in fact the case. I did Ordinary, because I was hacked off: I wanted out. I have some regrets about it because I had no idea that these things were regarded in quite the snobbish way that they are by people. I couldn't have told you what a Two One was, or a Two Two. And it was meeting Alison Cameron when I became a teacher that initiated me into the delights of these strange hierarchies and hurdles, and what this might mean for my teaching career. I hadn't known that. I still to a certain extent thought the world was a meritocracy. If you were good at something, people would know you were good at something, and they would just let you do it. I still don't really see the problem with that – apart from human psychology (L)! That mucks everything up, doesn't it? I still to a certain extent believed that, and I thought, get the degree and prove you can finish it – because then of course what my mother got me on, and she was quite right, was, you start things and you don't finish them. Get the bloody thing finished, get out of there, and get a job. So I went back to finish the quickest one, which was an Ordinary. I got out there to look for a job, (L) and I was unemployed for nine months.

IM Was that because there were jobs that you didn't want to take?

JG No: I was one of the first wave of students that came out and thought there were people waiting outside to say here's a job doing this – and there weren't. Not only that, but students were ending up on the dole. Big furores in the papers about waste of money and what were these students going to do, and brain drain. And I did two interviews to be a personnel officer. I didn't know what it was, but they were the only people that offered me interviews. I blew both of the interviews, in one because I was asked one question in particular that I thought was stupid and insulting, and in the other the bloke touched me up; so I blew both interviews (L) through being too sure of how I wanted to be treated, thank you! (L) I had a very near miss with a Society of Authors job, but they got somebody else with experience, and rightly so. And my mother eventually said, you still havenae got that job you said you were going to get, and the overspill of graduates coincided with a shortage of teachers. So the Teacher Training Colleges were running mid-term courses, from January till December, in a desperate bid to catch some of this overspill. And I got catched. At Hamilton College of Education.

IM Right. I was just assuming it was Jordanhill, in my ignorance of the West.

JG Jordanhill didn't run these. People at Hamilton were very sweet, actually: I still know some of the people who taught me there. And I liked it, because at last the guilt was getting off my shoulders, it was a proper job at last. It was not the job I would have chosen for myself. Few people do, because you want to get out into the world and do new things, because you feel you know what teaching's about because you've gone through that system. Of course you don't really, but you think you do. Going through teacher training college was in some ways a great experience. I've heard an awful lot of people say it was a waste of a year, but I learned a lot in that year.

IM There's something we left out. On the website, you mentioned 'a wonderful woman called Ms Redfern in the French Department at the university.'

JG   She's down there as Ms Redfern because I cannae remember her first name. [*Editor suspects this was Adrienne M Redshawe, and Galloway confirms the surname*]

IM   Did you do French as a subject?

JG   Well, yeah. I almost sat no exams at university, because if you get an exemption, you don't. If you go through school passing exams you quite like them! It's almost like a quiz. You quite enjoy it. (L) I'd never had that hassle that some people have; I would sympathise with it usually, having seen it in students when I was a teacher – terrible nightmares that some people get. It had never been that way for me. But I hadn't done the bread-and-butter subjects; I hadn't done Moral Philosophy, that you're supposed to do at Glasgow, and you have to do Philosophy somewhere if you're doing an Ordinary. And you have to do a language somewhere. And I hadn't done them, so that had to be my last year.

IM   That was what I was looking for. It was in your last year that you did French, and that this woman, out of the blue, suggested you should write.

JG   She had thought journalism, originally, because of what I chose to try and escape the botched job I was sure I would make of French Literature – and how frustrating to be handed a great work of literature and you have to tank through it with a dictionary, I couldn't bear it. So I did Social and Political Philosophy of France, which meant I read a lot of French journalism and French non-fiction texts, which I could thole more easily, with the aid of a dictionary. And because of the translations I had been doing of social history documents, she said, have you thought of journalism? I said no, and she said, do you write at all? I said no, and she said, well you should.

IM   That was good. I just wanted to put her in as a clear footnote. Okay. Hamilton was okay, but then comes the question of getting a job. Was it easy?

JG   Yeah. (L) That's the place where they *were* queuing up.

IM   And so, where did you choose to go?

JG   I chose the first post, because again I didn't really know anywhere. They said, where do you want to go? Again, reluctantly, home. Well, desperate to and reluctant to at the same time. You know that strange funk you get into. Well, I got into it bigtime. (L) Terrible mess bigtime. I'd been reared and told you're useless; and you're messy; you'll never be able to look after a house. I didn't have the confidence that I'd be able to find one, never mind look after it. (L) And didn't have the chutzpah to fight that enough. Plus I was worried about my mother. She was getting older. She was in her early forties when she had me. By this stage, she was still a robust woman but she was coming up to retirement, and that was quite a shock, that my mother was going to retire, and might have needs of her own from me. I thought I'd better be somewhere near home. I was at home for the beginning of teacher training. I chose the Ayrshire posting which was to Kilbirnie, a place called Garnock Academy.

IM   Was that far away from home?

JG   Not really. Maybe about fifteen miles from where I was living at the time. And the then boyfriend, the very staunch boyfriend, who had put up with my swithering and toing and froing about university, was still there, and he got a flat in Irvine, which was halfway to Kilbirnie – again sheer laziness and self interest (L) made me realise it would be good to move in with the boyfriend – it was halfway there, so that was my eventual move from home. (L) I don't imagine it's an uncommon story, but goodness, it's lazy. I think I also wanted him to lean on, just in case.

IM   Teaching. You've already mentioned that you met Alison Cameron when you became a teacher. She became an important person in your life. I'm thinking of the dedication to *Foreign Parts* [*1994*].

JG   Great friends, yes. Alison's had a dedication in most books, actually. We didn't hit it off right away, I thought she was quite an oddity to start with, and I'm sure she thought I was, but the two of us were the single women in the department, and ended up blethering together; isn't this hellish and isn't that hellish: it's nice to have someone to have a greetin' meetin' with. We're from very different backgrounds in a number of ways, and when my mother died, my friendship with Alison became even closer, because she was the person who said, oh look, I've got a car. It being a council house, we had to clear it: we'd three days. She drove me down; she took me from school, she helped me clear the house: – it was just so profoundly helpful.

IM   When was that?

JG   1982. It was just so enormously helpful at a number of levels, that very suddenly the friendship deepened into me going to her house more often; and she still lived with her mother. I still regard Margaret

Cameron as a kind of extra Mum, a kind of aunt, and Alison's younger sister Seonaid – I sort of became part of the family. If a group of people in that way – if a family in particular – see you through a difficult time, you tend to become absorbed in part of that family, and that was what happened to me. I lost my Mum, and found another family who were willing to kind of be the shock-absorber. They were all extraordinarily kind to me. Charles, that I'd moved in with, was a very, very nice bloke, but very keen to get married, and I didn't feel ready. So that relationship broke up, with no malice whatever – a great deal of sadness, but no malice whatsoever. (L) I was a bit stoney. I found my own place to live in. I didn't find it particularly easy to keep going as a one when you've been used to going as a two, on two salaries. Alison was keen to set up home on her own, so the two of us moved to Glasgow and found a flat-share – it was the only way we could do it; and in some way or another we've lived together ever since. That's a long time.

IM The idea of women friends is very basic to *Foreign Parts*. I'm not at all identifying either of you (L) with either of Cassie and Rona, but the dedication flags it up – what is it?

JG 'For Alison, my female friends, and all female friends.'

IM I think it's an important subject. The idea that you can have woman friends, and it's real, seems to me so important: it's one of the most important things your work has said. These days, people think you have to be lesbian, in order to have female friends: in my young day, women commonly shared flats: nowadays . . . (L)

JG Again, the press, bless it, is interested in that kind of thing. It's just boring to say, actually we're just pals – it's just tedious! (L) I have lesbian friends, who tend to be much more understanding of the fact that women like women, in a non-sexual way, as well as in their lives, in completely different ways. They tend to be very understanding of that. Virginia Woolf, was it, in *A Room of One's Own*, 'One must whisper it; let us whisper this: Chloe liked Olivia.' [*1929. Section 5: 'Do not start. Do not blush. Let us admit in the privacy of our own society that these things sometimes happen. Sometimes women do like women. "Chloe liked Olivia"'*.] (L) That again really spoke to me. I had seen movies from the Sixties when I was growing up, and movies which suggested that you had your women friends until the man came along. And I had seen pastiches of it – I'm a big fan of Doris Day, who pastiched so many of these ideas so beautifully, but so subtly that I'm sure some people thought these scripts were for real, they *were* about love everlasting, at a rather sugary level, it just became very important for me to take a look at that – I'm a great fan of looking at things that have been thrown away, that have been rejected, that have been made little of. And in the formative influences I had, which were mostly film and pop music, friendship between women, or how women reacted with each other, how women felt about other women, seemed to have been almost non-existent, or made awful light of. So that one has always interested me. And in fact in general, the women friends I have had have been very good to me. That said, the men friends I've had *too* have been very good to me! But how I tended to make most of my male friends in the early days was through having some kind of romantic liaison with them, then we'd *become* friends. Fortunately most of them still are. Like I say, my family seems to be quite sex-driven (L), and I think I've confused that sometimes in the past with just an enthusiasm for a man's intellect and how he puts the world together. I have confused that with a sexual interest. I'm much better at that now, I'm pleased to say; whereas the women – that had never entered the picture at all. So I was quite clear about women being friends.

IM You said interestingly a minute ago that with Charles you weren't ready for marriage. Are you ready for marriage now? I.e. are you the sort of person who ever would get married?

JG Yeah. I've got great respect for the institution. I'm no' much of a rule maker, to tell you the truth, Isobel. I think the less rules you make about your life, the more pleasantly surprised you can be by your life. (L) I've come round to that one.

IM I like it. (L)

JG I don't make hard and fast rules about anything. I'm sure under certain circumstances that would seem an extremely good idea indeed. Under other circumstances it would be a very bad idea. Under some circumstances it might be a great adventure just finding out. There are certain things about how the institution appears under law which I think are dubious, there are certain ways in which the institution has been treated over centuries that I find dubious; but what an extraordinarily noble ideal! The way the enterprise has been envisaged – *far* too much is expected of the institution in this day and age. I think that's why it's so often failed. In the past I think the institution has kept together largely out of a series of emotional and even physical blackmails, and certainly financial blackmails. There is much that can be said against how it has operated, but I think the institution itself is a noble ideal. No I don't have a hack against the notion of two people formally saying to each other and in front of witnesses, we're gonna try and be kind to each other and we're gonna try to stick with each other to make something together, instead of separately. I think that's a fine thing.

IM Right. You're teaching. You teach for ten years, but increasingly you don't like it: increasingly the form-filling and the expectations and the more bits of paper that come across your desk spoil the good times with the students.

JG Yes. It was the bits round about I didn't like. I liked the kids; always did.

IM So you're teaching, and you're looking for a way out, and you're thinking, maybe it could come from writing.

JG With an incredible lack of imagination, I didn't know what other people did.

IM Did you ever think of composing?

JG Naah. Cos there are so many tightropes, high-wires, trips in music. Don't start me on music. Music is such a locked-in world in many ways. And there are still formal set-ups whereby it's almost *de rigueur* to have a mentor, and it's almost *de rigueur* to have someone who will regard you as a protegee, and who will teach you personally, one-to-one, that you don't necessarily pay, that you might pay, to have someone who teaches you the craft of composing is almost essential. I only know one person who hasn't done it that way, and that's Sally Beamish. She's the only one person I know. I wouldn't have had the imagination to think, I can do this all by myself. I don't anyway think I have the talent to have gone down that particular route.

And I hadn't been involved with music for a number of years. The sort of grief I fell into when Ken wasn't such an intense part of my life – he came through the illness that he was suffering from, and got a lot better but was never again quite the powerful man that he was, in many ways. After Ken died, I just hadn't been able to deal with music, so deep was the feeling of loss from what I had had, I couldn't listen to it without feeling the opposite of what you should feel when you hear music; you should feel consoled. I just felt harrowed. I couldn't listen to music for something like ten years. The idea of composing would just have been anathema.

IM So I suppose choosing the subject for *Clara* indicates a coming to terms with all of that, and a moving on. You said in Aberdeen how much you'd been listening to music, and been moved by it.

JG I'm able to listen to it again, but there are still times when I need to put it off. It gets a bit too close. There is nothing quite like music to invade the memory banks, to invade the feelings, and carry them to a level. It's also got to do with my son's Dad, Graeme McNaught the pianist. And to have the piano continually in the house was like getting a gift back; wonderful. The house was just a storm of music. And when Graeme was no longer in the house, it was like losing the damn thing twice; I couldn't listen *again*, which was very difficult to deal with. Then I thought, oh, this is stupid, depriving yourself of one of life's greatest pleasures, and I fought it, assiduously, and I'm getting it back. And I'm getting my contact with musicians back: working with Sally was good in that respect. I could get in contact with music that wasn't quite so in my face. And just to talk to someone in a rational way about it, instead of it being such a powerful emotional thing; that was useful. And through that I've met the singers who were involved in the opera that we composed together, and have made very good friends with one in particular, who's teaching me to listen to music in another way, is teaching me a different repertoire of things to listen to, which doesn't involve the same memory-banks. Yes, I'm certainly back into listening. And writing *Clara* was cathartic, certainly.

IM Let's talk about starting to write. The first thing you wrote was 'it was', which is printed as one of the short stories in *Blood* [*1991, pages 32-5*], and it was making sense of a dream; is that right? Were there lots of other things at the same time?

JG No; not really. I remember writing 'it was'. This was a very, very strange dream indeed, about finding a face buried in the ground, and I wrote it down. And I worked on it, and worked on it, and worked on it. It was extremely therapeutic. I think people do turn to writing – I associate writing with emotional extremity. An amazing thing how when someone is bereaved they will suddenly begin to read poems, when they've never had much time for them before, can't be arsed with them, don't see much point in them, even. Suddenly poems acquire significance. It's extraordinary how common that is, poetry in particular. Or when people are in states of anxiety, sometimes they will begin to write, as a means of exorcising the anxiety. Some mental illnesses are notoriously associated with writing. It's a way of getting something out of the system. And I think that applies to human beings in general: they will attempt to self-express, or some will. It's the most direct, the most hands-on way they can think of to do that. They could sing – but they'd tend to be singing someone else's words. The idea of composing on the spot so you can sing your own words – that's tough. (L) It's easier for most people to write. It's a lousy time, and I think the sheer act of forcing these words to try to make some sense of something that doesn't make sense, that seems a very important thing for me to do, (L) make sense out of this mess. And dreams are by their very nature a mess; I was trying to make sense of it, so that the mess would make sense to someone else. It was extremely therapeutic: I did that for a couple of hours every night for a while, and eventually got a sense of what I could make it. Oh, I'll have to write something else now, (L) I hope I have another dream, I thought. And started making it up, without having the dream bit, but having the waking dream, which is what writing is. You go into a kind of trance, and imagine things, and imagine people, and imagine talking. That strange, trance-like state. Being able to evoke that is a kind of invitation. I'm sure that's partly what impels the process, when people begin to turn to writing – unless it's been that 'I want to be a writer' thing. People just kind of fall into it. It's somehow a desire to think something clear, and make something right, whereas what is round about might possibly not be. And that was how that started. It was one thing at a time, and it was for the sheer enjoyment of *editing*, more than communicating: it was the editing that turned me on. And still is; the creating bit – I loathe it, I hate the blank page. Once I've got a number of pages that have been written *on*, *that* is when my interest reaches.

IM   Let me ask you, with reference to that, about the scenarios – oh, what are they called? Those bits in *Blood* –

JG   'Scenes from the Life'?

IM   What's this about, these numbers? Do all the ones you don't print exist? 1, 2, 3, 4, 5 . . .? [*In the book we find 'Scenes from the Life' Nos 29, 26, 27.*]

JG   Nah. Private joke. I have an extraordinarily low boredom threshold. (L) To keep myself amused, from time to time, just for me. I think it was after being at a James Kelman reading: I went to hear Jim Kelman reading at the Third Eye Centre. He was reading with Tom

Leonard and I don't remember – oh, it was Norman MacCaig! Damn fine reading it was, too. Very well lit, and all three gentlemen had extremely striking faces. It was quite an evening to be at. And I remember Jim reading something out, and someone asking why did you call it that? And he said you've just got to call it something, and I was very impressed with this answer – just necessity – (L) something doesn't always mean something profound: sometimes it's just a means to an end, to get you over a hump, to get to the profound things. And they had to be called something.

IM   They're different in the way they're written, from other things. It's almost like you're taking someone round a film set, which is why in my mind I called them scenarios.

JG   Yeah. Well, they are! I've always liked the idea of playing with forms: again this is closer to editing than breaking a white page, I think. I like the idea of saying, well, this is possibly how a play might be written. This is how a play is supposed to be written. But wouldn't it be interesting if you wrote a play that actually wouldn't work as a play, you couldn't do it as a play? A page-bound play – what would that be like? Would that have any validity – is there a point in it? And because you're partly editing, what you're doing is editing a form. (L) I think that's where my interest in form comes from, because then you can regard it more as editing: I don't feel I'm totally on my own with a white page. Because I've got a ghost of a form somewhere in my head that I'm playing with. And I did that quite a lot, to begin with. And I also wrote 'poems', in inverted commas, that didn't look like poems. They looked like chunks of prose – I like that. I like that kind of thing. And I like sometimes breaking up what is quite clearly prose – breaking sentences in funny places as though it were poetry. That kind of thing enthuses me. And that was partly playing with what a play might be, what a play might not be. The idea of writing a play that couldn't possibly be a play excited me a great deal. (L)

IM   Some of them could be films, which is why I kept coming back to that. It's almost as if you've got a camera that you're training and sometimes you've got an audience that's there that you actually talk to in the course of the piece, and sometimes not. And I was also interested in what came first, the 'scene from the life' about the health visitor, or the health visitor episode in *The Trick is to Keep Breathing*. [*1989*]

JG   The health visitor in *The Trick*. I think. (L) Possibly they were contemporaneous; possibly I had two versions of how the health visitor in *The Trick* could go, and one is possibly built from out-takes of the other. I couldn't tell. (L) I'm very economical. The home background is always there, not to waste anything. I would never, ever chuck anything away. Peter Kravitz used to laugh. [*See Autobiography on website. Peter Kravitz, editor of* Edinburgh Review, *was JG's first editor at Polygon.*] I don't waste things. Give me that back! I know you don't like it, but I'm holding on to it. (L) You're so lazy! Not lazy: I'm being economical. I would use things again. When I was writing *Trick*, I wasn't consciously writing a novel: I couldn't have said, I am sitting down to write a novel. I would have frightened the shit out of myself; I didn't do that. I was just writing a something. I had to fool myself: I knew someway it was a novel, but at the conscious level I was assiduously telling myself it was a something, and could finish at any stage. I can't do that thing – the BBC used to phone up and say, we need something two thousand one hundred words. Sorry, you've got the wrong person. I don't know when they're going to finish. And I didn't know when this 'thing' was going to finish. I thought it was just pieces, and it's possible that what became the 'scene from the life' of the health visitor had been one of such pieces, and I thought, that doesn't belong in there, it belongs over there. I couldn't pin it down for chronology, but I think the health visitor in *The Trick* came first.

IM There's another one that fascinated me: that's the story of 'David' in *Blood,* which is the David out of *Trick.* [Blood, *1991, pages 36-39*]

JG Who is quite certainly related to the David in *Trick.*

IM And the names are the same, even his friends' names are the same.

JG Yeah. I don't really see the point in changing the names.

IM Again I wondered whether that, the further developing of the relationship, or how the relationship with David happened, in the story in *Blood,* was something that had got cut out of *The Trick.*

JG I don't think that was an out-take case. I was very new to writing, and didn't know the craft you learn, whereby when you shut the computer down, or you put the pen down, or however it is you do it, you leave it behind. It was very difficult to begin with. Plus, I didn't have children, so I *could* be self-indulgent and walk about with ghosts and fantasy people in my head, I could do that. I didn't change the names. I *knew* that that David I was writing about was the same David, but just the character interested me so much, I wanted to take him and do something else. That was all. I didn't see the point in changing the names. It was the same bloke; I could tell it was the same bloke! (L) Oh, to hell with that, I'm not changing it. That happened several times.

IM So my question's silly?

JG No! Why?

IM Is it silly of me to wonder what the connection is between the one David and the other David?

JG They're the same bloke, is the answer to that. It was just someone who was living in my head. At the time, I wasn't consciously saying, I will now write a short story: I was just writing bits. And occasionally they would round off and I would work on them. Those things were worked on again and again. An assiduous editor goes on for ever. With publishing of extracts, Robin, my publisher, has learned to take stuff off me (L); it's the only way he can get it. [*Robin Robertson of Cape*] It was the same with these stories, and it's partly because it's still that green thing in my head; it's still the enjoyment of editing, and having got that character, and finding he could do something else – I knew it wasn't part of *Trick*, because what David did in that book was sort of done, but I knew it was him. It's not a silly question: what you're asking me is about process: how do you in fact write? What do you do? Do you sit and make up characters appropriate to the story? No. The story doesn't come first: the characters come first. And if I've been interested in somebody who just happens to have been somewhere else, I have no compunction about saying, I'm still interested in that man; I'm still interested in that woman: they're coming over here now, while I do something else with them.

IM How about the typographical devices and things? At what stage does that happen? Those famous 'o's! (L) Have you ever regretted them? Have you read some of the amazing things that critics have said they mean? [*Some sections of* The Trick is to Keep Breathing *are separated by* '*ooo*']

JG Someone once wrote to me, a student, – I get letters from people who've been forced to read my stuff –

IM They do it willingly!

JG And one asked (L), are the 'o's vaginas? They're 'o's! They're 'o's!

IM (L) I get the vagina bit in classes all the time!

JG No! *No*!! The 'o's just struck me as a good idea. Also the sound, oh, oh, the exclamation of surprise I think had occurred to me. How anybody would think – No! It was certainly not conscious. People are free to construct whatever theory they like – of course they are. It had never occurred to me. I don't know how tenable that is. Why would you cover a book with fannies?!(L)

IM   Well, Alasdair did a whole book binding with y-fronts, remember. [*Alasdair Gray's* 1982, Janine, *Cape, 1984, had its binding embellished in this way, and was also very typographically innovative*]

JG   (L) Aye, but he can draw. I have to use an o because I cannae draw.(L)

IM   But at some stage, you had to realise that *Trick* was going to be something mightily like a novel, if it wasn't going to be a novel. It was going to be a long book where the bits all connected. Is that when things like italics here and non-justified text there and the wee bitties on the margins that were trying to fall off in the Polygon first edition got decided?

JG   They weren't keen: they weren't keen! The number of problems we had with that, with the typesetters. The typesetters must have got really pissed off. (L) I would proof-read the damn thing, and it would come back with different mistakes in it: a strange thing. I think he was just pissed off, the bloke. I should have spoken to him personally. I kept saying should I go and speak, but Peter thought not. It never actually did sort itself out. The American edition of *The Trick is to Keep Breathing* is as close as it gets to what that book should look like, that isn't full of mistakes somewhere. It's quite fun. I don't mind that at all. But they are different. People have again had to study the thing, and have voluntarily read several editions of the same thing. And there was a series of drawings that I did do that got missed out. Just blank spaces. So it's never really looked the way it's supposed to, that book. I don't mind; that's part of the fun of that book.

IM   But the various devices that you chose to use, were they there from the beginning, or were they . . .?

JG   Kinda yes, kinda no. Again, wee private jokes or tricks to keep me going, was partly what the italics was about, and the words dropping off the edge of the page, it was partly that. There were also different ways – sometimes they were up the side; sometimes they were hand-written, and I think I did ask Peter Kravitz, can I have that in hand-writing. He took everything very seriously, which again encourages you to go further in that direction, when someone says yes, there's really no reason why you shouldn't have it. You begin to look for more serious ways to do this thing, and more practical ways to do this thing. I certainly knew that the text shouldn't look as ordered as text looks normally. I knew that. Partly that was from the experience of having read *1982, Janine*, and seeing this was feasible. You have permission to do this. It was mind-opening. The 'o's again: there's an edition of James Kelman's *The Bus Conductor Hines* [*1984*] that has little 'o's' dividing the sections: I've never heard anyone say his are vaginas. (L)

IM I've never heard anyone ask him either!

JG I've seen this. There is an edition that has these. A trap from the gender of the author. Or maybe it's to do with the gender of the main character; I don't know. And I think at some stage it's possible I've just said to myself, I want that, because it sounds like an exclamation. And it's used in others. This sharing, this was one of the great things about writing at that time, to a large extent that is not necessarily any longer there. But there seemed to be writers who were writing at the same time as each other who were perfectly content to share: you read something, and you think, bloody hell, that's a great thing to do: that opens my head up, I'll have that. And it's not like Alasdair's pastiche that he does in *Lanark*, where there's a list of plagiarisms, it is more or less saying, look for Christ's sake, this thing's out there in common for everybody. [*Gray's satirical 'Index of Plagiarisms' is found in the Epilogue to* Lanark, *1981*] This is what writers do. This is what anyone creative does. And you don't know half the time where the stuff's coming from, but it's something that's opened your head up at some stage, and you take it and you do your own thing with it. It's not plagiarism: you take it away, and you do your own thing with it. And there was a huge feeling of sharing at that time: I read Tom Leonard in the same avaricious way, about how you break the sentences off: I read Kelman in that way: I read Alasdair Gray in that way. [*The three together applied for, and jointly obtained the post of Professor of Creative Writing at Glasgow University, 2001*] Certainly when Duncan McLean started writing, there were things that Duncan did with titles that blew me away. I think Duncan McLean is a short story writer like no other in Scotland. [*See eg* A Bucket of Tongues, *1992*]

IM Example?

JG 'After not having eaten for three days, I finally got my hands on some liver'. How's that for a title? (L)

IM It reminds me very slightly of that one of yours, *'later he would open his eyes in a strange place, wondering where she'*.

JG   Exactly! Exactly. (L) You find something that somebody else does, and think, bugger me, what a good idea. I made it part of the story. We all felt in it together, and you wanted somebody else to read your stuff and say, oh, that's for me. And I have seen the compliment coming back; I've seen it in other writers' work, where something echoes me. It was somehow a kind of common good. It would be going too far to say there was a deliberate communality of writers, but we certainly knew the other ones were there, and you knew what their names were, and you knew who you were interested in. And I'm absolutely sure that we know what we've got from each other, by and large. [*See also the Cathy Boyd factor, pages 43-4, 48-9*] Now, because there are so many – thank the Lord – there are so many visible writers in Scotland, that clear process of reading each other, and huge mutual support I think was there as well in those earlier days when a whole almost like a new wave, a new band of writers was becoming very apparent, it has just become the normal thing that it is for most other countries' writers. Because we have such a splendid, wide range now, the fact that we're all there for each other has now become just a commonplace: it's just how things are: it's part of the normal currency of being a writer in Scotland And before it wasn't.

IM   I want to ask you about *The Trick is to Keep Breathing*, just in simple, human terms. Joy is nae weel. She's some kind of not well.

JG   I don't know she's ever convinced she's not well. She's certainly experiencing deep unhappiness.

IM   She's not well about eating.

JG   Ah! Yes, she's certainly punishing herself.

IM   And she is eventually taken into hospital. And I know what I think about this, (L) but I'm interested in what you think, does she 'get better'? Does she improve? Not 'get better' in the sense of better, but is she improving, is she going forward, at the end of the novel?

JG   Yes.

IM   Right. Does the hospital do any good?

JG   Yes. Not necessarily intentionally. (L)

IM   But it's possible: one often gets students saying that the hospital and the doctors are just all negative, futile, hopeless. And while I think they come over as pretty sad, I think, some of them come across as *knowing* there's not much they can do, but is it possible that they know that she needs to be in a place with other people in a safe environment and on pills for a while, and that may help?

JG What hospitals in general do is they provide an environment where
some one will at least attend to a certain amount of your physical
needs. And if someone is suffering from some kind of psychiatric disorder or simple grief, whatever it is Joy's suffering from, she's certainly suffering. I don't know if I'm convinced she's mentally ill,
neither are the psychiatrists, but then the psychiatrists can't agree (L)
as to what the hell is wrong with her. How do you agree as to what
the hell is wrong with someone, when it's largely a matter of perception? How do you gauge what that is? There are some forms of
mental illness where it's very clear what they are, because the
behaviour patterns are so coded and categorisable. Joy could simply
be in a state of grief, and not very sure if she wants to go on living.
And because of that she's choosing lots of ways to sabotage her health.

What the hospital does is get some of the guilt off her back, that
she's having to be dealt with by the people she regards as innocent
people. Like poor Marianne, who's miles away, and sending these
kind of hopeless little letters, poor old thing; Marianne's mother
Ellen, who thinks food is medicine (L); and Joy clearly feels a
complete shit for upchucking these lovely meals. David, who occasionally will come round and will try to glue her together, but he's
a *boy*: what is he supposed to do in the face of this damned thing?
Sam, who's trying to take her for runs on a motor-bike. Everybody
is made to realise how impotent you are in the face of something like
depression, where it's a perception.

And more than anything else, what I wanted to do in that book was
get across the feeling of what that was like, the intense depression that
comes from grief, whether it's clinical or not. It might be clinical in
Joy's case. The fact that that renders everything hopeless and helpless. The way some people have interpreted it is somehow that the
world is a pile of shit, and this is a very cynical commentary on it.
But I don't think it is at all. I think somewhere she's got enough
perception to see these people are trying, but they can't get through
the glass wall, and what hospital does, and why she's so keen to get
there, is she gets rid of some of the guilt that people she clearly feels
for, and who clearly feel for her will not feel so helpless, if they know
somebody else is roped in. And these people are paid to be roped in:
these people will know what to do: somehow they will have the resili-
ence to cope with her when we can't. She lets her friends off the hook.
Enjoyment is too strong a word, but the feeling of relief that she's

able to get from that in hospital, allows her to sink into the dark a bit, where she can feel, is this really what I want to do? Is this really what I want to do? I think that is the case with depression. Somewhere your psychology has the feel, this is as bad as I can feel about everything: this is as lousy as I can feel about life. Do I want to do anything about it or don't I? The struggle to get back up to where the oxygen is is intense, and the motivation has to be intense. And what the hospital does for Joy I think is let her get down to the bottom. She thinks, these people can cope with me in this mood: I can go further, go further: and she can choose whether to kick off the bottom, which I think she does, not with a huge amount of energy, but there is a kick (L) – that's what I think.

IM But perhaps the pills are important and necessary because the bottom can be too much? She's safe when she's in hospital: it's only when she comes out that she has that decision that she can't cope and she's not going to kick, and if David didn't come around presumably she would finish it there.

JG It's also possibly her way of getting to the bottom. I think there is something in the ritual of suicide: very few people commit suicide in an unritualistic way. I'm fascinated by that – again, making sense of something that doesn't make sense. Why should a human being, who's designed for survival, choose to fight every instinct in their physicality, which is to get rid of itself? What is that about? And having looked at forms of suicide, and read umpteen reports, and spoken to people who work in psychiatric hospitals, and friends who work in psychiatric hospitals, about the ways people commit suicide – it's almost unheard of for there not to be an element of ritual. And I think part of what that ritual is – someone like Cleopatra, you go through the scenario about killing yourself with the asp so often, you hardly believe it's for real, when she does it. And she gets dolled up in all the finery, and she does the whole thing. And I think has to confront herself with that question, is it for real this time? I have gone through with all the ritual: do I want to take this any further? And decides yes. Bit of a limp position. Leaves it up to the snake whether it's going to bother. (L) But she does actually do that ritual thing. It's the same as taking pills. You leave it up to the pills, whether they're going to bother. Do you want to finish me off or don't you? A lot of people do this ritual; they line pills up, or they line bottles up: I had an aunt who committed suicide and went through the most extraordinary ritual of laying all her outfits out before she killed herself. I think that's part of getting yourself to the bottom, privately, of finding out whether you want to go ahead with this thing. I'm absolutely sure that some people commit suicide almost out of a strange feeling of self respect: I've taken it this far: I'd somehow let myself down, be seen to be a shallow person, if I've taken it this far and not go through with it. I think that's partly what she's doing, is getting herself there – I couldn't tell you what would happen if David didn't come to the window. I just know it occurred that he did. I don't know if she would have gone through with it.

IM   It just seemed to me that she was going to, but as you say it's left open. But it's fairly clear to me that she is a lot, measurably, better, at the end, just from the picture of her at the very beginning, sitting sort of away from herself in the room, dark and wet, and then the Christmas lights and so on, the music, and the decision to learn to swim. I thought that was really quite significant.

JG   Powerfully significant. It's very clear to me at the end. The signal piece I look for, when I've got a depressive member of the family or a friend who's in trouble, is some sort of physical proof, you know; the house should be tidier, or their clothes should be different, or something like that. She also does change appearance; she does this haircut thing, and she's gonna get her ears pierced, and she makes up her mind she's gonna make a physical sign. But that's part of the reassurance, the physical sign. It's a mental corner you need to turn, when you're suffering from depression, and as far as I was prepared to take the reader was that mental corner: I *will* do these things. I loved Michael Boyd's stage version; I thought it was just wonderful, because what he had Joy do was put on a different colour of dress. He made it a big upfront physical sign: all the three Joys changed the colour of their dress. I think it's quite clearly there, and for Michael doing that production it was quite clearly there, and I hope it's quite clearly there, but a lot of people reading this book seem to be young: it seems to be a younger person's book: young people seem to go for it in a big way. [*Michael Boyd, founding Artistic Director of the Tron Theatre Glasgow, adapted* Trick *for the stage, and it was performed in Glasgow, London and Toronto. He is now Artistic Director of the RSC*]

IM   Anorexics go for it in a big way. (L) Bulimics ditto, I have to tell you.

JG   I see. It's possibly because they tend to be younger persons' illnesses.

Maybe that's why I associate it with the younger reader. They often
don't see the positivity at the end.

IM No. I've started teaching *Foreign Parts* to third year, and *Trick* to
fourth year, because I think even the one extra year they've got helps
them not to be the 'young person' reading it. It's all very subtle: it's
difficult to pin down. But they all hate Tony!

JG (L) Do they? Joy even says, look, Tony's a nice man. She says that
herself.

IM Absolutely hate him. Because – well, he's pretty loathsome, actually.

JG Well yeah. He's trying in his own way.

IM 'You should have said more'; 'why didn't you?' after he's had sex with
her and she's crying.

JG Yes, he's pretty selfish, but he's making an effort in the way he can;
it's just that the way he can's not very admirable, possibly.

IM This is very true.

JG Even he's making an effort for her. I don't think anybody is being
lousy to Joy.

IM Were you conscious, when you were writing *Clara*, that it was going
to be a lot bigger than the others?

JG I became conscious of it. Writing that book was an extraordinarily
painful, slow business. I'm a painfully slow writer, but that was just
unbelievable; painful and slow. At one stage I said, if I hit page 260
I'm stopping: that'll be fine, that'll do. Then I reached page 260, and
realised that they hadn't been long married, so I thought you can't
stop here. So I thought okay, I'll speed it up now. To me a book
moves at the speed it moves at. I don't know how some people can
begin novels – apparently some people do – saying, this is going to
be a 260 page this, that and the next thing; it'll take me a year and
a half to write, and it will be with you by. . . They can give you
delivery dates: they can give you word counts. That's a totally different mentality from mine. It takes its time: it does what it feels like:
it's like the book's in charge and I'm not. And I just get allowed to
work at the chalk-face: I get allowed to chisel and chip away, but the
book itself knows the shape it's going to be and the size it's going to
be, and I'm just allowed to keep cutting at the stone.

IM But you don't necessarily know the size it's going to be? I noticed
that, both when you spoke to us at Aberdeen Ottakars, and when you
spoke to that lady for the *Edinburgh Review* [*Cristie Leigh March and
Janice Galloway*, ER *Issue 101, pages 85-98*], when you were in the

middle of writing it, you started off by talking about Clara's whole
life, and what happened to her, and how all those years after Robert
died, how she had to work, how she supported her children and her
children's children, and one of her children died in an asylum.

JG One of them died in Colditz, which at the time was a mental asylum.

IM Yes. But none of that comes into the novel as we have it, and I
wondered whether at one stage maybe you thought it might?

JG At one stage I thought it might, and then I'd always had the idea of
basing the novel on *Frauen Liebe und Leben* ['*Woman's Love and Life*'].
And the Chamisso text for the Schumann song cycle *Frauen Liebe*
begins when the woman who is singing the song meets the object of
her affection, the man who'll become her husband and the father of
her child or children: '*Seit ich ihn gesehen*', When I first laid eyes on
you'. A woman's life begins when she first lays eyes on the man she
loves, and it finishes when he dies: '*Nun hast du mir den ersten Schmerz
getan*': 'Now for the first time, you have caused me pain'. That is
where her life ends. And it occurred to me how the chapters were
going to work out – I knew there were going to be eight chapters.
At the time I did not know they were going to be so vast, (L) I knew
there were going to be eight chapters, which could be of indeterminate length, because there are eight songs, and each of the eight
chapters was going to be called after them. Then what I had to do
was find what I thought were proportions of the life that would fit
within that heading, giving the name of the song a completely different resonance to the resonance it had in the song cycle – if indeed
anybody knew it: it should be possible to read it and not know the
song cycle from a hole in the wall!

IM It works; I assure you it works!

JG That's fine. Again, this is the private joke behind it: this is the thing
that keeps me going. Nobody else needs to know it. (L) Knowing
what that means in the song, it's just a song about seeing someone
for the first time, feeling his heart swell for the first time, and what
that refers to is actually her father's hand in her life, and then you
move on to the second one. And it should have been possible to do
the whole life like that, and find out, partly serendipitously, where
the divides were going to come for the songs, and then chisel the
chapters to fit that title. Then I discovered how slowly and labori-
ously I was going through that life, and how much the detail of it
fascinated me, as opposed to the big shapes. The big shapes are

certainly there, I hope, but I didn't want to just have the big shapes. Something had to give. Either there had to be fewer big shapes so I could do more details, or I was going to have to concentrate on the big shapes alone. I've got a great love of detail, lists, tiny little things that are remembered or happening in the background, and I wanted them. I thought, it will end, then, where the song cycle ends. It will end with his death, and somehow I will need to imply there is a forty-year widowhood stretching out during which she popularises his music and the rest of them are carried by herself, which is what the roads at the end are meant to symbolise: they're all running into this place and also running back out of this place. The rest of her life was touring: the rest of her life was popularising his music.

I couldn't do what I initially thought I was going to do which was, where the book begins, a sort of pre-chapter, she's getting ready for the funeral, which is extraordinarily like getting ready for a concert, putting on the black, and waiting till the people come and get you, and take you out to perform. At a funeral, if you're the widow, you're certainly performing. People watch you.

And I had in mind also the extraordinary scenes – I went to Dallas two years ago, and went to the Kennedy Museum, and watched some extraordinary footage of Jacqueline Kennedy at that funeral, where she's certainly performing, and making the children perform – harrowing, utterly harrowing – and I had that in my head, looking at Clara putting on the outfit and knowing this was what she was going to have to do, that was for a performance. That *was* meant to come back at the end, and take you right through to Robert being buried, where the influence of the forty years to come could have been much stronger. But I chose to finish it where I did simply because I didn't want to hammer that home in any way. I wanted it to be a book that was available to the general reader. I'm not writing for music scholars: I'm not writing for people who know the esoteric ins and outs of the Schumanns' lives: I'm not necessarily writing for academic experts on *Frauen Liebe*: people who've spent a lifetime studying that song cycle: it would be nice if they could get something from it.

But who I'm writing for continually, I'm very clear now, I was never sure, I know I want to write for just people who're interested in people, the general reader. I have a high opinion of the so-called general reader, and that's who I want to write for, and I thought, all this is hammering something on that people don't need to know. It is clear enough from the roads reaching out, that she's going on a long time. That is sufficient, and I don't need to do the funeral; I don't need to do the fact that he was on unconsecrated ground; a legal lunatic.

IM   That is perfectly fine: but I wondered whether there might be a sequel.

JG   At the moment, that makes me want to jump out of a window. The very idea! (L) It appears to have occurred to a couple of other people as well. I certainly wouldn't put it totally out of the picture, but the idea of having to immerse myself in Clara Schumann again for another six years is like trying to draw my intestines down my nose with a crochet hook! (L) At the moment there are no plans in that direction.

IM   Yes. And Clara's later life can be read as saintly heroism. And I just thought, it obviously is heroism, her next forty years, it's extraordinary. I get so angry with a woman like Caitlin Thomas, Dylan Thomas's widow, who called her autobiography, *Left-Over Life to Kill*. He was dead: that was the end: there was nothing more. Clara wouldn't have put up with that for a minute. Of course something had died in her when Robert died, but she had left-over life to *live*.

JG   She had stuff to do.

IM   She had left-over life to work, and she was such a strong worker. I'd quite like to read even a short story? (L)

JG   That's my old pattern, I'm interested in that person so now I'll write some more stuff and see where it goes. I might. The thought of the research! But I might. There's Brahms. Brahms just appears at the end as a boy – all of Brahms' life is still to go. And Liszt's most astonishing transformation into priest, (L) the naughty boy, and Wagner, Wagner was still to turn into a serious composer: at the moment he's a joke, and nobody likes him very much, and he's a pain in the arse, a difficult, horrible man. And there are all sorts of directions that could come from it, but in a way I'd be worried it would be more of the same. I admire survival, and I admire people with life to live, the books are all about that in some ways, about this idea of endurance and keeping going, and even when you feel lousy you must find stuff to do, because damn it to hell, you *are* only here a short time, and you should do something – it's a social duty, almost, to do something constructive with this.

[Tape 2: 23/7/02. Personnel as before.]

IM I want to start today by asking Janice about what we can call her non-fiction, the things she's done out of the line of fiction, and very often with collaborators, in particular Anne Bevan the artist and Sally Beamish the composer.

JG The first thing is that I like collaboration. You have more fun with more people, in my opinion, and it's nice to work with people. I think that's why the work looks different. I'm quite interested to hear you saying it's not fictional: I regard everything as fiction. I regard the things that look like poems in the *Pipelines* collaboration as fiction. [*Anne Bevan:* Pipelines, *with Janice Galloway, The Fruitmarket Gallery, Edinburgh, 2000.*] Otherwise I guess I couldn't write them: I've got a self-consciousness about anything else.

IM Okay: they're all fiction!

JG It's like the form thing again; when I think in terms of a form, I feel very restricted, whereas fiction seems to me such an open word. So it's a form of self-deception, I suppose, but it's intriguing to hear it described in that way. The *Pipelines* collaboration I think would be the first formal thing I did in collaboration. Anne Bevan is a sculptor, an Orcadian. I had seen some of her work before, on holiday in Orkney, and had bought a postcard of one of her sculptures, which I had next to the computer in my workroom. I was quite surprised to get a letter from Anne just saying, could we work on something together? This is what I have in mind. I immediately wrote back, saying, I've seen some of your stuff; in fact I've got the postcard sitting right next to me now. Let's meet up and talk about it. And it just worked from there on in. I think I'm very lucky, in that the two people I have collaborated most with I get on with very well. I don't think it would be possible to collaborate with someone I didn't feel on a wavelength with, because I need to be with them, I need them sitting in the same room as me, at least at some stages, so we can talk, we can have a laugh. If you can share humour with someone, if you can share a laugh with someone, if you can share an empathy in that way with someone, if someone can feel at liberty to come in and say, I had a fight with my boyfriend last night and this is how I'm feeling this morning, you've got a place to begin work from. You've got a share of something together, and you can trust that

person more, somehow. It's an extraordinarily vulnerable-ising thing
to do, to show unfinished work to someone, and say, if you think it's
crap I'll start again. It must make them feel extraordinarily awkward
– I know I do, if Anne shows me something she's half way through:
I don't know what to think at this stage.

IM Is it significant that these are both women?

JG I don't know. Sally was more or less self-selecting. [*Sally Beamish
    wrote the music and Galloway the libretto for* Monster, *an opera about
    Mary Shelley, the author of* Frankenstein, *which had its premiere on
    28 February, 2002, with Scottish Opera*] No other composer has
    offered: Alasdair Nicolson has worked on material of mine: there's
    a song cycle called 'Five Card Trick', which is songs taken from *The
    Trick is to Keep Breathing*, which I've heard only once, and on a tape,
    because I wasn't able to make it to the performance in Perth that it
    had [*1994*]. I'm sure I could have worked with Alasdair. But Alasdair
    is a very reserved person, and also lives very far away, so it wasn't
    possible for us to be in the same room. I sent him words and he set
    them.[*Nicolson is based in London.*]

    The two women I've collaborated with seem to be keen to get into
    the same room with me, to talk to me, to share a joke, to share a glass
    of wine, and talk about what we're going to do, and I've found that
    more amenable. Whether or not, social set-ups being the way they
    are, it's a more difficult thing for a man to do or feel relaxed with,
    whether or not it's just not feasible because the men I've worked with
    have always lived far away – how much of an accident that is, I don't
    know – it seems to be accidental. But one never knows what one is
    engineering subconsciously.

    Certainly Anne was the one who wrote to me, and I was delighted
    to hear from her. We met up, discovered that we got on, and thought,
    well that's a good sign. If we can get on at a social level, we can
    probably get on at a work level: our work empathies may not be too
    far away. And she'd read something of mine; I had seen something
    of hers. We both responded to the work of the other: it seemed a good
    idea. Her idea basically – it's called *Pipelines* because I called it that:
    Anne called it *Undercovered* – and what she wanted to look at was the
    water supply that runs from the Borders of Scotland to Edinburgh.
    She's Orcadian, but she's lived in Edinburgh for a great number of
    years. I've never lived in Edinburgh; I know bugger all about the
    Borders. (L) It just struck me, well, this is Anne's baby, this is Anne's

idea. And *what* a break for a novelist! For someone who has total control over the material, and the only collaborator you have is the material itself, is the subconscious, that's the only thing that can push or divert you or your mood when you wake up. The weather can sometimes help: but you're at the mercy of so many things, and appear to have to control the whole show yourself. I can't tell you what a relief it is, to get into a room with somebody else, who is so clear-thinking as Anne Bevan. And who says, we're going to do this, this, this, this and this; we're going to do it in that order, (L) and you just say, yes. And you go along with it, and your eyes get opened. You don't even have to find the material: she goes out and she finds what she's interested in, and she shows it to you. It's a wonderful balance that Anne has of certitude and generosity. She knows what she's interested in; she knows what she wants to do, and she'll give it to you. She doesn't put her arm round it like the school homework so you'll not see what she's done: she'll show it to you and say, this is what I really fancy doing: how do you like it? And you get to walk into what interests her. That was wonderful, and I've worked with Anne three times since, and I feel I could work endlessly with Anne, because of that generosity and that clear-sightedness.

IM When you've worked with her three times since, have you published anything?

JG Nothing's been published in book form, except *Pipelines*. How we worked tended to be very come and go. She took me down – again, I wouldn't have dreamt of doing this – a stay-at-home novelist wearing usually high heels, it's highly unlike me to put on a hard hat and want to go down a ladder and see what sewers look like. (L) How many people do that? Apparently sculptors do! It's quite normal in their world, and it was very energising to be taken into that environment, feel so totally thrown into something, and have to respond. You don't have to respond in a situation that's very alien to you; you just begin responding anyway. And I showed her the words I'd come up with; we simply talked through the ideas I'd come up with: she said, oh, it's funny you should say that, because I've already thought of doing this. And the points of coincidence we merely deliberately veered towards. The points of non-convergence were maximised as well, because you need that vivid contrast. We got together regularly. The blessing of the Internet is that she could send me J-peg files: she could send me moving pictures, even little videos of the stuff she was doing as she was doing it. So we could collaborate even when we were not in each other's company.

IM So it really couldn't have happened before it happened? Ten or fifteen years before you were setting about it, it would have been too impractical.

JG Unless one or other of us had more time to spend a great deal of time on the train. It would have needed to be me, because the word person has to carry fewer materials. But because I've got a wee boy to look after, the amount of time I can spend ferrying to and from Edinburgh on the train is minimal. Anne couldn't do it, because she had all her materials in her studio where it was, so that was the solution we found. I think one of the great things about that is it frees up women with kids to get involved in proper collaboration. If you wait until the kids have gone to bed, you've got that stretch of time. The phone is not going to ring; you can have a genuine, real time conversation with somebody, typing, or you can get on the phone, and when you get off the phone, what you can do is you can send files to each other. And that was again partly how Sally Beamish and I were able to work. She has three children, she lives out in the middle of the country: she stays just outside Aberfoyle.

IM How did you come across her?

JG Ah! For my sins, I used to be a music critic, for *The Glasgow Herald, The Observer, Scotland on Sunday* – it's such a long time ago, and I'm so embarassed by the tag thing. A horrific experience in some ways. Michael Tumelty was kind enough to allow me to flex wings in that direction. I suppose it gave me a certain confidence that I could write fast if I wanted to: you'd to turn in the reviews on the night. And the first thing I heard of Sally Beamish's was the *Magnificat*. Now I am not a person of a conventional religious bent in any way shape or form. Sally is profoundly English Catholic, and I wouldn't have thought our empathies would have been too terrific, simply from knowing that: that seems to be a fundamental difference. Actually, it's not that fundamental, because one of the things that women with kids do is talk about the kids. (L) So we found we actually had a lot to talk about when we met up. I can make her laugh: she can make me laugh. That's such an indicator of capacity to get on with someone, the ability to make them laugh, and the ability to laugh at what they find funny. We got on very well. I always thought at one stage – I had trained in music, a little bit at university, and significantly at school, and had played all sorts of *instruments*, and had sung at one time, and composed in a very desultory kind of way myself – I'd thought, one day we'll do something. Again it was Sally who energised it: I seem to be shy of approaching people, or simply it doesn't occur to me; maybe I don't have the imagination, or feel I haven't time to do it seriously. Whatever reason, it seems to be the other people who approach me, and thank goodness for that. And Sally said to me, could you write us a text for The Chamber Group of Scotland, about four women composers. And it was very straight down the line; it was about the lives of four women composers, and pieces of the four women's music. [*The text of this event, staged at Mayfest 1995, is now available on the website.*] And we enjoyed that so much – well, I enjoyed it once it was written; it was a complete bloody nightmare trying to write it, and the amount of research was unbelievable – once we'd done that, we wrote a song cycle based on the life of Clara Schumann, which was a precursor, away before the novel, before I'd even thought I would write a novel about that woman. And eventually we wrote a piece for the Scottish Chamber Orchestra, who paired us together because we had worked before, and then I wrote the opera libretto for Sally [*For* Monster, *first performed 28 February 2002*]. And as with Anne, a high degree of active collaboration. I'm not remotely interested in the phonecall that says would you write us some words and send us the words and then leave us alone, and we'll do something with your words, and we'll give you an invitation, and you can come and see what we've done with them at the end. That doesn't interest me. There's no companionship, there's no exchange of ideas; there's none of the things I want to escape from in my other job, which is as a solo novelist. What interests me about collaboration is to get out of that, and bounce ideas off another individual, and find yourself and your own ideas energised, and sometimes completely turned over, to find how you prioritise shaken a bit, and when you shake something, usually bits come down, you shake a tree and some leaves come down, and some fruit if you're very lucky will come down, and you've got more things than you suspected that you would have before to work with. Collaboration, to me, is extraordinarily freeing, enlivening, and something I very much want to do. I'd like to do more of it with the two women I've already done it with, but I'd like to broaden it out and do more of it.

IM   Can you remember who thought of *Monster* first?

JG   The idea for the opera? Well, that was . . . Well, who thought about
     an opera was clearly Scottish Opera: somebody has to come to you
     in this day and age: nobody in their right mind sits down and writes
     an opera, and then starts hawking it round opera companies, saying,
     do you fancy putting this on? It doesn't work like that. Music is an
     incredibly old-fashioned world. I became sharply aware of that
     during when we were working on *Monster*, dealing with musicians
     and with music institutions again. They're still raddled with a
     nineteenth-century mentality and thinking. It's a very hierarchical
     world; it's very much you still take the apprentice on – we talked
     about that yesterday with composing. Even the composition of an
     orchestra has them arranged in desks, and the back desks don't get
     to do anything without the agreement of the desks in front. It's
     extraordinarily hierarchical. And when it comes to composers, the
     commission system, as it was in the eighteenth and nineteenth
     centuries, is still very much the norm, because of the huge expense
     of putting on something like an opera. You can't just write a piece
     for orchestra, and somewhere an orchestra will materialise. Someone
     has to buy that orchestra in, and pay them. Rehearsal time has to be
     found; a space has to be found; 'mike-ing' has to be found; a
     conductor has to be found; a concert hall has to be found; tickets have
     to be printed – it's *vastly* expensive. And because of that, partly
     because of the set up of how music operates in the way it gets to the
     public, and because of the grand-scale thing, which is largely
     nineteenth-century, and which kept it in the secure grip of a kind of
     ruling class when they were in danger of losing it to the small chamber
     concert, these big, grandiose concerts have to be commissioned. And
     a composer cannot simply say, I feel I've got it in me to write an opera;
     I want to do one: that's not going to work. Somebody has to say, we
     are giving you the chance. And I was astounded at how grateful Sally
     Beamish was expected to feel at being given the chance. Whereas in
     the literary world, because it's so self-driven, because it's so artist-
     driven, I was quite appalled by the way she was expected to almost
     wear livery at times.

IM   But did they say, you can write an opera, or, you can write an opera
     about Mary Shelley and Frankenstein?

JG   They said, you may write the opera. Now once someone has said, you
     may write the opera, she has to find a librettist. She was already

working with a very fine playwright called David Pownall, and approached David first. Scottish Opera were not interested in David's idea. Then she said, I have worked with Janice: maybe we could do something. They seemed to be interested in that, but who can tell how these things work? Again they need to approve the idea. And she came to me, and we sat on the floor, with a bottle of wine, saying, I dunno; what do you think? For a substantial length of time. (L) And then she said, the one thing I'm sure about is I want to write about grief and losing a child. She came with that idea. That's what I want to do: I feel I've got something to say. And I said . . . Mary Shelley. We'd had a few glasses of wine: you don't know where things come from, even if you're stone cold sober. And I wasn't far off stone cold sober, it's just that kind of ease you get into, with expressing things you otherwise wouldn't say – Mary Shelley came out my mouth. I've never really questioned where that came from, just knowing a little bit about the story, and about the loss of the baby. She said great, I don't know much about it: she wrote *Frankenstein*. I believe we both watched Kenneth Branagh's *Frankenstein* movie – oh, how we laughed! (L) And she said, yeah, I think we can work with this. She went to them, said it's going to be about Mary Shelley, and they said, oh, she wrote *Frankenstein* – the very mention of the word *Frankenstein* was what sold that opera to those people, I think. It was Mary Shelley herself who sold it, because it wasn't anything remotely approaching an idea at that time.

IM   And is there, or is there going to be, any form of CD or video?

JG   I doubt it. I *think* they made a video, but Scottish Opera are extraordinarily protective of what belongs to them: they make videos for their own archives, but not for general release. BBC videoed some of it for a programme they put together, which has been networked, and there is a CD recording of it available at the BBC, but again that is BBC property. I can't see it being recorded in a hurry, which I think is a great shame, because the staging of it I don't think worked. That doesn't mean to say that I think the director was a poor director; I just think he was the wrong choice: in many ways Mike McCarthy is a good director, but I don't think he was the right choice for this. And we ended up with a production that nobody was particularly happy with. Mike wasn't very at ease with it; the designer wasn't very at ease; the lighting engineer wasn't very at ease; and Sally and I were profoundly ill at ease with what ended up happening. But the way that opera seems to work, or the way that Scottish Opera in particular seemed to work, is that everyone is meant to stay in separate boxes, and not talk to each other. And that's not at all what any of us had wanted. I think Mike very much wanted to come to us and say, what would you like here? Sally in particular had *very* particular ideas about how she would like the thing staged, and was never able to effect that. And we ended up with an incredibly uneasy compromise, and I think it came across: I don't think it was a satisfactory production. That really shakes your confidence a lot, and you think, is it just the piece that doesn't work, and the two of us sat and listened to the radio version, and when we couldn't see the production, we couldn't see part of the distraction the production was, the both of us agreed – and we're not easy people to satisfy about our own work – that we think it actually works as a piece. We're sure it works as a piece, it just didn't work in that form.

So it would be lovely, especially to have a sound version of it, where I think it works best, and at some later stage, let a different imagination loose on it, and possibly turn it into something different. We had interest in making it into an opera-film, but I think opera-film is such a rare taste, and such a rarefied taste, a lot of people even who enjoy opera would not watch it in a film, because the excitement is the live thing, that they had to be absolutely sure that they were on to a dead cert, and Sally and I both had to be honest, and say, well, we don't think this is necessarily the production. So they re-thought, and I think wisely in the end pulled back from making a film of it. If we get the chance to do it again, I'd love it, but that again reflects the way both of us like to work: we wanted to work in collaboration with the director. And that's just not how Scottish Opera do things. It was just very unfortunate how the whole thing fell out for all sides; nobody ended up very happy with how the thing worked out. But it was a great opportunity to work with singers; a great opportunity to work with an orchestra, and I can't tell you what pleasure that was. So a very mixed experience; I wouldn't say it was a negative experience, but I'd *love* to see somebody else having a crack at it. It's very rare in contemporary music, to give someone a second bite at the cherry. When I think of the pressure that poor Sally Beamish is under; it has to cut ice one time, and usually on one hearing: when the critics come is first night; that's it! And something that's taken her two or three years to put together – minds are made up like that!

With a book, I'm very fortunate. People can return to it; people can make up their own minds: it's there on the shelves, if people want to come back and buy it. Sally, she has to make an impression first time out, or that piece may never be heard again. It's like me writing a novel on spec, a publisher might be interested. One does that with a first novel, – or one used to! I'm forgetting, (L) times have changed *very* drastically in Scotland! People can get advances for first novels, (L) which was unheard of twenty years ago in Scotland in particular. It was generally taken for granted we didn't really have writers, we had people who did it part time, and sometimes if they were very lucky, they got a book into print. People can do that now. Sal can't do that.

IM   But you are pursuing the next idea with Anne Bevan, and as I recall, it's your turn to choose what you're doing.

JG   Oh yes. *My* turn. And just out of sheer badness, I think. She had taken me down these tunnels and pipes and into outlandish places, and in a way it was as opposite as I could get! It was so opposite it was a mirror image. I decided we would go for gynaecological implements, and imply different tunnels entirely. And she was very wary; (L) she was very wary indeed to begin with. Anne is so external, out there, flamboyant, out into the world, open, energetic, whereas I'm much quieter, much more introspective, darker, I think, in general, and I think she felt a kind of strange cloy of being drawn in to – much the same as I felt very strange going down these tunnels and sewers and lord knows what all. I think she found it very strange to be drawn into the territory I felt at home with. You enter that territory and let it shock you. [*In January 2002 Galloway was awarded a Scottish Arts Council Creative Scotland Award to work on a collaboration with visual artist Anne Bevan. The project to incorporate text and sculpture, 'throwing a new perspective on the medical processes surrounding women,' it resulted in an exhibition at the Hunterian Museum in Glasgow in 2004, and the book,* Rosengarten, *by Janice Galloway and Anne Bevan, platform projects, 2004.*] She's taken very much to it now, but we're having extraordinary trouble – ah ha! Medicine seems to be quite nineteenth century. The permissions! We can't get permissions to get into obstetric wards! This is private information; it's a private subject. It's very cloaked. Even when we'd explained who we are and even when we'd got a letter from our patron, as it were, saying this is a bona fide project and they're not just random nutters, looking for cheap thrills: let them in: let them see the equipment: it's a hellish uphill struggle. So we've got almost nowhere, at the moment. I think it's just the secrecy of information: it tends to work that way with medicine. I have fought very hard to acquire this rather abstract esoteric information, and I'm damned if I'm going to let it go this easily. (L) We'll get round it somehow.

IM Right. New tack: how important is it when you put together *Blood* and *Where You Find It* to theme the book?

JG Not at all.

IM So it's the publisher who announces, this is a book about love? You just count the stories and see if there's enough for a book?

JG Yeah, the first time I did: with *Blood* it was just there was enough. The book was very well received: a lot of people said good things about it. People said perceptive good things about it, which is very pleasing. At the same time, a number of people said, and rightly so, there's no theme in this book. I didn't see what the theme thing was meant to be about. That seems to me to be a marketing ploy.

IM I think it was jackets and things I got this notion from.

JG Aye. I don't know how much of a myth it is, but publishers tell you till they're blue in the face, don't write short stories; short stories don't sell. And I think what they're trying to do, if they theme the thing, it somehow sounds more like a novel chopped up into wee bits. It's unified somehow. Don't worry. It's not really short stories. Robin Robertson, who's my publisher at Cape, and has been for thirteen years now, is very generous, in that he doesn't suggest themes; he doesn't push ideas at me, he doesn't even push me to finish things, which I believe is very rare in a publisher. (L) He knows he's on a hiding to nothing, if he tries to push me, because stuff just finishes when it finishes, and he knows that. Also because he's a poet, and a very fine poet himself, I think he has more insight into the creative process than many publishers do. You're not entirely in charge: although it looks as though you are. A thing takes its own time. So he didn't suggest, make it about something, but it was quite clear to me when the stories for *Where You Find It* were coming up, he said, are you likely to have a theme? I said, what do you think? Possibly because that had been at the back of my head, that question, many of them did seem to be love-stories of one kind or another. That said, what is not at some level about love in some shape or form?

IM   What a wonderful cover it did produce, with the heart-shaped sand-
     wiches!

JG   It's great when the book-designer has actually read the damned thing.
     You get some people who say, what's it about? And then cobble
     something together. I think it was a good cover.

IM   You mention Robin Robertson, the shadowy godfather of modern
     Scottish literature. (L) What about agent? What sort of relationship
     do you have, agentwise?

JG   I'm very, very, very fond of Derek Johns, my agent. I knew I needed
     to have one, because I was so intent on not dealing with the money
     when I first started. It made me nervous, and if people said, what do
     you expect for this? I had no idea, it was just so alien. Again, having
     come from a background where you applied for a job and you looked
     at the rate of pay, I was under the impression people suggested to
     you, and if they didn't, I was flummoxed, and felt, in that way you
     do, when you begin being freelance, almost embarassed asking for
     money. I found it sticky and difficult; I knew I would have to get over
     it, but suspected I wouldn't get over it quickly enough, and an agent
     might be the best way to do this. A friend of James Kelman's and
     Jeff Torrington's was Cathy Boyd, and Cathy Boyd wanted a crack
     at agenting, because she knew a fair old handful of Scottish authors,
     and more seemed to be appearing – they were popping up like weeds
     at the time. Or people were becoming more aware of the fact that
     people who'd been there for a long time were in fact there. And Cathy
     wished to act as agent for them, because there was no agent living
     in Scotland at the time: there was no such thing. One had to find one
     in London, often they hadn't read the work; she was aware that
     Scottish taste in writing can be very different to English taste in
     writing, and saw that some of these people would not be represented
     otherwise. And had a go at it. I'm not sure whether her heart was in
     it, but I admire the fact that she had a go at it. [*Elsewhere, Galloway
     refers to Cathy Boyd, widow of playwright Eddie Boyd, as Cathy
     Thomson.*] But dealing with London publishers, when she lived so far
     away, when she was out of that circuit of agent talk, when she was
     out of that circuit of literary lunches and dinners, where a lot of the
     whisper campaign and the who's in the know, and who knows what,
     and who knows who got what for what book, which gives you a scale
     on which to judge your own clients, she was outside of that, and it
     must have been extraordinarily difficult for her. Also, she sounded

completely different to any other agent, that anybody in London I
think had heard. Very crackly, bark in the throat voice, Cathy.
Everyone liked her certainly, but I don't think she was taken as
seriously as perhaps she should have been, partly because of the
distance, partly because people knew she wasn't on such a sure
footing, hadn't been part of the background. Cathy did a sterling job
for a wee while, but it got a bit too much, understandably. She was
first representative for Alan Warner, for Duncan McLean, for me,
for Jim, for Jeff Torrington, for Tom Leonard – an extraordinary
group of people. And we all had a meeting at Jeff Torrington's house;
Margaret made us soup; and we all sat round the table eating our soup
and Cathy said, I just cannae do it any more: what do yous want to
do? And we decided to disperse at that point, more or less. It had been
wonderful having Cathy as the lifeline, saying Alan's working on this;
we knew what each other were doing: that was nice, and we were
going to lose that, which was quite scary. At the same time, there
comes a stage when you have to do that, it was like adolescence was
finishing, and we were all off now, we were all going off out to proper
work. (L) And we wouldn't necessarily know what the others were
doing. We still had the same publisher, who was Robin Robertson.
So I spoke to Peter Kravitz, the sainted Peter Kravitz, who had been
my first publisher at Polygon, God bless Peter Kravitz! So many
people would not have the confidence to keep writing, if it hadn't for
Peter, and wouldn't have been published for the first time, if it hadn't
been for Peter. And I would just trust him with anything, anything
literary to do with my life at all.

Who do I need? I asked him. He said, I met an awfully nice man
last month. A lot of agents are kind of sharky; they don't contact you
very often; I think this is just a good man. You need to speak to him.
Derek was prepared to come to Scotland to speak to me, which at
the time, again, was kind of outlandish; one was expected (L) to go
to London and be grateful! If anybody was prepared to give you the
time of day. I said, how often are you prepared to come to Scotland?
I guarantee I'll come twice a year: I'll probably come more than that,
and I can certainly phone you once a fortnight. I said, make it once
a week and you're on. And Derek has phoned me once a week. I have
since learned through speaking to other writers in other countries,
English writers, Irish writers, that an agent contacts them when they
haven't heard from them for a while to see if they're working on a

book: then gives them a lot of attention when the book is coming out, kind of hand-holding stage, and then melts again. I couldnae be doing with that! I need somebody to pass the time of day with, to share a joke with, feel grounded with, and certainly I would call Derek a friend of mine. I need somebody who's my friend, because otherwise it's a vulnerable thing to say to someone, I'm working on this idea, but I don't know if it's stupid: what do you think? You need to trust the answer.

IM So when does he see what you've written?

JG When it's finished, and not before. Almost nobody sees stuff before it's finished, unless it's my collaborators. I would trust another artist to work with, because one has to be flexible, and you have to change it; you have to stay in that plasticine stage for a while. But you can't ask an agent to look at a piece of half-finished work and tell you if it's any good: that's too much. You're asking for a literary judgment there. Both the gentlemen who look after the publishing and agenting side of my life are friends, people of whom I'm very fond.

IM You have a book that is now coming out in November, partly inspired by young James.

JG It was Hamish Whyte, whom I've known for yonks and yonks. I was the first female editor of the ASLS's *New Writing Scotland* with him. Hamish is just such a sweetheart. He nursed me through the difficulty of trying to read all these scripts. Again, very easy to collaborate with, on what was going into the book. But Hamish is also a poet, and publishes: he's Eddie Morgan's publisher, and publishes poetry by lots of people, and has been first time publisher for lots of people who've gone on to other things. And he does beautiful wee books with the Mariscat Press. And every time he was putting an anthology together, he'd ring up and say, you want to give us a poem? No. But he's never given up. It must be fifteen years I've known Hamish: that's unbelievable. He kept saying, I know you've got them; I know you've got them. And eventually I think got me on a weak spot: I think it was survivors' poetry he wanted something. And a weak spot for me is always like a charity asking what seems to be a very reasonable question, have you got a piece lying about that's never been published, and we'll put it in our book and it'll help to sell the book. You feel such a bloody mean-minded person, saying, No! Again, I don't think of them as poems; I think of them as prose that breaks in funny places, or, different ways to use language, or as experiments on the way to poetry. This is not because I disrespect poetry; it's possibly because I've too much respect for poetry, or because I'm scared of it: I don't know. But they seem to me to be prose-ish pieces and eventually I accumulated enough, partly on commission: there were things lying about from ages ago. But also, Fruit Market Gallery had asked me to write something for their exhibition which was about children and parenting, and what seemed to come out was discontinuous sentences. Bookworks, a wonderful organization in London who continually pair sculpture, visual art and words, had asked me to do something ages ago and what came out was very fractured, very broken. I think I was responding to the idea of visual art and making it visually interesting, as well as attempting to mean something. I put those together: there are pieces like 'Six Horses', which occasionally just come out as a kind of fractured, prosey poetry kind of mish-mash. [*First published in* Where You Find It, *1996*] And he said, well, I would like to do them. And eventually he kind of persuaded me. And that's coming out in November. I'm not quite sure how I feel about this. I'm apprehensive, for some reason, about this book, I think because they're such unclassified and unclassifiable pieces, it's such a mixed bag. I've no idea what the reaction if any to it will be. [boy book see, *Mariscat Press, 2002*]

IM   There may be very little, of course, because a wee book such as you describe might easily not get reviewed.

JG   A bit like *Pipelines*. That was the first book that I'd had words in for something like five years, and I was not apprehensive about it coming out, because I thought, oh, this counts as visual art: nobody will give a tuppenny damn. It's amazing what the press choose to be interested in and what they choose not to be interested in. (L) It was quite a relief, bringing that out and thinking, well this is just for me and Anne, and the people who'll buy it. And I don't have to confront that bloody, you know, that damnable wall of critical reaction. You sometimes feel like you're struggling over it. It sometimes can give you a boost, but either way, it's not part of what you wrote the thing for. It was nice to get that out the way with that one and just enjoy it for what it was. This one might be the same. I don't imagine there'll be a huge amount of interest or uptake in it, apart from people who have a scholarly interest.

IM   I don't know where I got this – I think it was you, in Aberdeen, the time before last, you mentioned this forthcoming book, and you seemed to connect it to James.

JG   There's a bit called 'boy book see', which is quite definitely about him.

IM   That's right; that's the thing you were telling us about. I just ask about that because of that amazing, splendid piece you wrote about your chosen year, 1992, when you were pregnant.

JG   We're getting into territory I normally don't talk about, for superstitious reasons. But the next novel is probably going to be about children. This is just a wee oddity.

IM   Okay. Well, 'wee oddity' is something *Clara* is not. I'm good at links today! I just want you to talk about it, but you dropped a line in Aberdeen, again, at Ottakars, about a relationship it had to Scotland. I don't know how serious or how important this was; you were talking about Scotland being off-centre, as it were, and Clara's world being off the musical centre. Is that important?

JG   It's not wildly important. But it's extraordinary how there is still – Scotland is a mass of fucking contradictions kind of country – some of the finest writers in Britain live in Scotland at the moment, and I think the populace in general, certainly the academic population I've come across, seem interested and enthused by this: but there seems to be in general an undercurrent of press reaction that is almost embarrassed by the fact that we have this seam of fine writing and enthusiasm, and indeed a seam of fine visual art, and a rich seam of fine contemporary composers as well. There's a kind of embarrassment about it, as though – the performer's anxiety – at any moment the whole country will be tapped on the shoulder and told, it's a scam you've been getting away with, and I hope you're bloody ashamed of yourself for trying to do this! World class, my arse! Get off the stage! There's a strange embarrassment about the fact that we're exhibiting ourselves in this unseemly fashion. (L) And swearing and things.

IM   The top thesis in our year this year by the top student was a study of how contemporary Scottish writers, yourself included, use the word cunt. I didn't manage to read it, because I was off, (L) but she came to see me when she was planning to do it, and you featured.

JG   Oh yes, doubtless. Whether or not that's a manifestation of the embarrassment, I don't know, but it sounds as if it's slightly more centred and at home with the idea. But one does find this strange

worry about the too big for the boots thing, and I guess – it dawned
on me, part of the way through writing *Clara*, I thought, oh shit,
somebody at some stage is going to say to me, what right have you
got to write about something that's not Scottish? Who do you think
you are, writing about something not Scottish? And I thought, well
I can see that's stupid; but why don't I ask myself the question, what
right have I got? And of course the answer that is there is what Ken
Hetherington gave me: that man opened up to me the very best of
the very best in his head, as to what music could offer, and said, this
is for you. I've never doubted since then that the very best of the very
best is there for me. I have been asked only once, at least only once
to my face, why on earth should you want to write about a dead
German: why should you not want to write about a Scottish composer? Well, there's no reason why I shouldn't want to; I just
happened to wish to do this: the impulse was there to do her. It's like
this argument that comes back periodically, they're always thrashing
the writers for something, by and large; why are our books all so
doomy and gloomy? Why are our books all about the working class
and leave out middle-class people? There's always this daft fucking
cycle one has to go round and establish somehow that writers aren't
quite doing what we'd like them to do. (L) Ye cannae tell writers what
tae do: it's no like plumbin': ye cannae say, this is the pipe that needs
fixed; could you fix it? (L) We're not the national plumbing service;
we're not national psychiatrists: we're not politicians. You write what
you want to write. You've only got to say what you've got to say. What
the country gets is the accumulated body of that work, what has come
out of being nourished in this country and being nourished by this
environment, or indeed not being nourished by it, which is also
something to address. You don't drive the material: the material
drives you. Clara Schumann seemed to self-select, in much the same
way that Mary Shelley seemed to self-select.

IM I don't have any problem at all here; I was just fascinated that you
made this remark.

JG I think that was partly where the remark came from, which was that
it was helpful to for example have been to London with Cathy Boyd,
whom I mentioned earlier, and experienced the reaction to Cathy's
voice at literary parties. It was terribly interesting and entertaining.
(L) It has been very entertaining or interesting since, to have people
for example phone me up, not knowing even, that I was a Scot, to

talk to me about the Clara Schumann book. And assume I was not the author. Because I came on first, they would ask to speak to Janice Galloway. I would say, I am, and you would hear this re-registering going on, almost as though it was mildly outlandish, that someone Scottish should choose to write about this. Therefore I have been made conscious of my country of origin, as indeed throughout my life at times I have been made conscious of my sex, suddenly, that people would not be expecting – when I went to Jordan, for example, the University of Jordan, I was more acutely aware of my gender than I had been for a long time in this country, because there were certain things it was not permissible for a woman to say on a public platform. I had a little induction course on what I could and couldn't say, and the British Council to their credit, made it quite clear that I would be treated with the respect that just 'an author' would be treated with, and they were to ignore the gender question, I would be permitted to say whatever I wished to say, and in the end I was not allowed to appear, because British Council said, she's not going to make guarantees. So I ended up not appearing. At times I would be made aware of my nationality; and being down south with Cathy was one of the things that helped me think of Clara Schumann going to Paris, which was then the centre of music – that's where you had to cut ice – and being laughed at because she had a heavy Leipzig accent, and her father had an even heavier one, and thinking, I know this one. There were times where that dislocation of being off-centre was genuinely useful. I don't think it's a major focus of the book at all, but it was one of these things I found helpful. I singled it out I think at the reading because at an earlier one someone had asked what it was legitimate for Scottish writers to write about. Then you ask what's it legitimate for women to write about; what's it legitimate for men to write about: writers are writers are writers.

IM But I so much recognised throughout *Clara* the woman's situation, between the domineering father and often the dominating husband; it just seemed to me that women's stories sometimes don't change because of the nationality.

JG No, they don't. The most powerful driving influence I think behind my perspective on the world or one of the overwhelming things that interests me is gender; how people treat people according to slight differences. Mental illness interests me because of that as well, the way one person will be treated one way, and another person will be treated another way, because of a presupposition about their mental state. Gender is a hard one to conceal. Colour interests me, but I feel such lack of authority and voice in that area; I think that's probably better left to people who are much more motivated at dealing with that thing from the inside. Religious difference interests me; but again because I'm not a religious person I wouldn't feel on a sure enough footing. I've been a woman all my life; I feel on a sure enough footing there. That's a territory where I can express that fascination about the way people get treated and about the responses they are likely to have, and what might be effective because of certain facets of how they appear in the world. And gender is one of these things.

IM   Yes; gender is a very important thing in all of your writing. It's more important, I think, than Scotland.

JG   Massively more important.

IM   Or class.

JG   Although class certainly is an interest. Again, that's to do with the fascination of the differences – I think it's register in the end that interests me more than anything else. If you want to level all this out. How people respond to how one appears. The one time Ken Hetherington said something that shocked me. He was an Englishman, Yorkshire, but he had a kind of flat accent; you couldn't tell where he was from. I remember him saying this girl had come to him wanting to play the trumpet. She was a lovely girl, how pretty she was. And then she opened her mouth. Gawd's trewth! I remember him saying, she had one of these really guttural Paisley accents. I remember being shocked by this; somehow this had made her less pretty! It had made her less pretty. I managed to link it in later life to Orwell – is it the Wigan Pier book? – talking about knowing perfectly well intellectually that the working classes don't smell, but actually, they do. (L) It's how he puts it. [The Road to Wigan Pier, *1937, section 7: 'Four frightful words which people nowadays are chary of uttering, but which were bandied about quite freely in my childhood. The words were:* The lower classes smell'.] You can know something intellectually but what's bred in the bone about certain class things, especially in this country, is very, very difficult to get rid of. I always had this residual reaction – I seem to have gotten rid of it through extraordinarily hard graft – if somebody told me they were a Catholic, suddenly it made them alien! It made them like a wee green man from outer space! Because they were the ones we chucked things over the wall at, we shouted 'Slugs' at, that was what was bred in the bone with me.

And through the application of hard graft I have managed to get rid of that, but it's extraordinary how many of them go deeper, and Orwell extremely nobly I think confessed that he had this difficulty with 'the class question'. And where else do you get that – you can get it from certain aspects of clothing – but more than anything else you get it from people's voices. And it's that thing about register that interests me. My own voice is extremely flexible; I can do all sorts of accents because I've got a musical ear, and will do, I'm glad to say very seldom wickedly, just to see what you can lead people to believe, because I would trip myself up sooner or later. But you will notice that in certain situations a lot of Scottish people are good at this; they can flip register at the drop of a hat. Interview voice; phone voice; with your pals voice; out for a night on the town voice. (L) You have this repository of voices at your disposal, in order to influence how people react and behave towards you.

Gender is a very difficult one. You can do things with clothes; a woman in a low cut dress will elicit different responses from a woman in a high buttoned blouse. A woman wearing make up will elicit different responses from a woman not wearing make up. A woman with obviously dyed hair will elicit different responses. That is fascinating, because there's such a repository of them with gender, but class interests me by and large through the expression of voice. And of course all writers must be obsessed with voice. You can't not be obsessed with voice; it's what you're dealing with. I don't know if I would call it class; but I'm interested in how people express, the way that is perceived, and what is going to accrue to you as a result of how you speak, how you dress, how you express, and your home background. You know that creepy feeling of how you take someone back to your house for the first time, wondering how they assess your belongings, how they assess your taste, how they assess the street you live in: that's all aspects of the class mentality in Britain. And I would say, yes, I am terribly interested in that, but not the conventional class warfare set up, not the Marxist analysis of class and how that applies. It's more the details. Everything is in the details.

IM I want to get you to talk more about *Clara*. I'd like you to say a bit about the men. I don't have any difficulty – well maybe *you* have difficulty, being too charitable – but *I* have no difficulty in seeing Clara's father as the ultimate pain in the neck; I'm not so sure about Robert. How responsible is he for what he does?

JG   Well. I don't know, to tell you the truth. I think one of these things about living with someone is that by loving someone who suffers from a cyclic mental illness . . . It's very difficult to see what Robert suffered from, what the name of the actual illness was, because the range of possibilities in those days was much more limited, and any insight into calling this disease was certainly much more patchy. Germany, however, was one of the great movers and shakers as concerns advancing psychiatric knowledge, and where he ended up, at Bonn Endenich, was supposed to be one of the best asylums in Europe, with people who were supposed to know their stuff. That said, Richarz, the person who was looking after him, could never make up his mind what the damn thing was, and they didn't have terms like mania. Peter Ostwald, who is a musician and psychiatrist, has written exhaustively on the subject of what it was Schumann might have suffered from, and seems to come down firmly in the area that it's some form of mania. It could be schizo-affective disorder, which means it's like mania allied to schizophrenia, it could be mania, which he'd had all his life, which became conflated with some form of syphilitic mental illness later on in his life; it could be something else entirely. Nobody's very sure. One of the things about mental illness too is that it morphs – it changes according to the person who experiences it; because it's not just acting on an empty milk bottle; it's acting on a human personality. Therefore it's going to look different every damn time, because what it makes you do or not do, what it brings out in you, is going to depend on what is there to bring out in you in the first place. So this is a perennial problem for anyone, for any psychiatrist certainly, and certainly even more so if you love someone who suffers from a mental illness. It's awfully hard knowing where the mental illness stops and starts, and where the person you love stops and starts; how much you need to love this mental illness because it's an intrinsic part of that person, how much you need to separate it, and love what's left over when you take the illness away: that's hard: it must be even harder for the sufferer. And utterly debilitating at times to know what's you, and what's something you don't really want to do, but seem impelled to do from the outside. Because it's working in the inside of your head. How can you ever separate that from your feeling of you-ness? Yet it is separate from your you-ness to a certain extent. So because I don't know; because I'm damn sure Robert Schumann didn't know, what was him and what was illness, I'm absolutely sure, with unshakable conviction, that Clara hadn't the faintest idea what was going on half the time, with how he was reacting, but was such a dutiful woman that she had signed up. For richer for poorer, and better and worse.

IM In sickness and in health?

JG I don't think she would even have called it sickness; I think there were just rotten times and there were good times, as far as she was concerned. I don't think she thought of it often as a sickness. But having lived with someone who suffers from a form of mania – James's father suffered from bouts of intense manic behaviour, and occasionally we experienced horrible psychotic episodes – I know there is not a lot you can do, and what you really must do is tell yourself they don't mean it: occasionally they will say things that are unbearable, because they know you; they know your psychology. They know how you are put together and if what the illness or whatever it is the way they're feeling from the fallout of the illness, whatever it is, whether it's deliberate or whether it's not deliberate, I imagine it's a bit like being drunk; you've got not much control over what's coming out, and the next day you think, oh my God, did I really say that? Now people would say – my mother used to say that, and I think she's wrong – it's the truth that comes out when people are drunk. I don't think it's the truth; I think it's gibberish that comes out from the recesses of the subconscious and beyond, when people are drunk. I'm sure that's what happens in psychotic states; gibberish, nonsense, rubbish, paranoias, just pure delusion, come out, and at times I'm sure he must have sunk his head in his hands and thought, what have I done, what have I said, and again in common with manic people possibly developed a tendency to rewrite history, and make out he didn't say that at all. That's not what we said; that's not what was meant, to preserve his own dignity, forgetting that what that's likely to do is drive the person you're living with cuckoo, because they remember it. What are they supposed to do with that, if that erodes their dignity, your attempt to get yours back erodes theirs. So having seen just a little bit of that, although by no means am I saying that what you can do is extrapolate from your own experience and apply it to fictional characters, to a certain extent one must do that.

But I tried to empathise with Robert to the degree where his confusions would become apparent on the page, and the fact that he doesn't know where he stops and starts, and doesn't know what he's responsible for, especially since the two of them were living in the nineteenth century, where men in particular, creative men behaving bizarrely, was almost seen as par for the course. Liszt did it on purpose! He notched up nutty behaviour, and in private wasn't necessarily erratic or strange at all. The flamboyance was part of showmanship at the time. And I think also there has traditionally been a get-out clause for creative people to behave badly to people they love, and it's all right because they're creative: they somehow can't help it. Rilke was an utter bastard to the people he loved, and seemed to think this was his entitlement. An awful lot of creatives do that. Gertrude Stein was apparently *appallingly* behaved towards people who loved her, but she was a creative genius, so that was her entitlement. I think this is just a lousy excuse for lousy behaviour. I've got no patience with it. (L) If you can find people who are prepared to put up with it, that's your business, but I think it's a lousy way to behave.

And part of what I wanted to do in the book was try and look at a man – I think Robert Schumann, from everything I've read about him, was trying to behave well, but couldn't control well, and couldn't control his perceptions of how he was behaving, and didn't know what the hell was going on with him half the time, but somehow he conflated his creativity with his strange behaviour, and was almost afraid to get rid of his strange behaviour, until he became aware of the fact that he might damage his wife and family; and it was he that asked to be put into an asylum. Now I think you can have nothing but respect for that. Very few manic people ever admit they're ill; the blow to their dignity is too much. There are many manic people out there in business; it's a driven behaviour, a behaviour that treats other people like pawns in a game, and can sweep them out of the way when it suits. That's almost lauded in current society as well; that's being singleminded and fighting your way to the top, and actually sometimes it's just being a bastard. And we need to be more upfront about saying that, that how you treat other people signifies in this life. And Clara too is trying so hard; I think that's one of the things that united them, they're trying very hard to be good, worthwhile people. And I think she can see, that despite his trying he was not succeeding, and it's one of the reasons why she didn't blame him. And one of the reasons why she manages to keep loving him, despite the fact that, almost beyond his control, he continually hurts and damages her, makes her doubt her own perceptions of herself.

IM So what about Clara's father?

JG Well again, I'm not keen on putting people in a corner, and putting a chalk line down the middle of the book, and the bastards are on this side, and the good guys are on that side. With Joy in *The Trick is to Keep Breathing*, right from the first, I wanted everybody to be comprehensible. Even the people she thinks are treating her badly, she's partly aware that it's just a perception, and the self-obsession of depression is making her see people in that way. But she can also see the human side of why they do what they do. To some extent this was extraordinarily important with Wieck, because throughout history he's just been seen almost as a cartoon baddie with a wax moustache, who's tying her to the railroad tracks. (L) Where does that come from? What makes people behave so possessively, so tyrannically, towards their own children? What does that? But it's not a book about him, and I didn't want to end up writing – it's so easy to write about bad guys, or indeed bad girls, because that's such a source of human fascination, and you can get drawn into it, and you can play-act and get into that dream-state where you can just write and write and write. What was hard about writing *Clara* was writing a good girl without becoming dull. We so associate duty, trying to be worthwhile, trying to do right by everybody, with dullness.

IM And hard work, don't forget hard work!

JG Yeah, the whole thing. I had to crack away continually, crack ice on keeping the good girl being the focus of our interest. It would have been all too easy to divert and start ranting about Wieck for ages and ages. Although it was very tempting, and I found those the easiest bits to write, writing Wieck was a dream. Those were the fun parts, writing Wieck. But a little of his history was put in, just to show the kind of poverty and the drivenness of where he'd come from. I'm sure he thought he was doing his daughter a favour.

IM Those letters that he writes when he's getting back in touch with her, is that him or you?

JG She's to come to Dresden and bring the quintet? That's him. (L) That's actually him. He was clearly a creature who wanted the limelight, too. I was reminded at times of the mother in *Gypsy*, the musical

Gypsy, where Gypsy Rose Lee is played by Natalie Wood. I forget who plays her mother, but she's one of the all-time great stage mothers, because *she* really wants to be the one who's out there on the stage; she wants to be the one who's doing it, but she's past an age where people are prepared to tolerate a woman of her proportions on stage, therefore she does it through the daughter [*Rosalind Russell*]: I'm sure that was part of Wieck's thing.

IM Oh yes; I think so.

JG And when he cut the daughter off, the rage at losing control of her, I think he also realised he cut off his chance to feel it was him walking out on the platform. And it took a few years. Because of the pride, it took a few years, but he wanted to get back in touch with that.

IM And he tries to replace her with Marie, who isn't good enough.

JG Good old Marie, who just was not good enough, who was really not a top notch talent. You feel that poor old Marie was always going to be not much at all. A candle next to this chandelier that Clara was. (L) And then later on he tried to do it with a singer called Minna Schultz, and to spite Clara called her Minna Schultz Wieck. Continually trying to relive his glory years. I think those years he spent as a touring dad, with a teenage daughter who hadn't yet become unmanageable, were the best years of his life. And he couldn't quite get over the fact that it was gone; he just kept trying to repeat and he got stuck.

IM What is the story about Clara destroying some of Robert's work?

JG Oh, this is later on. After he died, she and Brahms were the custodians of his work. They suppressed some of it. It's said that she actually burned some of it. All of this was done in tandem with Brahms, – the violin concerto that he wrote for Joachim is still regarded with enormous suspicion as the work of a diseased mind. You get some people – Yehudi Menuhin is one – who say, this is a great work, this is a wonderful work, and people regard it as the product of a diseased mind simply because they know he was ill, and they're superimposing disease on the work: in fact this is a finished work. And other people are saying, no, it's a mess; it doesn't sound right; it doesn't sound good; it's not structured; you can relate it to nothing else of Schumann's really. Again, how do you know when the illness starts and stops? How do you know where the warp begins?

Clara and Brahms had a big problem on their hands. They both worshipped him, and wanted his memory to be revered. Now the nineteenth century attitude to mental illness – it was tainting. She had become tainted by it; people avoided her in the street; people would sometimes refuse to give her bookings – it was almost like a catching thing, or at least embarrassing to have her on the stage or to acknowledge her because she had been associated with this man. With other people it turned to blame! Probably nothing wrong with him; there's no such thing as mental illness really: it must just have been the dreadful life that she led him. Even today, you will find people with extraordinary repositories of blame directed toward Clara Schumann. This is common experience with people who live with folk that suffer from mental illness. It's very common; it's still prevalent. Again with my interest in mental illness, I know people who've been through this mill. The easy thing to do is blame Clara. On the other side you find people who see her just as a kind of saint, who only nursed Robert, and this was the primary purpose of her life. She was neither of these things; she was just a woman making the best she could of an appalling situation, and that was all I wanted to get across: she was trying to put something together.

Now the second book you talked about; if that went on, that would mostly revolve, I guess, round the dilemma that she and Brahms had. We revere this man: people are going to call him an idiot and an imbecile and are going to trash the music. Her primary purpose in life and what was going to drive her forward was making the music in the public's eye into the thing she felt it to be; playing it, and having people listen to it, as something pure and beautiful, which is what she thought it was. And what she and Brahms did was they got together and decided: the public must not hear anything that is possibly flawed, that genuinely has been something that he's cobbled together, or shows traces of psychosis. Now how on earth you decide which music shows traces of psychosis? I have no idea. These were the two people who knew him best in the whole world. I reckon I'm prepared to trust that they did what they did under those circumstances.

I find it bizarre that music purists come along with a holier-than-thou thing, and say, how dare she have done it. You might as well say, how dare she have popularised her husband's music. Why didn't she just leave it, and see what fate did to it? It would have sunk without fucking trace. She did what she did, and if some of it means losing some music, so what? Some Bach was found wrapping meat in a fleischmarket. The ephemeral nature of music is one of those things about it. Clara Schumann said it, 'I destroyed some of the music because I thought it was substandard' – to blame someone for being honest (L) – bizarre behaviour, but you do find it. He suppressed some of his own in hospital too.

Books by Janice Galloway mentioned in the interview

The Trick is to Keep Breathing, (novel) Polygon Press, Edinburgh 1989: currently Vintage, 1998

Blood (short stories), Secker & Warburg (London) 1991: currently Vintage 1998

Foreign Parts (novel), Jonathan Cape (London) 1994: currently Vintage 1998

Where you find it (short stories), Cape (London) 1996: currently Vintage 1997

Pipelines: mixed-media text with sculpture by Anne Bevan and photographs by Michael Wollchover Fruitmarket Gallery, Edinburgh, 2000

Clara (novel), Cape (London): currently Cape 2002

boy book see (poetry and prose pieces), Mariscat Press, 2002

Rosengarten, by Janice Galloway and Anne Bevan, platform projects 2004

JOHN HERDMAN

JOHN HERDMAN HAD known Bob Tait since at least 1970, and a large part of the interview dealt happily and at length with literary and cultural life in Edinburgh then, when Herdman was a member of the Heretics, and Bob Tait edited *Scottish International*. But as Herdman has dealt with this scene in *Pubs, Poets, Polls and Pillar Boxes: Memoirs of an Era in Scottish Politics and Letters [1999]*, interested readers are referred there, so as to leave more space here for the discussion of Herdman's work. Isobel Murray caught up, with the publication of *Memoirs of My Aunt Minnie/Clapperton* in Aberdeen in 1974. In 2002 he came to Aberdeen for a weekend, to be interviewed at their home. On the first day, the conversation was generally about John and his ideas and experience: on the second, we looked more systematically at his writing.

Since the interview he has remarried [*2002*], and he and his wife Mary run a rare and secondhand bookshop in Blair Atholl, 'Atholl Browse'.

St Machar Place Aberdeen. Present, Isobel Murray, Bob Tait, John Herdman. Date, March 2 2002.

IM John, tell me what you like about your early days and your social background.

JH I was born in Edinburgh in 1941. I suppose my family could be described as upper bourgeois, but mercantile rather than professional. Most of my family were in commodities, one way or another. My father was a grain merchant. My mother's family were in the tea trade, and I suppose my ancestry was a mixture of Highland and Lowland, predominantly Lowland, but established in Edinburgh and Leith for a few generations.

IM Upper bourgeois in the sense also that there would be family money by this time?

JH Yes, there was a bit of family money, more on my mother's side than on my father's, because my father was in the grain trade and quite successfully at one time; they traded with the Baltic. But I think the

changes in the grain trade as a result of the war – as a result of the war the home grain trade became more self sufficient, so my father's business went into a decline after the war and he wound it up when I was about thirteen or fourteen, after which he was around the house a lot of the time.

IM Were you an only child?

JH No, I've a younger sister, five years younger than me [*Mary*]. I was educated privately, first of all at a prep school in Edinburgh for about five years [*Angusfield House*], then at St Andrews where I was not happy at all.

IM Were you boarding then?

JH Yes, I was boarding, at a school called New Park, where I got a good education, but I didn't enjoy myself very much.

IM You were a bit of a cuckoo, coming from this background, with the intellectual interests you were going to develop?

JH I was, yes. I was very interested in books from the very word go – I suppose you could say precocious. I started writing when I was about seven, and wrote a lot between the ages of about seven and twelve, I would say.

IM Let me ask you now. Is any of the child's writing in *The Sinister Cabaret* [*2001*] genuine?

JH It is: it's absolutely genuine. (L) It's written by me at the times specified. I also had ambitions to be a composer at that time – I was always going to be a writer or a composer. But I didn't really have any natural musical ability apart from a good ear, I didn't really have any outstanding musical ability at all, and I realised that fairly soon. So I went back to writing. But when I was thirteen I was sent to Merchiston Castle School, a public school (in the English sense) in Edinburgh where I was again a boarder. And during that time I was rather diverted from my basic interests: I was rather forced into a mould. I thought at that stage that I would probably be an advocate: that was what I wanted to be.

IM So more and more one is beginning to see little bits of resemblance between you and Donald Humbie? [*Protagonist of* The Sinister Cabaret]

JH Yes: he is I suppose what I could have become had I taken the path marked out for me (L) in my teens. I think my father was very keen that I should go in that direction: I think he would perhaps have liked to have been a lawyer himself, but his elder brother was killed in the

First World War, and he was more or less forced to go into the family business. So I think he thought of me as carrying out the ambitions which he had had.

IM Did you get on well with your parents?

JH Not particularly, no: particularly not with my father. My father was probably quite a difficult man, a frustrated man in quite a lot of ways, and drank more than he should. I don't think my parents had a very good relationship at all, and my mother tended to smother me a bit.

IM So you went to Merchiston Castle, and I know that you were to go on to read English at Cambridge. Was that always what you wanted to do?

JH I initially went to read History – I won a History scholarship, but I decided very early in my career there that I wanted to be a writer, and changed to English at the end of my first term at Cambridge, partly encouraged by winning a prize awarded by David Frost as editor of *Granta* in a freshman's short story competition (L). [*David Frost, ed, Plain Words, Cambridge, June 1961*]

IM Wonderful! Do you remember the name of the short story?

JH Yes: it was called 'Rat's Progress'.

BT Why Cambridge? Why not Edinburgh, or St Andrews?

JH Because I was pushed that way, very much so. It was very much the public school idea: the best pupils went to Oxbridge if they could, and I was groomed for that and at the time didn't have any objections. I never regretted going to Cambridge, because I think it was there that I became aware of having a Scottish identity for the first time – although as a child I was very interested in Scottish history. But Cambridge was a completely unexpected experience for me in the sense that having gone to this public school I'd rather been expecting that it would be an extension of my previous experience, whereas it turned out that I felt quite alien there. I enjoyed it, actually, but I felt kind of foreign, and I didn't feel that most of the people there were the sort of people that I was used to. At the same time I began reading a lot of Irish literature. I began to feel that I had an affinity with Irish literature that I didn't feel with English literature, particularly Joyce – I got quite obsessed with Joyce for a long time – Joyce and Yeats –

IM Not necessarily to the exclusion of Scottish, but more than Scottish?

JH Before I came to Scottish really, because I wasn't exposed to either Scottish literature or history at all at school, really, although just as a private reader I'd read at least half Scott's novels by the time I was twelve or thirteen, and I'd read a lot of Stevenson as well. But that was just because they were in the house. Irish literature really turned me on, and then I discovered MacDiarmid, and all this with feeling alien in Cambridge determined me toward Scottish Nationalism.

IM   At Cambridge?

JH   Yes.

IM   That is interesting, because in several of your books we're just given it *as* a given that the main character, Clapperton, or Pagan or Duncan Straiton, that they are just different, that they are Scottish, and they vote Nationalist if they possibly can, but it's never explained why they are Nationalist.

JH   That's true, yes. I start at that point usually. But it was also for me definitely associated with feeling a much stronger affinity for other literatures than for English literature. (L) I always felt part of a European tradition, and the writers I was interested were primarily European and Irish rather than English.

IM   Did you have any particularly memorable teachers at Cambridge?

JH   Yes. There was a chap called Arthur Sale, who died only a couple of years ago, that I always kept in touch with. He was a maverick in Cambridge terms: he'd been educated in Nottingham, and had not risen through the Cambridge system at all. They'd needed an extra supervisor at some stage and he happened to be living in Cambridge while he was working in the university library editing texts for I think London University Press, and he was recruited to help out at Magdalene, the college I was at. Over the years he became an institution, but he was really excluded from a fellowship because he didn't come from the right background. Subsequently he became a cult, because he taught many people who later became quite well known in the media. He was a strong influence. [The Double in Nineteenth-Century Fiction *is dedicated 'To Arthur Sale, Teacher and Friend'*].

IM   After Cambridge, what did you mean to do?

JH   I was determined to be 'a writer or nothing', as Eugene O'Neill put it (L). To begin with, I thought I might be able to combine that with an academic career. I got a Double First in English, and I hovered as to whether I would do a PhD. In fact I went back after three years and did start one, but immediately in the years after Cambridge I travelled around a bit, as I had just enough money that was in a trust for me to maintain myself, although I did other temporary jobs as well, anything from teaching English in a school in Switzerland to washing dishes. But basically I could just about get by, so for those three years I was coming and going. I went to America, I went to Switzerland, I went to Germany, but I was coming and going between Scotland and other places. Then in 1966 I did go back to Cambridge and start a PhD on Hogg, whom I'd actually discovered just before that. I was writing by this time: I started writing short stories again seriously when I was at Cambridge.

IM So you started this Hogg PhD, but discontinued?

JH Yes. I was being taught by Ian Jack, who was assigned to me I think purely because he was a Scot. He was an expert in Augustan satire, and had no real knowledge of Scottish fiction. I think I knew much more about Hogg than he did when I started, and he told me at the end of one term that he didn't think there was enough material in Hogg to write a PhD on, and he asked if there was anyone else I might be interested in. I came up with Grassic Gibbon, and I wrote to his widow, and she wasn't at all helpful, and I didn't really think it was the right topic for me anyway, because although I admired Grassic Gibbon he didn't interest me in the way that Hogg did. To be honest, I'd partly been doing this to pacify my father, and to mark time, and to get some kind of grant (L), and I abandoned it after a year.

IM It's interesting that you went back to Cambridge, that you didn't think of doing your PhD at a Scottish university.

JH Yes. Looking back on it, that was a huge mistake. I always had a tendency to go back to places that were familiar, and in the academic context it was Cambridge that was familiar to me. I think that's mainly why I did it. A mistake, though I made a few lasting friends during that year. I also did a lot of work in that year around MacDiarmid and other modern Scottish writers. That stood me in good stead.

IM You came back to Edinburgh after this?

JH Yes. I came back in 1967. I more or less settled down for quite a number of years after that, and plunged into politics – Nationalist politics – at that stage. Previous to the Hamilton by-election I had espoused Nationalism really rather as a lost cause. I hadn't really thought there was a realistic possibility of it happening. But after the Hamilton by-election, which was in November 1967, I joined the SNP and got involved at a local level. ['. . . *a breakthrough. This came*

*in November 1967 when, on the back of extreme dissatisfaction with
the Labour government, Winnie Ewing was triumphantly successful in
the Hamilton by-election'.* Poets, Pubs, Polls & Pillar Boxes, *1999,
p 16.*]

IM What kind of involvement? Were you to be a candidate?

JH No, I was never going to be a candidate, but I was on the hustings
and helping with the elections, and I was Vice Chairman of my local
branch and by this time I'd begun to write also for *Catalyst*, which
was a nationalist publication of rather extreme views; militant nationalism: a lot of very strange people involved in it. When I say 'it' I
mean the 1320 Club which published *Catalyst*: I was never invited
to become a member of the 1320 Club, but I was eventually asked
to edit the journal, and I got involved in a lot of controversies over
that.

IM So you did edit it?

JH I edited two numbers of it only.

IM So the nationalism which developed in Cambridge because you
essentially get a feeling of your own difference from the civilisation
you're in, becomes much more practical.

JH Well I suppose my actual active involvement in politics was fairly
short, maybe about three years when I was actually working at branch
level, so I was never really a natural politician. I was interested in
politics as a means to an end, and Nationalist politics mainly in
cultural terms. I was of course somewhat left of centre as well. I never
took any strong Socialist position: I didn't feel that with my
background and my living on a private income I really had much right
to assert myself in that sort of way, but as I say I was always left of
centre.

IM But very often in what you write I sense that the political dimension
is almost pushed away. There is a tremendous concentration on the
individual, whether it's the Truth Lover, or Horatio Pagan or who-
ever; one of them – I can't remember which off-hand – actually
specifies this, that politics doesn't mean much. [*In* Pagan's Pilgrimage, *'individual action alone was meaningful', pp 23-4.*]

JH Yes, I think that's right. I was a very isolated individual in my early
twenties particularly, very inward-looking, very neurotic (L). It
wasn't fun. Very concerned with questions of individual identity and
will. I was also interested in religion in a kind of abstract way.

IM What was the background you came from as regards religion?

JH   Church of Scotland.

IM   And was it active, believing, living, talking Christianity, or was it just what you did on Sunday?

JH   It was more or less what I did on Sunday. I suppose I got interested in religious issues in my last two years at school, when we were taught what was called Divinity quite well, and I did quite a lot of work for the school Divinity Prize, which I won on two occasions (L). But I abandoned Christianity when I was about nineteen, but got interested in Eastern religion, as many people did in the sixties. In particular I was very interested in Hindu beliefs for a long time – the Bhagavad Gita and the Upanishads and so forth in my mid-twenties, and some of that goes into some of my earliest writings – I was concerned about these kinds of questions. And questions of will: I read people like Nietzsche and Kierkegaard, and I was interested in confessional writers, Rimbaud, Rilke, Dostoyevsky. He came a little later, I think.

IM   But he is of course perhaps the most important. You say you abandoned Christianity when you were nineteen, but you were never really sold on it before that?

JH   No.

BT   So at that stage you describe your interest in religions as somewhat abstract. Can you explain that a little more? You were drawn in some way. It was more than an academic interest, wasn't it? Academic or detached?

JH   Yes, I was interested in meaning, the meaning of life (L), the ultimate questions, yes I was.

BT   And so alternative religious traditions which seemed to lead to the ground of things?

JH   Yes, an existentialist position, I suppose. There was a lot of it around in the sixties. It fed kind of seamlessly into literature as well, the people I was interested in.

BT   Sure. That helps me to get the connections.

IM   In your first book, *Descent* [*1968*], which I must say I find extraordinarily difficult, there is this quotation: the daily work of the artist, 'one who lived always in a strange limbo, that borderline world where the artistic impinges upon the religious life' [*p 22*]. Do you think there is a sense in which your writing is very much like a religious quest?

JH   Yes, I think that's true. In that quotation that you're referring to, I think I was picking up something that Rilke said, that the artist's quest is essentially religious, but – the essence of it was that insight gets in the way of love, and I felt that I had to take the way of insight.

IM   Yes, there's an opposition that comes up, so that Horatio Pagan, for example, sees himself as essentially hard, where other people are essentially soft.

JH   There is of course a lot of self-delusion in that.

IM   Would you like to say anything about the way in which you relate to Duncan Straiton and Horatio Pagan? How close are they to John Herdman?

JH   Well Duncan Straiton in the *Truth Lover* [*1973*] is I think pretty close, although not all the things that happen to him happened to me. By the time I wrote *Pagan's Pilgrimage* [*1978*] I had realised that I had to find a way of distancing myself from my characters much more decisively than I had in *Descent* and *A Truth Lover*. *Descent* is written in the first person as myself, really. In between them I wrote *Clapperton*, which was a kind of break through for me in a way, first published in *Scottish International* ['*Clapperton: A Day in His Existence*', *November 1972*] and that was the first place where I think I gave humour a central role, and humour is a way of distancing the author from the protagonist, particularly, and *Clapperton* had elements of Dostoevsky's *Notes from Underground* in it, as well as quite a lot of Beckettian influence. I think that reductionist comic mode was a way of distancing: I became interested in ways in which narrative voice, even in the first person, could be distanced from authorial voice.

IM   My notes, even on *Pagan*, say that this is funnier than the *Truth Lover*.

JH   Oh yes, it has definitely taken that road. There are funny bits in the *Truth Lover*, but it's not meant to be a comic novel primarily: it's meant to be a *Bildungsroman* really, whereas *Pagan's Pilgrimage* has influence from people like Flann O'Brien as well, and that anarchic kind of humour, but at the same time I was interested in the same problem of the will, of the protagonist who asserts his will, and in *Pagan's Pilgrimage* I wanted to ask the question what happens when, unlike Raskolnikov, or the Justified Sinner, the protagonist finds that he can't carry through his intention, in this case of a holy murder, what happens to him.

BT   I wonder if the humour had another role in your life at that time. You mentioned earlier that in your early twenties you were introspective, and I think you actually used the word neurotic, and it wasn't fun, you said. Was the humour also unintentionally therapeutic, enabling you to handle some of the things that were giving you the *angst*?

JH   Probably it did, yes. It certainly gave me the feeling that there was a mode in which I could function as an artist, and which I hadn't entirely found before.

BT   It must have been quite a discovery, then, a very reassuring thing.

JH   (L) Yes. In my earliest work I had style but I had to find a voice. So I think it was with the comic in *Clapperton* and then *Pagan's Pilgrimage* that I actually found a voice that I felt was my own for the first time. That was the voice of a persona, of course: it wasn't my personal voice, but it was the voice of a persona.

IM   Did you tend to know where your writing was going? Your work has been described as eclectic. It is very strange: as we've been doing, it's quite easy to make it all seem to fit a progression, but this is a way of making your literary career sound perhaps tidier than it is so far. Did you know that you would write about Bob Dylan, or that you would write a book about the double in nineteenth-century fiction, or that you would produce parts of the Statistical Account of Scotland? Or are they all accidents?

JH   (L) They are in a sense accidents, but they are all – except perhaps the Statistical Account of Scotland – fairly central interests. I was interested in Bob Dylan from the appearance of Bob Dylan, really: he seemed to me always to be an absolutely individual voice and clearly a genius. I also had lots of literary interests in common with Bob Dylan actually (L): we were both very interested in Rimbaud, and I was interested in Brecht at one time and so was Dylan, and we were almost exactly the same age, (L) so I felt in some peculiar way that Bob Dylan and I had developed in parallel, though thousands of miles apart.

IM   He was a double?

JH   He was a kind of double, I suppose, yes. And of course I was interested in the double. I realise that I was interested in the double because of Hogg, but I realised that it was something that was inherently of interest to me. So in a way all these things do tie up, although I wouldn't say that I'd ever have predicted that I'd have written either of those books, although I might have predicted the double. Whether I'd ever have got round to it under my own steam; but in fact someone asked me to write it.

IM Ah, did they? A publisher?

JH No, John Orr, who was a sociologist at Edinburgh University, but also very interested in literature. He interviewed me once, I think for *Cencrastus*, and he became one of the editors of this series, 'Edinburgh studies on culture and society', and he invited me to write this book about the novel.

IM That is very interesting, because from outside one can see entirely why you would write it, but you probably wouldn't have written it if he hadn't invited it.

JH I almost certainly wouldn't have, because I'm afraid I'm lazy by nature (L). I tend not to take things on. In certain senses I'm lazy, I can work extremely intensely for short periods of time, and write very fast actually, but I tend to need a prod to start a big project. The Bob Dylan book had a slightly different origin, because I did write – I think it was for *Akros* – Duncan Glen was doing a series perhaps on music and literature, and I wrote an article on Dylan for that. [*'Attitudes to Bob Dylan'*, Akros *30, April 1976.*] And then I was kind of provoked by Dylan's temporary conversion to Christianity in 1979, and just for my own interest I wrote this chapter about Dylan and religion, pursuing religious themes through his earlier work. I couldn't think what I could do with it, it was too academic for a rock magazine, for instance, so I decided to make a book of it and I approached Paul Harris, who was an up and coming publisher at that time, and he and Trevor Royle, who was working with him, thought it would be a good idea to publish this book for Dylan's fortieth birthday. In fact it didn't come out in time for that, but not through any fault of mine (L).

IM Were you yourself a Christian at the time when you were interested in Dylan becoming a Christian?

JH No, I wasn't, but I think I was hovering on the verge. In my late thirties I went through a psychological crisis of some kind. It would be quite difficult to trace its origins, but part of it was to do with religion, and part of it was due to anxiety about the world situation, an apocalyptic dread. I found Dylan's conversion to Evangelical Christianity very disturbing, probably because it was touching on things that I was edgy about at the time. It was just after that that I underwent a conversion experience which ended up with my becoming a Catholic. I'd always been interested in monasticism and medieval Christianity, and I'd now almost totally rejected Calvinism.

So when I felt drawn back to Christianity for a lot of complex reasons, I was sure that I didn't want to go back to the Church of Scotland.

IM It was always whether Roman Catholicism would fit, because that was the obvious one?

JH Yes. And at that stage I felt quite strongly drawn toward monasticism. It was to do with things in my personal life as well. I was very unhappy and I suppose I had an impulse to withdraw from the world, and from literature as well. I did actually withdraw from literature for a long time, from fiction, although I wrote most of my non-fiction works, the Dylan book and the double book and another book which wasn't published, which was a sort of spiritual autobiography, during that time. But I did have an impulse to withdraw, and become a monk.

IM Yes: you actually considered this twice?

JH I once thought about it seriously, but didn't in the end, because I got married instead. (L) And then later when my marriage had broken up, I did actually try to become a monk. I was far too old by that time.

BT There are all sorts of kinds and aspects of monasticism. What were the aspects that had such a draw? There's the monasticism that's about submission and service, usually of a particularly subservient kind, and there's the kind of monasticism that's related to a life of prayer and contemplation. Would I be right in thinking that it was the latter?

JH (L) Yes, you'd be right. I was interested in the mystical side of Hinduism and Buddhism for a long time, and I came to realise, which I hadn't until then, that there's that in Christianity as well, which most obviously found its home in the monastic tradition. I was always interested in the Middle Ages, and I suppose there was that kind of romantic attraction to it – future monks are drawn to this side of Catholicism. My conversion to Catholicism had a lot to do with monasticism actually.

IM Can we put a year on that?

JH Yes: the very beginning of 1980 was when I had this experience which made me decide I was going to become a Christian. I don't want to make that sound too evangelical, because I was always a sort of existentialist Christian really. I decided to follow a path, and I decided that was the path I was going to follow.

BT Kierkegaard was always there.

JH Yes. I don't think that I would ever have said that I subscribed in too exclusive a way to Christian doctrine and to no other: I never abandoned feeling that there was truth in Hinduism, Buddhism, many other systems. But I wanted to follow that path, and I felt that I had to follow some path if I was going to get anywhere along the mystical road, which I think in the end I wasn't suitable for. I was received into the Catholic Church in June 1981. I went to do a course in Medieval History at St Andrews, so that's why I was received into the Church there.

IM Not wishing to be intrusive, are you still in the Church?

JH I would say that I'm probably mostly lapsed now, although I still keep a connection with Pluscarden Abbey, where I tried my vocation, and I still find that a spiritual home, very much so. I've gone back more to the position I started in: I still have a belief in an ultimate spiritual reality which lies behind everything. I think that all religious discourse is metaphorical or symbolic. I don't feel that I'm able any longer to sit so closely to the Church as I could.

IM Did you have any problems when you were received, with papal infallibility, or with some of the social or doctrinal teachings?

JH Yes, definitely. I'd always thought that papal infalliblility was basically un-Catholic, unhistorical (L) and non-apostolic and everything else. And yes, I felt alienated by a lot of the moral teaching. However I did remain a Catholic and I was away from the sacraments for a couple of years and then I was allowed back. I got a bit disgusted by some of the casuistry that was involved. (L)

IM Can I take a leap which is either a big one or a very tiny one? Putting God on hold for now, what about the Devil?

JH Ah, the Devil. One of the big bridges between my previous position and Christianity that I found very useful when I was becoming a Christian was Jung, and I read a huge amount of Jung around that period, and I've always been very interested in his idea about good and evil being polar opposites which require each other, and the psychological and other problems that are caused by the repression of the dark side of the personality. In that sense I suppose I believe in the Devil as a necessary balance in psychological terms, a figure that has to be recognised because he represents something that would otherwise be in danger of being repressed, which again fits into my interest in the double: most of the characters who are overtaken by a double are people who have repressed the dark side of their personality, which has then erupted with disastrous effect. So I believe in giving the Devil his place. I also remain open to the idea of there

being spiritual forces negative and positive in the universe, which
could be understood either psychologically or spiritually or both.

BT   What would that mean? What are these spiritual forces?

JH   I don't know what they are; spiritual entities, or beings: these questions depend on whether you think that matter or spirit is primary.

BT   Or whether you think that spirit is a meaningful category when you
are talking about entities at all, which I don't, which is why I'm
puzzled.

JH   The reason I'm using the phrase was that I tend to think that the
ultimate basis of reality is spiritual, and that spirit generates matter,
rather than vice versa. Rather than brain, for instance, generating
consciousness and spirit, I think that consciousness generates matter.
Or spirit generates consciousness, and consciousness is an aspect of
spirit, and consciousness generates matter. This is what I like to hope.
(L)

IM   So good and evil are both equally real.

JH   A necessary polarity.

IM   Where do you find yourself geographically when you're looking
back?

JH   My grandfather on my father's side came from near Dalkeith; he was
the son of a tenant farmer there. My mother's family also came from
round Dalkeith, but with ultimate origins in Napdale. My father's
mother's family originally came from Lewis, because my great great
grandfather was a shore porter in Leith and had come from Lewis.

IM   I don't know why exactly, but this leads me to ask about the Statistical
Account.

JH   Well, I was living in Berwickshire at the time, after my marriage
broke up. I went to Berwickshire, primarily because I found a very,
very cheap house there (L). Patrick Cadell, my old friend and school-
mate, whom I shared a study with at school, was the Keeper of the
Records for Scotland until recently. He was the editor of the West
Lothian volume of the Statistical Account and the editor of the
Berwickshire volume had dropped out, and so they were looking for
someone to fill that gap, and as I was living in Berwickshire he
thought of me, and that's how I came to do that. Subsequently the
same thing happened to the Roxburghshire volume, so I did that as
well. It was mainly at that stage a question of collating the contri-
butions and rewriting some of them, and getting the photographs and
apparatus.

IM Did you enjoy it?

JH I did, actually: it was tedious at moments, but it was an interesting
thing to do. A useful thing too: the Statistical Account has a long and
honourable history: it's a very useful tool for local historians and
social historians.

IM Would you do it partly as a deliberate distraction?

JH Yes; I think I was casting around for something to do at the time,
because that was the time I'd decided I was going to write fiction
again but hadn't quite found the direction, and I had a session at
Hawthornden, the writers' retreat, where I wrote most of the book
about the double, and at the end of that period I suddenly wrote my
story 'The Devil and Dr Tuberose', which was the first substantial
bit of fiction I'd written for about ten years, and I was really carried
away with that: it suddenly just came to me. I think it was reading
all those Gothic novels that reignited my interest in writing and it
came so spontaneously that I thought, there must be more stuff here:
I'm not as played out as I thought I was.

BT Had you thought you were played out? Was that the reason for the
shift in direction to non-fiction?

JH Yes it was. It was a variety of things: my intellectual interests had
shifted so much from literature to religion for a time, religion and
cultural history, and also getting married at a fairly late age, and as
it turned out fairly traumatically, I wasn't able to concentrate all that
well either.

IM Let's throw a date and an age in here if you can do it.

JH I got married in 1983, I think just after my forty-second birthday.
I was married for ten years but we lived together for only about six.

IM (However I should add for the future reader that relations with your
former wife are very good. The last time before today that we saw
you and indeed her was when she was preparing a fabulous lunch for
your sixtieth birthday last summer.)

So it's after that that we get *Imelda* and *Ghost-Writing*, and you
really found that quite easy: the inspiration was coming back?

JH It suddenly came, yes, I would have to describe it in those terms. I'd
tried to write a novel before that, which was to be a kind of *Pagan's
Pilgrimage* volume two, (L) but it didn't work at all. And then I
suddenly got an idea which turned out to be *Imelda*, at least a combination of two ideas, some of which came from a dream, and I wrote
it very fast: I wrote it in a month. I'd had a pattern of writing fast

since *Pagan's Pilgrimage*, which I wrote in six weeks as well. I wrote *Imelda* at a very stressful time, because my mother was dying, and I had the Writer in Residence job in Perth, and I was also going up still to Blair Atholl where my wife was. I was moving in three different directions, to Edinburgh, Perth and Blair Atholl, and I was living in St Andrews. And yet I somehow managed to write this book in four weeks. It just all jelled, in a way I'd never known before.

BT Well that is the point, isn't it? The way you did it shows that there was an awful lot there, and also, anticipating possible later discussion, there seems from there on in to be more variety and complexity in what's going on in your stories. So the fact that it is all fitting together is a wonderfully good sign.

JH That's right. I think in some ways the staying away had freed various things, because I'd always had great difficulty with structure before, I could write well episodically but I didn't feel that ideas came to me whole: I felt that even my best work had been a bit episodic.

BT It's a very solid structure, *Imelda,* formally, just in terms of the architecture of the thing and it's nice and clear, but more interestingly, it's got very complex structure, in the sense that all sorts of things have to just fall into place as the story progresses at precisely the right time and with the right weight. To me it's a beautifully structured story.

JH I surprised myself, because I didn't even know what direction it was going in till half way through, I decided that the character Affleck was the villain, it became clear to me that that had to be the answer. Really it's structured for rereading, so you go back knowing the truth or what purports to be the truth, because I also of course was leaving questions open of what the truth was. I suppose I was almost taking a post-modernist stance at that point, although I abhor post-modernism as a theory, but I think some of the practice is very interesting. Ideas of the elusiveness of truth interest me a great deal. I'm a stubborn anti-relativist; and I don't believe in the relativity of truth, but I believe that truth is extremely difficult to determine, and I'm very interested in the ways in which reality can be interpreted very differently by different people. I'd been reading Wilkie Collins also, before I wrote *Imelda*, and I was interested in trying to write a whodunnit, in a way.

BT That might cast light on something I'd been thinking about *Imelda.* Your chosen tone of voice has a certain period flavour to it.

JH Yes, Wilkie Collins will certainly be there: very much so. It was turned down by a publisher whom I won't name on the grounds that the tone of voice was incompatible with a mid-twentieth-century setting. Though in fact, I imagine that Berwickshire in the 1950s might not have been as far removed from Wilkie Collins as that publisher might have imagined. But anyway, I've always loved pastiche, and pastiche is part of the point of it. And I like incongruity as well, and the incongruity of setting a nineteenth-century-flavoured novel in the mid-twentieth century also appealed to me for its own sake.

IM Dreams are important in all sorts of ways. Are they important to you, personally?

JH Yes. I've been interested in dreams particularly ever since my interest in Jung, and I came to realise that they're a great source of images. At a number of crucial points they've been quite important in my writing. I think *Imelda* had its origin in a couple of dreams, and *The Sinister Cabaret* is almost entirely structured on dreams and dream images, a journey made in terms of dream imagery. I've always been fascinated by what happens in dreams and the way in which dream imagery expresses things with sometimes extraordinary accuracy and inwardness. And also of course the incidence of the flow and the striking vividness of dream imagery is a great source of inspiration.

IM And the accidental. You were saying *The Sinister Cabaret* is based on dreams: I suppose that for example the wonderful pachyderm Russian in the Mountain Dew might come from a dream?

JH No, I think he comes more as a parody of Dostoevsky, but some of the characters in the Mountain Dew. Though actually, dare I say it, the Mountain Dew is a real pub in Wick, which I visited when I was performing in the Wick Festival. What's described in the novel is not very far from the truth, but it might easily come out of a nightmare (L).

IM It's not fair: the most unlikely apercus come out of almost unasked questions (L): I don't know which other ones not to ask! Music. On the one hand, there's obviously Bob Dylan; on the other hand there's the kind of music that Horation Pagan hears, which actually seems to be part of what stops him in his mission.

JH Yes, I think the music in *Pagan's Pilgrimage* is influenced by David Lindsay: the David Lindsay of *Arcturus*. He uses music in that kind of a way, as being kind of metaphysical or spiritual movements: I think it's in his final book *The Witch* that the protagonist moves through different musics which represent metaphysical states. [*David Lindsay, 1878-1945, published five novels, the best known of which is* A Voyage to Arcturus, *1920. Often ghettoised as science fiction, but a cult audience has always seen it as a spiritual and philosophical allegory*] Music's always been important to me, yes, because in a way I'm a frustrated musician.

IM   Yes, you were saying that like Donald Humbie, you had musical ambitions. So what kind of music is most important to you?

JH   I'm fairly eclectic musically: I have fairly conservative tastes in classical music, Vivaldi, Mozart, Haydn, I liked all that stuff very much when I was a child, and I also like certain aspects of rock music, Dylan, Van Morrison, certain individual artists, and I just love the pop music of the fifties and sixties (L), and I actually like country music as well.

IM   Second day! 3 March 2002. In Aberdeen. Bob Tait, Isobel Murray, John Herdman. And the first thing I want to do today is to iron out a wrinkle that came out of yesterday: John told us that he went to start a PhD on Hogg, but that he didn't finish it. He is nonetheless a doctor. How come?

JH   I got my doctorate eventually in 1988 under a system whereby Cambridge graduates can submit published critical work, and I discovered about this when I was in Cambridge doing a course on Theology, and I submitted my book on Bob Dylan plus about a dozen essays on modern Scottish writers that I'd written over the years for various periodicals. I was subsequently examined orally by Eddie Morgan, who was my external examiner, (L) and the only person I think who could be found who could deal with both Bob Dylan and contemporary Scottish literature. And I got it. So that's how I'm a doctor. About twenty-two years I think since I originally set out on that false trail. (L)

IM   Right. The book that I think John and I are farthest apart on, because as I've said I don't understand it, is number one, *Descent* [1968]. Tell us about the circumstances of writing it and getting it published, which was a little unusual too.

JH   Well, I was interested in confessional literature at that time, and also in short prose forms. I was particularly interested in Rimbaud in those days, and I think I modelled *Descent* on *Une Saison en enfer*, which is a very densely written book and quite obscure, if you don't know much about Rimbaud's life. *Descent* follows that sort of pattern in an inferior mode (L) but I was also interested in Jung at that time, and I think the idea of the descent into oneself was from Jung's *Psychology and Religion* – his short book on psychology and religion which I'd just been reading. And Rilke's *Notebooks of Malte Laurids Brigge*, I think. [*The fullest and most sympathetic account of* Descent *is found in Macdonald Daly's Introduction to* Four Tales, *Zoilus Press, 2000*]

IM No wonder I didn't catch all the implications! (L)

JH It was originally longer than it is in the published version, and I pared it down later because some of it was very self-indulgent. Probably what remains is as well, but not so severely. I tried about sixteen or seventeen publishers with it, very naively, because its length alone would have precluded its being published separately, and a number of magazines. Eventually I decided to just issue it myself: it's about ten thousand words long I think, and I got Callum MacDonald to print it. It cost me £70 in 1968, three years after I wrote it: I wrote it when I was twenty-three. I just hawked it around the Edinburgh bookshops and a few Glasgow bookshops, and sent lots of copies to friends.

IM *A Truth Lover*, to me, is like the reader's version of *Descent*. (L)

JH (L) Yes; that's what it was meant to be, really; it was an attempt to make much more concrete the ideas that were very abstractly presented in *Descent*. Somebody once said that abstraction is one of the modes of modernism.

IM I just have this childish appreciation of story, and development, and a beginning and an end, and seeing a process, because here there is a process. I think the blurb said he makes a partial self-discovery. Do you remember whether you wrote the blurb?

JH I think I did, yes. (L)

IM So Duncan does actually advance a bit in self knowledge. He actually spends some time in prison. Are his motives for going to prison excusable?

JH I think the idea was that they were an example of self assertion, which was inexcusable. Of course the metaphor there was that he imprisoned himself by his own self absorption and self assertion. Towards the end there's a movement out – I find in each of my books there's always been a movement, a journey towards a more redemptive position which is then kind of undercut at the end. It's not as effective as it at first appears to be. I've always turned away or eschewed the simple idea of a redemptive movement. I tend to think, from experience really, that psychological imperatives pull you back in the direction from which you've come.

IM Yes; that's a very helpful general statement. Immediately I think particularly of *Sinister Cabaret*, because it happened so recently. When Cant turns up again at the very end –

BT Here we go again! I think the ending of that book is just an absolutely brilliant stroke.

IM But you took a word out of my mouth, as it were, John, when you said there that each of your books has been some sort of journey. I was thinking quite literally that journeys are quite important.

JH Yes they are: a questioner at a reading recently asked why in all my books except *Imelda* there is an actual movement usually from Edinburgh into the Highlands and back again, and I couldn't really provide an answer as to why it took that particular form, and I'm not sure that I can now.

IM In *A Truth Lover* the point about the journey seems to be that it doesn't get you anywhere at all: what he has to do is to descend, to go into himself, and floating around Europe doesn't get him anywhere at all.

JH Yes. The journey that appears to be a bit redemptive is the journey to the Highlands towards the end, where he undergoes some kind of insight into his own inner condition, but again, if I'm remembering the ending clearly, it's undercut, when he has some sort of a reaction which indicates that his supposedly redemptive journey hasn't been as effective as it might be.

IM But it isn't completely undercut.

JH Not completely, no.

IM Because that would be a very cynical thing, if you were always setting out to undercut, but it's much more that any victory is only partial, and impermanent, and you don't finish with a victory, and you have to conquer yourself every day, every time.

JH Yes, absolutely yes.

BT What you were saying about the journey to the Highlands, that you haven't actually worked out why that happens to be the case: it does happen, though, to have certain echoes in literature. In Scottish literature the Highlands is a place of wilderness, of wildness, where you can find the dark side, and something that is restorative can also be found. Is that not true?

JH   I suppose that is what it is. It's the movement away from the city which could represent civilisation towards something more fundamental, more primitive, something that lies underneath it.

BT   But it fits in very neatly I think with what you were just saying: it's not a place where any conclusions are reached: it's an ambiguous place.

JH   Yes, you've put your finger on it, I think.

IM   And it's a place which often has Gaelic names. I'm thinking especially at the moment of *Sinister Cabaret*. I was going to ask you whether you have Gaelic in a big way?

JH   I have some Gaelic, not in a big way. (L) I've taken a number of classes over the years, starting in the sixties. I know enough to read poetry, to know what it sounds like. I can pronounce reasonably well, and so I can know what poetry sounds like, and working with a dual text, that's very helpful. I'm particularly devoted to Sorley MacLean's poetry, and that's been a great thing for me over the years. His very intense sense of reality, both emotional and political, and the utter straightness with which he faces every question, emotional and metaphysical, I just find incomparable, to use one of his own words. And the music of the poetry as well: I know enough Gaelic to appreciate some of the music. Also it's very useful for place names and their derivation, and so on.

IM   I asked you I think off-tape whether I was missing any jokes or points in *Sinister Cabaret* in the Gaelic names, and it was quite interesting, the name of the village that a lot of the action happens in.

JH   Yes: it's Cul an Duirn, which means the back of the fist: it's a violent place (L).

IM   People get slung out of pubs all the time. A lot of violence happens. Actually it's quite interesting how much violence occurs casually in your books.

JH   Quite a lot, yes.

IM   Why do you think?

JH   Must be something in me (L).

IM   If it were something sinister in you, you would dwell on the violence and make it more graphic: it's casual, quite often. Even in *Sinister Cabaret* when they destroy the cabaret people, it's over quite quickly; it's not detailed.

BT   But it is explosive, and very brutal. Explosive, brutal episodes of violence keep happening.

JH   That's right. That brings to mind a very interesting comment that
     was made on *A Truth Lover* by Douglas Eadie in his original review
     in *Scottish International,* where he said the style reminded him of a
     man who suddenly loses his temper, and then regains it very quickly.
BT   That's exactly it.
JH   So it's to do with control, with an eruption of violent emotions under
     a controlled surface, which I think is something I've used in my
     writing a lot. People suddenly begin to behave in extraordinary and
     exaggerated ways, grotesque ways, sometimes, out of a very
     apparently calm surface. And bringing things which are repressed –
     repressed emotions, repressed feelings – everyone knows how they'd
     sometimes like to behave in a certain situation but actually don't –
     making characters behave in that way is something Dostoevsky does,
     I think. I'm probably influenced by that, but I also think it's
     something that comes naturally to me (L) as well.
IM   I'm trying to remember: *Clapperton* comes next?
JH   Yes. *Clapperton* comes between *A Truth Lover* and *Pagan's Pilgrim-
     age.* There was another novel between them, but it wasn't pub-
     lished.
IM   I think you are unjust. *Clapperton* you seem to be happy to own, and
     I should think so too, but you're very dismissive of *Aunt Minnie.* You
     rarely mention it.
JH   I suppose it's just because it's so short, really: it seems less substantial
     than *Clapperton,* but it's only what, 2700 words long.
IM   It's the most sustained picture of a woman in your fiction (L).
JH   Perhaps it is (L). No, I do like it; I think it's fun; it's more of a jeu
     d'esprit than anything else.
IM   But a very glorious one, and an early example of Herdman finding
     out how funny he can be.
JH   Yes. Those two, *Clapperton* and *Aunt Minnie,* were published
     together originally by Rainbow Books in Aberdeen [*1974*], and they
     both came out of much the same little impulse of discovering ways
     in which I could use humour and grotesquerie as a way of distancing
     myself from my material, really.
IM   I will never forget you reading *Clapperton* at the launch at Aberdeen
     Art Gallery – people crying with laughter. It's very hard these days,
     for a writer who isn't a good performer: you're lucky   in this way,
     of course, you've even put out a CD of readings. [John Herdman
     Reading, *Zoilus Press, London*] I was intrigued going back to it this

time particularly – by the illustrations. Tell me about the illustrations. You didn't ever do it again.

JH   No. They were I think the idea of Annie Inglis, who was much involved in that publication, she certainly had a lot to do with it. [*Formerly a lecturer in drama at Aberdeen College of Education, Annie has been for many years a central creative and dramatic presence in Aberdeen.*] She found this young artist called Moira Spence, who I must confess I've never heard of again. I don't know what happened to her. But they were extraordinarily just like the way I imagined the characters, very effective.

IM   I think they're wonderful. I was scared you were going to say they were just put there to make it look long enough to be a book. Because I think they're so good.

JH   Yes. They fit very well with the grotesquerie that's there: they point that up very nicely, I think.

IM   And this again is one of the places where hotels are important, *Aunt Minnie*.

JH   Yes. I suppose I've spent a lot of my childhood holidays in hotels, Scottish Highland hotels mainly, and I always found them interesting in that there were most interesting characters in them, and if I remember rightly, Enright was based on a hotel porter in Gairloch – maybe I shouldn't say that (L), but I can't remember the date. Hotels are interesting places, because they are places where people come together that have no knowledge of each other and stay in the same place for a length of time, and their lives kind of intertwine, and then there's the background of the staff who are there more permanently.

BT   Scottish Highland hotels tend to be superannuated and remodified Big Houses, and the architecture tends to be dark, and brooding, and there are all sorts of very private obscure places in these hotels. And people come and go with horrendous tortuous private lives – it's a bringing together of places which are private and dark and hidden with suddenly the public faces as well.

JH   That's right. They're a kind of Gothic. A Gothic image in a way, yes.

BT   They're not all singing, dancing, modern jolly intercontinental ballistic hotels.

JH   No: I think I was attracted to hotels, for these kind of reasons that Bob puts his finger on: I find them fascinating places in some ways.

IM   So this is the first funny book, and it's very funny, *Aunt Minnie* and

Clapperton. And I suppose it would be a very broad generalisation to say that *Pagan's Pilgrimage* unites the new comic Herdman with the old serious purpose, from the *Truth Lover*, so that it's a whole new ball game really. What were you doing when you started it?

JH It was in the mid-seventies when I was quite heavily involved in the Scottish literary scene, and there's that element of parody of Scottish literature in it, references, jokey references to various previous Scottish novels and that sort of thing. I'm not sure that the two strands that you are talking about sit altogether easily together in *Pagan's Pilgrimage*. Certainly it was the first attempt to bring these two things together.

IM I think they come together very well, and the anticlimax which is at the centre, Pagan having taken on this serious assassination mission and then being fated not to do it, anticlimax is almost a comic mode in itself.

JH Yes, that's what I hoped would work. I'd been looking at the double again, my perennial fascination with the double from Hogg, and just before I started the novel I'd read Hoffmann's *The Devil's Elixir*, which is another very Gothic novel in that mode, which also has a crazy monk who becomes a killer. I think that's what sparked it off. I wanted to investigate these possibilities of anticlimax, and the failed assassin, and the double theme as well, just a whole assortment of quirky influences came in, bits of Beckett and bits of Flann O'Brien.

IM I think it works on both levels from the very beginning. The first sentence is: 'My imagination has been haunted by the wrinkle-nosed laundryman for as long as I can remember.' You've got this series of dreams that goes on all the way through, and they're sinister, and they're frightening, but it is essentially funny, even when you're taking it seriously. It's not until near the end that he manages in a dream to push the laundryman off the roof.

JH That's right: he kind of exorcises this bogeyman, demon.

IM But he is essentially a comic bogeyman, demon.

JH Yes. There are elements where the protagonist is in a sense the victim of the narrator's humour, though of course he is the narrator himself, but he's not entirely conscious of poking fun at himself. The author is poking fun at him through the medium of a first person narrative. I've always been quite interested in the different ways in which first person narratives can be manipulated to yield something which is at a distance from the character. While the character continues to speak in the first person, there's nonetheless an authorial distance somehow effected.

IM Yes: the author by using the narrator's own words obviously can nonetheless communicate with the reader over his head in all sorts of ways. That's something that very much happens here. Why is he called Pagan?

JH It is a real name: people don't realise that. I was actually at school with somebody called Pagan. I suppose Horatio is a pagan. He's the son of a minister, but he's somebody who's rejected his parental religion, and I think that has something to do again with this theme of wilfulness and self-assertion: he's not someone who's prepared to acknowledge any authority above himself or his own will. That's again the same metaphysical or psychological problem that's in the *Truth Lover*.

IM And the similarities with Hogg's *Confessions* are very striking. But it's interesting that the Gil-Martin figure, as it were, Wraith, doesn't tempt Pagan with a religious message: it's a purely 'philosophical' one. Robert Wringhim is told to go and kill good ministers because this is an excellent thing to do, a religious thing to do, and he glories in his religion, whereas Pagan has an assassination message that is much more random.

JH Yes. The idea is that he should kill this exploitative landlord Teuchtershards, who is the sort of figure that was being poked at a lot in the Scotland of those days, a hate object. But the psychological climax comes when Pagan realises that an actual human being lies behind this stereotype, and he has this sort of semi-conversion to something more like a movement of love inside his soul. Which is then questioned afterwards again.

IM Yes. But he does realise for example that the stereotype isn't that simple, that Teuchtershards or Gadarene has been particularly loving, forgiving towards Nanny, for example: he isn't a simple brute: he's got a personal life and has done admirable things. What do you think of the ending, then? We were talking about making progress and then taking it back again; is it just that possibility in the last sentence that if Wraith came back again he can't be sure he wouldn't go along with him?

JH Yes: he wouldn't 'find the key turned against him in the lock'. [*p 80*] He might go along the same path that he appears to have turned away from.

IM I think it is considerably less worrying as an ending than for example *Sinister Cabaret*.

JH Yes. With *Sinister Cabaret* you get the feeling that the character, the protagonist, may be locked in a movement which he can't break out of.

IM What comes next?

JH The next book that I wrote after that was my critical study of Bob Dylan's lyrics.

IM Going through the books we've talked about so far, there was a kind of progress seen, and this just seems a very unexpected thing to happen. A big proportion of the book is about the love songs, and the conversion songs, but that politics and protest don't seem to come in so much. My original picture of Dylan was 'Hard Rain'. Is there a sense in which you played down the protest?

JH Well, I think Dylan turned away from that very quickly actually: it's what he's most famous for among non aficionados of Dylan, but he turned away from direct political statement very quickly. I did talk quite a bit about that in my chapter on the religious themes, the apocalyptic side of 'The Times They Are A-Changing' and 'A Hard Rain's A-Gonna Fall' and these kind of songs in that context, but he was always a bit ambivalent about his own sincerity, even (L).

IM He went on singing them.

JH He went on singing them, in new versions. He's always recreating his old songs.

IM You refer to both a novel and a film: what about them?

JH He wrote a novel called *Tarantula*, which he was commissioned to write: it's very, very difficult and very obscure. I wouldn't rush away to find it. There's also the film *Renaldo and Clara*, which I think is wonderful. It's had a lot of criticism, but I think it's a tremendous film. It was based, if I remember rightly on his Rolling Thunder Review tour, which he did with Joan Baez and various other people. There's some marvellous live footage of concerts in it, interspersed with dramatised incidents and documentary stuff: it's a strange mixture, but I think it works very well.

IM So the useful message is: forget the novel, and try to see the film.

JH (L) That would be my advice, yes.

IM Much more traditional, is the book about the double. Covering quite a wide area of nineteenth-century fiction.

JH Yes. I start off with the religious and philosophical background, and

then I move on to early Romantic examples of the double. And then
I deal with various individual authors, like Hoffmann, Hogg, Poe and
Dostoevsky and Stevenson. I don't actually talk about *Frankenstein*
in the book, because I felt that *Frankenstein* had been so fully dealt
with by other people, so though it can be looked on as a double as
well, I shied clear of it.

IM It's a very male tradition that Mary Shelley doesn't quite fit, I feel.
Why did you stick to the nineteenth century?

JH Well, I think that is the era in which the double is most clearly a
theme. I make some perameters. In the twentieth century the double
theme is still around, but it isn't nearly as much a genre theme: it's
more that it creeps into works of fiction that are perhaps not primarily
about the double. And also I thought that in the nineteenth century
there was an understanding of it. I was interested in the way in which
religious understandings and psychological understandings kind of
came together. It seems to me that the double is a theme, the primary
theme in which you've got a possibility of understanding human
behaviour in either a pyschological or a moral/spiritual way, and that
when these two can be seen as aspects of the same thing then you've
got a fruitful metaphor there. But I think that at the end of the period
I'm describing it's less easy for writers, because of scientific advance,
to hold these two things together. Stevenson, for instance, has some
difficulty in projecting the split between Jekyll and Hyde as something that occurs in a laboratory, but also something that occurs
within the psyche. Whether this can be understood in a moral/spiri-
tual sense or whether there's a more deterministic sense in which for
instance in Chekhov's *The Black Monk*, he is reduced to thinking of
the double that appears as purely a hallucination, a form of mental
disease, rather than a significant event in the psyche that has a moral/
spiritual dimension.

IM If you had to choose one. . . .

JH I think it would have to be Dostoevsky. He operates on so many
different levels, on such scale.

BT Can I connect the double theme with Bob Dylan? I'm trying to put
my finger on why you're so drawn to Bob Dylan. You said earlier
on that Dylan turned away from writing lyrics which were overt
public protest about targets which were easily identifiable, public
targets, he could write about them in 'Hard Rain' or 'The Times they
are A-Changing', in ways that were easy, literally, to understand. The

referential quality of those lyrics is very simple. But what he does in songs like 'Maggie's Farm' or in 'Rolling Stone' is he creates a world in which people are grotesque. It's as if the real life people around us have an alter ego which is a grotesque one which lurks below the surface and in this world you find yourself trapped, 'trapped inside a mobile', and trapped on Maggie's farm, or 'like a Rolling Stone', and there are all these geeks who are threatening, and suddenly they come alive. I'm wondering for a start if that's one of the reasons you're attracted to Dylan, the creation of these fantastic environments, but environments which in your work and in Dylan's work are also godless, unsettling relations to reality that we're all familiar with, so it takes you just over the boundary between real and unreal. So the alter egos are kind of unreal, or freakish, or belong to contexts like cabarets and carnivals –

JH   Absolutely.

BT   And yet at the same time are in the end deeper and more real.

JH   Yes, I think that's absolutely right. And the cabarets and carnivals – both Dylan and I have in common an influence from Rimbaud. Rimbaud was one of the writers that greatly influenced Dylan, and the gaudy carnival, the parade, is something that's there. Yes, his use of grotesques and the way in which his insights are projected through grotesques and the way he can use grotesque projections to say things that are more difficult to say directly about non-grotesques. (L) I think he is actually interested in the double as well – lines come to my mind: I think it's one of the *Street Legal* songs:
> 'I fought with my twin, that enemy within,
> Till both of us fell by the way.'   [*Where Are You Tonight?*]

BT   Yeah. Facing the deeper, lurking, carefully repressed, which at some point has to be acknowledged and addressed.

JH   So I think there are a lot more things I might have in common with Dylan than might immediately appear.

BT   Exactly: that's what I was realising.

IM   What's next?

JH   *Imelda* is the next, after a long gap, during which I didn't write very much fiction. The story which brought me back to fiction really, decided me I wanted to write fiction, was 'The Devil and Dr Tuberose', which I wrote just after writing the first draft of my double book. In a way it's a kind of update of Dostoevsky's novella *The Novel*, set in a contemporary Scottish context.

IM   I am impressed by that and the other stories, but I was overwhelmed by *Imelda*. I think the story is wonderful.

JH   Yes, I still think it's closest to being my most perfect work, and the one which came unbidden, completely from nowhere, without thought, and was written very, very fast, and had to be revised almost not at all. Usually I find with most books that I have to go back because there's some structural flaw which I am not willing altogether to recognise when I've just finished the first draft. Then you show it to friends, and they put their finger on the thing that you felt vaguely uneasy about and you realise, I've got to do something. With *Imelda* it felt right from the start.

IM   And it's really quite complex; it strikes me as quite surprising that it was so quick, because it's so complicated. And the frame works so well, the whole idea that this girl wants to know about her parentage, and she never does.

JH   It formed itself as I wrote, because I wasn't clear about the structure when I started out. I had a general outline in my head, only about a page of notes, and at every point where I inserted a clue, it just suddenly came to me that that's what I had to do at that point. I remember it just rolling, in a way I had never experienced before. Almost really as if the unconscious was writing it, that there was a subliminal understanding going on there. If I'd sat down and worked out a plan, it wouldn't have worked.

IM   Do you think there is a sense in which Affleck and Restoric are sort of doubles?

JH   Yes. There's quite a number of doubles in the book; the two brothers are complementary opposites; Restoric is the dark side and the henchman of Affleck and the one who acts out his impulses to some extent. He does his dirty work for him in terms of the plot, but he's also Frank's dark alter ego as well.

BT   Exactly so. That's an interesting case, because here we have an alter ego who is the shared double. And that's a real twist in the double theme; I don't know if anyone else has done anything like that. That's fascinating; this character who is actually shared between the two. The idea that in spite of themselves these two who are antagonists essentially actually have this connection.

JH   That's right, and in a sense it's an indication that they too are doubles in a way, Affleck and Frank are antagonists, and they see in each other what they hate in themselves.

IM   And you never know whether to trust Frank entirely because he's
      obviously deluded in some respects, but you believe this appalling
      scene when he finds Restoric and Affleck *in flagrante*. It's a foul, hor-
      rible little scene, brilliantly done. Is it the only time we've had any-
      thing homosexual in your work?

JH   Overtly, anyway, I would say. No, I think there's a scene with a
      homosexual in the *Truth Lover*.

IM   Yes, but not . . . Is it a metaphor?

JH   To some extent perhaps, yes. I think Affleck is someone who's
      capable of anything. (L) He's capable of all kinds of perversion.
      There's also a hint that he's having an incestuous relationship with
      his sister, and of course with Imelda he has an abusive relationship:
      that's the central point. But he's someone who has a kind of un-
      focused perversion in his nature which can go in almost any direction.
      He's a grotesque – and yet I didn't feel that that was unlikely.

IM   You're probably right about it being the nearest to perfect; it's
      Herdman-length, in a sense as well. I get the sense that you're never
      going to write a great big fat novel.

JH   No. (L) Though on several occasions I've thought I had the material
      for a full length novel, and it's never worked out that way. I think
      it's partly something to do with my style, that there's very little
      padding.

IM   There's an economy.

JH   I think I naturally write quite tight sentences, and I seem to have an
      energy span too: I'm a sprinter rather than a long distance runner.
      I work very intensely for short periods. And I'm quite tired by the
      time I'm finished a novella actually, because I'm temperamentally
      impatient as well. I get anxious about all the things that can go wrong
      if I don't finish something; once I've started I want to finish as fast
      as I can. Also I like novellas; I've always liked that length. It's a much
      commoner form on the continent in French, German, Italian litera-
      ture than it is in English literature.

BT   In a sense it seems to me that you don't write novels. Your work
      characteristically explores what happens in a phase, or a moment, or
      with relatively few people – you're not really interested in the whole
      background of all the sorts of mundane everyday things that they
      might do and all the rest of it – that's sketched in. You get enough
      of that to make the characters credible as real characters. But really
      what you're interested in is some moment or phase or crisis, and as

soon as that has been explored – that's it! Primarily you're focused on that moment.

JH   Yes, that's right. They're not big social spreads at all.

BT   That's why I say in a sense you're not a novelist.

JH   But I think the novella is my correct length. I've written a few short stories, and I think my best ones are my longest ones, the ones that come closest to being novellas. So it's short novels, long short stories.

IM   And you also let nothingness operate in your favour, as we said a few minutes ago: a twist at the end which suggests that the whole thing may have to happen again is – you're letting the blank pages at the end of the book work for you.

JH   That's a nice observation: yes, I like that. (L)

BT   *Imelda* is also the work which most makes me want to talk to you about style and voices. The voices of your narrators: first of all I don't want to give the impression that I think there is one sort of voice only, because it's very clear that in fact you subtly vary it. For example, in *Imelda*, there are certain tonal connections between Affleck and Frank and even the Major; but what you get is that Frank seems to write in a remarkably clear, perspicacious prose: he seems to think in that, and there's not many cliches, whereas you get to Affleck and you find the cliché count goes up, and the Major's just full of banalities (L). But what is striking in *Imelda*, and I think it would be fair to say in other works too, is you have a penchant for early twentieth-century or late nineteenth-century voices, in terms of what carries as the vehicle for the story, and I wonder if that is a way in which you make a distance between the characters and the ordinary, everyday world of modernity.

JH   I think so. I don't think I sit altogether easily in contemporary modernity.

BT   But you're perfectly capable of producing beautifully rendered demotic speech; modern speech when it *does* come in is very convincing.

JH   Yes, I can do that. In Scots, anyway, Scots demotic speech. I suppose what I'm less at home with is the looser English style that you get a lot of contemporary novels written in. Perhaps because of my reading, I always felt myself situated as you say in late nineteenth century into modernism, also a bit of late Romantic. I think my social background as well was Edinburgh bourgeoisie, situated even at the time I was growing up, a stage further back in social history.

BT   Exactly. The world that that belonged to and the world your char-
     acters live in is already slightly disconnected from what most people
     would take as ordinary everyday life.

JH   I think that's probably one of the reasons why I haven't caught on.

BT   And people have got used to going to fiction for a kind of instant
     feeling that yes, this is rendering *our* immediate sensibilities and
     realities: but here's a man who's producing characters – who are they?
     They're not quite real. But to me actually, this is one of your
     strengths. Your world has got all sorts of complexities and resonances
     but it's a world which is past, or a world which is not quite of the
     present.

JH   To carry on from there leads into *Ghostwriting* a bit. I felt I tried in
     Ghostwriting to be a bit more contemporary. I don't know if I really
     succeeded but there was that intention there. The prose style I
     thought was a little less mandarin.

BT   Mandarin is one word for it, but with the kind of voices which we're
     talking about and the periods of literature which we're talking about,
     there's a very high element of surface control, and you mentioned
     earlier that the nineteenth century was the one which was very much
     concerned with the hidden, potentially eruptive, evil within. So the
     voices you use are just perfect really for creating characters who have
     this superficial control over what they are doing but have a seething
     life within which is liable to erupt. And in *Imelda*, which is where
     I started from, Affleck is the personification of apparent complete and
     total control both over himself and over his world.

IM   Well let's go on to *Ghostwriting*. It comes after *Cruising*, but as John
     says, the fiction has a unified development. Tell us about *Ghost-
     writing*.

JH   I think the idea of the ghostwriting actually came from a newspaper
     paragraph about a man who was offering to write people's biographies
     on a commercial basis; insignificant people whose egos were a bit
     inflated, and they thought they'd like to have their biographies
     written, and that interested me, just as a snippet about human nature.
     But I was also at the time interested in the occult, and the dangers
     that I saw in certain aspects of New Age ideas. I think those were the
     two ideas that came together to produce this novel, and also some of
     my interest in medieval history and the Cathars, and that sort of
     thing. And Norman Cohen's books about the great witch hunts and
     about the pursuit of the Millenium [*See eg* The Pursuit of the

Millenium, *Oxford, 1970*] All these fed in together into a peculiar hotchpotch.

IM Did Leonard Balmain come first, or did Torquil Tod?

JH (L) Ah, now you're asking! They again are alter egos, so I think they were probably conceived in tandem. For those who don't know the book, there's an outer structure where Leonard Balmain describes how he has been recruited to ghost the history of this character called Torquil Tod who turns out to have a very dark past and to be possibly paranoid and crazy. I wanted to use the dual narrative: I'd used a dual narrative plus in *Imelda* and I wanted to use it again. I'd become very interested in the elusive nature of truth – I touched on this yesterday – and I wanted to make an anti-post-modernist theoretical statement (L) about how I don't believe in the relativity of truth. I think it's very important to hold on to the idea of there being objective truth somewhere, but also how difficult it is to reach it. So I think that's really what the book's about. I have a swipe at academic literary post-modernism at the end (L).

IM The power thing is also important. The shift of power between the two of them, when Leonard realises that he knows too much about Torquil, and therefore he's liable to be killed himself. You said off-tape that Abigail, the woman in here who's also known as Annie, is perhaps your most fully rendered fictional female.

JH I think she probably is, yes, which isn't saying much, because she's not all that fully rendered, and again she is seen through the eyes of a male, perhaps entirely through the eyes of a male. I've found it difficult to find the confidence to write from within a woman's mind. As I said also off-tape, I think the best portrait of a woman that I've done was Cynthia in my play *Cruising*, because I felt confident about how a woman would speak: I feel less confident about trying to enter the consciousness of a woman.

IM Yes. This is a different genre. Although I think you've got a real feel for it, you haven't written anything dramatic that wasn't suggested by someone else?

JH That's right, yes. With the exception that I did write a screenplay of *Imelda*. I've always found just the idea of trying to get a play staged has been so daunting that I think that's put me off. But I would like to write more if the opportunities were there. But I'm getting very tired of hitting my head against brick walls and writing things that turn out not to have an outlet. But *Cruising* [*1997*] was something I really enjoyed, because it was different and it was using a different medium. And I find dialogue comes fairly naturally to me. Again I wrote this work very fast, I think in less than a month.

IM   I think we'd better assume that the reader has not seen or read it.

JH   Well it's actually about a cruise. Two elements: I once went on a cruise with my mother and a friend of hers and the friend's son: I can't remember how the idea of a cruise as a subject for a play came into my head, but that element came together with the experience I had when I was moving into a new house in Perth. There was this wee guy who supplied furniture and restored furniture, and I needed some new doors, because the previous occupants had taken all the doors out of the interior of the house (L). It was an incredible chapter of accidents, which more or less is repeated verbatim in the first scene of *Cruising*. I wanted the idea of bringing two different classes of people together in a situation and seeing how they intermingled. And at the end of the phantasmagoric interlude which the cruise becomes, how they revert to their previous stereotypical positions at the end.

IM   It's a nice, clear, simple message, if you see what I mean. This is why I think you should write more plays, because you can move so easily into this different world: it all has to be much simpler. The wee guy with the doors who turns up on the holiday with the titled pair having been established as the useless little door-fixer at the beginning, then turns out to be a sexual threat to Sir Hamish, the advocate –

JH   The QC. And he also turns out to be one of these amazing Scottish autodidacts who's highly expert in theology (L).

IM   He knows everything: people keep getting ready to patronise him, and then he turns out to know more about theology than the minister –

JH   And he talks about theology in Edinburgh demotic Scots. (L)

IM   Basically it's all either in bars or on deck. So the actual staging of it would be remarkably easy.

JH   And of course there's a kind of double theme in this as well (L), because in a sense Sir Hamish and Wee Davy, who become pals as well as sexual rivals, are also alter egos in some peculiar way. Complementary opposites, perhaps. One thing I should have said about *Ghostwriting* is that it's of course also a metaphor, about the theoretical idea of the death of the author. In this the death of the author is actually enacted in real life.

IM   We'll leave out your memoir of Edinburgh in the Seventies, because although we love going over it, interested parties can read it! Bob is desperate to get on to *Sinister Cabaret*, and given that we have talked quite a bit yesterday about that period as far as you were concerned, I think we should move on. Can I first of all ask you about the publisher, because it's a new label to me.

JH Yes. Black Ace is really a one or two person publisher and really it's Hunter Steele, who lives in Forfar, a novelist and previously a music publisher, and he set up Black Ace I suppose about ten or twelve years ago. Really it's him and his partner Boo Wood who looks after the art side of it. I moved to them from Polygon, who rejected *The Sinister Cabaret*, and I hadn't been very satisfied with the way they distributed my books, and Black Ace have proved to be extremely good, particularly on the production and editorial side. As a one man show it doesn't have great ambitions in terms of distribution, but I'm happier to be published by someone who does what they can within their limits than someone whose limits ought to be much wider, and doesn't do the job.

IM But anyone can order this from any book shop?

JH Any good bookshop (L).

IM So we don't have a problem of availability. Okay, *The Sinister Cabaret*. You said in passing that it comes from dreams.

JH Yes. I kept a dream notebook for many years – at least I still keep a dream notebook, but I only note down dreams that are very vivid, which tend to come in short bursts, in periods of change when you're not always aware that things are changing psychically, but they are, and you get a series of very vivid dreams. And over the years, I suppose starting about twenty years ago, I started keeping a dream notebook. I was really looking for a theme, because (L) I felt it was about time that I wrote something else, and I didn't have one. I suddenly realised that I'd used dreams a lot as you noted in my earlier books, and that it would be interesting to try to construct a narrative. I was interested in finding out whether these dreams could be made into a sequence that was meaningful, psychologically and in terms of a fictional narrative. I found that they slotted into place remarkably easily. So that was the basis of the idea.

IM It's a very playful book in some ways, the names, Sir Grossleigh Fatt, Mrs Henn-Harrier: that was why I was worried about the Gaelic ones, thinking I might be missing things, because it's such fun.

BT It's my turn to ask a question, and I'm going to threaten to annoy you:

I think this is your most postmodern book. I say that provokingly because I know how much you dislike postmodernism and pretty much all its works! (L) You have referred to the fact that you particularly abhor postmodern doctrines about relativity of truth. However, I think in some respects your work has been all along quite postmodern, and I referred earlier to the way in which you use an archaic set of voices very often, which has the effect of distancing, almost the alienation effect that Brecht calls for also. It distances the characters from the normal perceived lived-in reality of late twentieth-century life, and the characters are really made of text: they are woven out of that particular text, and some people find it so weird that they can't hack that, but that is a postmodern mode it seems to me, to do that.

JH   Yes, I think that's absolutely right; I don't have any quarrel with what can be called postmodernist practices in fiction, and I'm aware that I use them myself; what I more have a quarrel with is some of the theoretical positions that are derived or said to be derived from these practices, the conclusions. The downgrading of the position of the author really. I feel that I'm always in control of what I write, even though there are this and that cultural influences coming in.

BT   Right! Now, turning to *The Sinister Cabaret*, I'll be very forthright. I think it's among your most achieved things. It has a particular feel to me of being written by a writer who has truly, truly mastered his art, and is teasingly in charge of it all, and letting the reader find his way through this. There is an author there in the background, and a curiously knowing one, and that impression comes over in this particular book more perhaps than any other one. Do you recognise that impression? Would you say it was a fair one?

JH   Yes, I would. I think there's a more conscious distance between the narrative voice and the protagonist than there's been in any other. The way in which the protagonist is in a sense placed and laughed at – of course it's a third person narrative, rather than a first person narrative; my early novels were mostly in the first person. In *Imelda* and *Ghostwriting* there's a kind of ambivalence, but yes, I do recognise that.

BT   The particular postmodern feature which I find so striking in this book is the question of who – other than the author, who is master of his art and craft – is in charge of what here. I have the feeling that the protagonist is really not so much telling the story from the position of knowing what is going on, but is being carried forward by events, by a flow of revelations or disclosures in the words, in the text, he's a completely textualised person and identity. Would that be a fair impression?

JH I think it would, yes, because the text is created out of the unconscious in a sense.

BT Yes, exactly, which is connected with the theme of dreams. But what we get here is something which is really quite nineteenth-century, once again this preoccupation with the subconscious, the unconscious, and dreams, and how they can erupt into reality, and have to be faced and addressed in some concrete form, with this very postmodern, late twentieth-century notion of us all really being creatures of text, even if the texts are out of our own mouths and are being produced by us, but it's not as if we are as such creatures really truly creators: we are scribes. It's as if our moving finger is being made to write this by something we are not in control of, but which constitutes us, which produces us.

JH Yes, I think that's true, and it causes a difficulty for the conscious artist, because it's more difficult to reach a conclusion when it's being written for you, as it were, it's being textualised. And looking at it from the psychological viewpoint, if you're going with the unconscious, the unconscious is not amenable to neat roundings off, which I think is possibly the reason why for instance Kafka couldn't complete either *The Trial* or *The Castle*.

BT That's an interesting and very relevant observation. But it also has to do, hasn't it, with the character of dreams, and something else that we've discussed in these conversations, and that is the way in which redemption for you is never finalised; people never reach a full conclusion: there is recurrence, there is a recycling of something else in a slightly different form that will replicate and rehearse what has gone before. That's exactly what happens here.

JH In the final analysis the demons that are supposed to have been expelled reappear in an old but modified form, and you're not quite certain what the future holds for the protagonist: whether he has actually made any psychological/spiritual advance at all, or whether he's bound on an Ixionic wheel, and doomed to a Nietzschean eternal recurrence.

BT And that of course is a very postmodern thing: we are condemned to recycle in an endless spiral of signifiers, which in the end don't

get us out or liberate us, don't get us to connect with anything which
could be solid and allow us to get rid of what is controlling us.

JH   Yes. There are two voices also in this book. One is the voice of the
unconscious which is largely the voice of Donald Humbie, who does-
n't really know what's happening to him: he finds himself in a world
he doesn't understand; and then there's the voice of the detective who
represents the differentiated moral consciousness. The detective
warns Donald Humbie that he mustn't deal with his inner demons in
a way that belongs to them, and of course he doesn't heed the advice.

IM   'It's very important that you don't try to deal with them on their own
terms. If you do that, you may *think* you've defeated them, but one
fine day they'll come bouncing back.' [p 109]
      The detective's name?

JH   MacNucator? Actually no significance. It's just a name I found in a
dictionary of Scottish surnames that sounded right. It is a real name.
Various people have attempted to interpret it, but I'm afraid that
there wasn't any meaning there.

BT   But that in itself was interesting, because the detective of course is
the source of the answers and the meaning, or should be, and you're
playing a nice game again. And people will look to find some significance in the name, that which spells his identity, and there isn't any.

IM   Let's look at Donald as if he is almost real. He does win some vic-
tories, doesn't he? Cant turns up again at the end and that's serious,
but there is a sense in which I could say to a student, write me an
essay about *The Sinister Cabaret*, with the title 'A Bad Day for
Horses'. Tell me about the horses. Do they come from a dream, or?

JH   I did have several dreams about horses, and the dream about the
burning horse where the head emerges initially as a log, and then
takes the form of a horse burning on a pyre – I think I used that also
in a previous story, in the *Imelda* volume, called 'Original Sin'. And
then the other dream, again a double theme, in which two large
figures, one in the form of a monk, and one in the form of Billy
Bunter, who are doubles, identical twins. One is beaten by the other,
and the horse takes the blows. This is linked to an experience of my
own, I think, which is described towards the end of the book, about
a wooden horse that I had as a child. That really did exist, yes.

IM   Was it called Queenie?

JH   Yes. I realised a long time ago it had a great emotional significance
for me, that I'd lost this early companion.

IM Donald Humbie makes progress about all of that, when he eventually gets back and discovers his own younger self and understands about Queenie, and how the various horses in the book matter. He still has Cant to deal with at the end of the book, but he has beaten something, because he doesn't try to deal with Queenie on his own terms, he makes it with Queenie.

It may be based on dreams, but I was interested that it was constructed quite complexly: if he goes back far enough, if he dives into the past in the Alexandria mode, he will get to early truths about himself.

JH Perhaps I can bring something of that out. The journey theme is integral to it. There's an image at some point of – I think it's Mac-Nucator suggests this image to Donald – of life as an elliptical movement, not a linear progression or a simple return to source back along that linear line, but an elliptical movement from birth to death. I think the book is constructed in that sort of way as well. There's a return to the original situation, but it's a modified version. So one of the themes is coming to terms with ageing and death, I think, and I think you're right that he makes certain progress in coming to terms with his own mortality – that's one of the things he comes to terms with.

IM A great many things go back a long way; Queenie goes back a long way; Cant, Scrote, all that, goes back, and if he can come to terms with it in the past it's OK. Motion doesn't. Motion doesn't go back into the past.

JH No. He's a recurrent dream figure. I'm talking here about the genesis of the Motion image. He's a recurrent figure who has appeared in my dreams in the form of an impostor. Someone who looks a bit like Clark Gable, with Thirties sleek dark hair and one of these moustaches that looks as if a slug has crawled across the upper lip (L). I don't know quite where he comes from, psychologically speaking, why this impostor figure takes this form, but that's what his origin is. I'm not entirely sure what he represents, psychologically for me, but in the novel he is I suppose the part of Donald Humbie that's an actor. He's unwilling to come to terms with certain parts of himself, but prefers to act out a persona.

IM I find it strange, because as I say 'A Bad Day for Horses' can in a sense sum the whole thing up; it's so tight, but Motion doesn't fit, and I couldn't understand why MacNucator told his life. I couldn't connect it up, exactly. When he tells the life of 'Perpetual' Motion and 'Opportunity' Knox. Cant is so clearly brought from childhood and refaced.

JH Motion is an image of a part of Humbie, I think. A part that's acting a part, and is dishonest with himself.

IM Well then, if he dies, which he does, that's a victory for Humbie too.

JH Yes, he's one demon perhaps killed off effectively, but there are others still there. Again I find it a bit difficult to talk about this because there is a sense in which I did go to school with the others and it's not too clearly schematised, what exactly their role is. I trusted that if they had a genuine psychic importance in the journey I was trying to describe, which is in a sense my own, that then their positions in the novel wouldn't glaringly not fit. But it's not too schematised.

IM Oh no, not at all. It's just that –

JH There are bits of it that puzzle me as well (L).

BT But it seems to me that that should be the case in a story of this type, if it is to be an authentic story of the type. There must be still some puzzles.

JH,IM Yes. (noises of complete agreement)

BT The thing shouldn't be absolutely clear. When I said that I thought it was a masterful achievement of somebody with real confidence in their art and craft, I think the fact that you were able to do that with confidence and not worry about it, is part of that. It doesn't matter if this isn't absolutely neat, in the case of Motion, there should be elements like that in this story.

JH Yes that's right. To compare it with *Imelda*, *Imelda* is much neater, although it's still left open, and in a sense the neatness came to me intuitively rather than being carefully thought out. But nonetheless it is much neater. But with *The Sinister Cabaret*, the unconscious is a little more in control.

BT Quite. Exactly so. That's one of the things that makes me feel this is excellent, and gives it great power, I think.

JH There's a sense too in which the reappearance of the Cant figure – I think I had partly at the back of my mind at the point where he's thrown over the cliff and he thinks he's got rid of him for good, and then he returns – it's a bit like Holmes and Moriarty (L). In that case Doyle had to bring Moriarty back because they wanted more, but these figures have to return, they have to return.

BT Would it interrupt your flow if I asked a question? You mentioned

Cant, and names in your books are often very important. Cant is an old Scottish name.

JH   Yes it is.

BT   And it is also an old word for, basically, bullshit. Are we expected to see that?

JH   Yes, and canting was also moralistic bullshit.

IM   And you changed Pie to Scrote.(L) You had to actually write to me about that, because I had been using the proof copy to write a review. Scrote is a rather disgusting name. (L)

JH   Yes, it was one that actually didn't come from me; it was actually my publisher Hunter Steele who came up with Scrote, because he was a bit nervous about the use of Pie, because that was a real life nickname.

BT   Again the name Scrote; it's got the slightly disgusting connotations, but it's also police slang for a lowlife villain.

JH   That I must confess I didn't know. Though Hunter Steele may well have known it.

IM   I know everything doesn't have to mean something, but I feel the sea monsters mean something.

JH   That again was an incident from my dream journal, and a very powerful dream, which I still can recall the atmosphere of, very vividly. They seem to represent instinctual power, I felt, that was the dream feeling, great instinctual power, natural power, something belonging to a primitive, subterranean world. So I suppose it's an image of unconscious forces, confident ones.

IM   I was reminded, why I don't exactly know, of the Ancient Mariner blessing the watersnakes.

JH   Mmm. It's an image that I use in *Pagan's Pilgrimage* as well, yes, an important image for me, I think. That kind of moment that the blessing of the watersnakes represents is the sort of moment that Pagan experiences when he comes to see the humanity in Gadarene.

IM   '*Maybe God's not the person we think He is either*'. [p 61]. What are we saying about God in the book; does it have any meaning or is it personal wallpaper?

JH   No, the question of God is quite important and lies behind a lot of the book. It lies behind the question of a deterministic universe; the idea is toyed with that indeed Humbie may be thirled to a deterministic structure that he can't interfere with. On the other hand you've got the conventional idea of God as someone who intervenes in human affairs and may pattern our lives in a way which we are not aware of. So it's a question about whether there's a meaningful pattern in human lives. I think the position I'm talking about in that sermon, which is obviously a parody of a sermon, the serious point at the bottom of it is that it's apaphatic or negative theology; that I believe in the reality of God, but I also believe that there's nothing at all that can be said about God. And that all discourse about God is either symbolic or metaphorical or an approximation, and that the classic figure for this is Dionysius the Areopagite, (L) who is quoted in the grotesque sermon. But there's a serious point here about the unknowability and the inexpressibility of God, which I understand to be the ultimate truth of the universe, about which nothing can be said, because it's not contingent.

Books mentioned in the interviews

Descent, The Fiery Star Press, Edinburgh, 1968

A Truth Lover, Akros Publications, Preston, 1973

Memoirs of My Aunt Minnie/Clapperton, Rainbow Books, Aberdeen, 1974

Pagan's Pilgrimage, Akros Publications, Preston, 1978

Stories Short and Tall, Caithness Books, Thurso, 1979

Voice Without Restraint: Bob Dylan's Lyrics and their Background, Paul Harris Publishing, Edinburgh, 1982

The Double in Nineteenth-Century Fiction, Macmillan, London, 1990

Ed, *The County of Berwick: Third Statistical Account of Scotland, Vol XXIII*, Scottish Academic Press, Edinburgh, 1992

Ed, *The County of Roxburgh: Third Statistical Account of Scotland, Vol XXVIII*, Scottish Academic Press, Edinburgh, 1992

Imelda and Other Stories, Polygon, Edinburgh, 1993

Ghostwriting, Polygon, Edinburgh 1996

Cruising, diehard publishers, Edinburgh, 1997

Pubs, Poets, Polls and Pillar Boxes: Memoirs of an Era in Scottish Politics and Letters, Akros Publications, Kirkcaldy, 1999

The Sinister Cabaret, Black Ace Books, Forfar, 2001

See also *Four Tales*, 2000. A reprint of *A Truth Lover, Memoirs of My Aunt Minnie, Pagan's Progress* and *Clapperton*, for Introduction by Macdonald Daly and detailed bibliography

CD: – *John Herdman Reading*, Zoilus Press, London nd

[Herdman has a modest website at johnherdman.co.uk]

ROBIN JENKINS

Born 1912 : Died 2005

ROBIN JENKINS PUBLISHED his first novel, *So Gaily Sings the Lark*, in 1950. When we went to his beautiful house on a hillside on the Cowal Peninsula to interview him in 1985, he had published twenty-two books. I was, and remained, resentfully convinced that he was undergoing a period of unwarranted neglect, and that he was one of the most important of Scotland's twentieth-century novelists. Most of his work was then out of print, and unobtainable. He suggests in the interview that his foreign trips, to Afghanistan, Borneo and Spain, and his use of these countries as material for his work, may have contributed to this neglect. My suspicion that inadequate agents and cursory publishers may have contributed more to his neglect was only strengthened when we entertained him and his wife May to dinner where we were staying at Innellan. Over the meal, I asked whether there had ever been a film of *Dust on the Paw*, as the cover on my paperback resembled a movie-still. No, said the novelist, and there had never *been* a paperback! I disappeared upstairs, and returned to present him with the said paperback, produced by some disreputable conjunction of agent and publisher without his knowledge – or any royalties.

Although I had heard that he could be in unforthcoming mood, our interviews went well, and he agreed to let me edit and re-publish my favourite 'lost' novel, *Guests of War* [*Scottish Academic Press in conjunction with ASLS, 1988*]. He told us at length about the unpublished novels he kept in a drawer, because public demand was for more fashionable writers. I have cut this material here to concentrate on the published books he discussed, and because it is difficult to know how far these manuscripts were then in their final form, or how he may have revised them. He told us something about *Poverty Castle*, about *Just Duffy*, and others: of *Just Duffy*, then 'in the drawer', he said, provocatively: 'I should think it is probably the best book I have ever written.'

I wrote various articles, chapters and introductions about his work in

the years following this, but when I wanted to publish an edited interview on the treatment of conscientious objection in his work in a special Jenkins feature in *Cencrastus* in 1986, he was unwilling to let me quote the interview, saying he preferred to stand by his books as he had written them, and at the time I acquiesced. But I have treasured a letter he wrote me in 1989 which reads in part: 'If here and there, I am told that I am now "receiving the recognition I deserve", I know who it is I have to thank for it.' After our interview, now in a way a museum piece, he continued indefatigably, writing novels, keeping them for indeterminate times in the drawer, and then publishing them, and over the years we had a number of very rewarding but unrecorded conversations. I have now decided to edit this long-ago interview and publish it, because I still find his comments on his own work so stimulating. Try this:

> I don't see myself as a political person. I see myself as a moralist. I judge all political issues from a moral point of view. And in my books I'm pretty sure I sometimes over-steeped them in morality. (L)

Throughout the interviews, the novelist expressed and thought of himself as a strict and punitive moralist, and he repeatedly expressed surprise at our reading the novels in a more generous and sympathetic light.

In those early days we interviewed George Mackay Brown, Naomi Mitchison, Norman MacCaig and Iain Crichton Smith. All of these interviews have been published, and it would seem perverse to omit Jenkins.

Of recent years he received an OBE, and he received the Andrew Fetcher of Saltoun Award for Services to Scotland from the Saltire Society in 2002, and a lifetime award from the Scottish Arts Council and the Saltire Society.

Tape 1 27 June 1985 at Fairhaven, Robin Jenkins' house on the Cowal Peninsula. Present: Robin Jenkins, Isobel Murray and Bob Tait

IM   Robin Jenkins, I would like to ask you a little, to start with, about your childhood and early life. I believe you were born in Lanarkshire; is that right?

RJ   Yes, in Cambuslang – well, not quite Cambuslang, about a mile outside Cambuslang, in a small village called Flemington.

IM   That was a mining village: were your family in mines?

RJ   No, we had no connection with mining at all.

IM But you would see yourself in your childhood as being part, very roughly speaking, of a working-class environment?

RJ Yes, definitely!

IM From that angle, were there any difficulties, any social difficulties, when you went to Hamilton Academy and began to be an obvious swot and coming success?

RJ No, I don't think so. I had to travel a fair distance, I suppose, and therefore, like many others at Hamilton, we didn't know each other at home, and therefore we all met each other as sort of strangers. But I never found that. I may say, though you use the word 'swot', that I was quite a brilliant scholar, and was first, first, first, like that you see, and I suppose that would help to take away any other strain on me. (L)

IM Yes. Did you enjoy the working at school, or did you not even have to work to keep coming first?

RJ Oh, I had to work quite hard, yes. Things were fairly difficult at home, and I was aware even then that I was being given a chance and I had to make sure I used it.

IM Were you an only child?

RJ No. I've got a brother and two sisters.

IM So you had company, even for starters, at home. I asked, I think, partly because of some books – right enough, John Stirling isn't an only child, but one thinks of him so often as alone. [Happy for the Child, *1953*]

RJ Yes, well, I think to some extent you could say it's *Happy For the Child* that's autobiographical. Just to some extent, because I had friends later who said, it was nothing like that! It was nothing like that! And they knew me intimately. But they refused to believe it was as difficult for me as it was for John Stirling. I may say this, it was every bit as difficult for me. It was so very difficult for me that I'll never tell anybody about it!

IM Well, that's fair enough. So happy the child very often wasn't?

RJ Very often wasn't!

IM Very often wasn't. But school was some sort of consolation. And coming top gave you a certain satisfaction.

RJ Yes, and another thing, I was the star of the cricket team!

IM Ah, the all-rounder, then.

RJ I was indeed. And I had some difficulty, if I can put it this way, laying my hands on a pair of white flannel trousers! But I was the star of the cricket team, and I can remember to this day, my greatest feat in life is not writing any particular book, but having six wickets for two runs against Hutchie Grammar School! (L)

IM This is much like Gordon Williams telling Bob long ago that he'd rather have played for St Mirren Reserves than written *War and Peace*! (L)

RJ Yes. I certainly would never agree with that! (L)

IM I'm not entirely sure he was serious. So, one of the things that made the life of the child not entirely happy was a consciousness that money didn't grow on trees. That life was fairly hard?

RJ Yes indeed.

IM Can I ask again, without wanting to pry, whether there was a lot of religion in the background when you were a child?

RJ Absolutely none! Not a scrap! And the big influence on me was my grandfather, John Robin. My name is John Robin Jenkins. Robin is not a first name, it's a second name. My mother was Annie Robin. My grandfather was John Robin, and it's a pity he died when he did, because he could have been an even greater influence on me, and he was a very, very stalwart free thinker! And I can't think of any single person in my family who ever went to church, so utterly no religion, although certainly from my books you might think I had a strong religious background. Although *myself*, as a boy, I used to go to the Scottish Episcopal Church, I think it would be once a week in the winter, to pump the organ for this lady who was practising. And then I went to the Church of Scotland, and then I went to the Baptist Church. I was trying them all out! I must have been at this time about fourteen, fifteen.

IM Ah, but did you try the Catholics? (L)

RJ I never tried the Catholics. No, I did not! Because the Catholics were a breed apart, in as much as they went to different schools, which I think is a pity. Although, mind you, I used to play with Catholics quite a lot after school.

IM But essentially the grandfather was a Protestant freethinker, if you see what I mean?

RJ I would think he would be a Protestant freethinker. I may say that in the family they would probably tell you that he was a Jewish freethinker, because the joke was the name's not Robin, it's Reuben. Not true! (L) I think it's French in some way, because I can remember my daughter pooh-poohing this when I said I'm sure it's French. She was living in Diss at the time, down in Norfolk, and we looked up the telephone directory for that area: there wasn't one single Robin. Later, I came up with her again, this time in Paris (she's married to a diplomat), and I said, let's have a look at your telephone directory. There were column after column of Robins. So she was convinced!

IM Would you like to tell me any more about the grandfather, who sounds intriguing? You haven't quite said in what way he influenced you.

RJ Born in 1912, I was too young to know this, but I believe that he was extremely supportive of a local conscientious objector in the Four-teen-Eighteen War. He was a councillor too, on the Labour side, but was very respected, even by his political opponents, who turned up at his funeral, right enough. So yes, I think that he would have had even greater influence on me. I think the family think of me in terms of him in some way.

IM And did he actually interest you in reading about freethinking?

RJ Oh no, I would have been too young, I think, then to be influenced in that way! I would be influenced in the way a sensitive child is, watching from the background. People often ask me how did I ever become a novelist? I was listening to Jessie Kesson and Alasdair Gray on the television recently, and they were being asked about them-selves as storytellers when they were young. I would never in a million years have regarded myself as a storyteller then: I was a sort of sensitive recorder in the background, watching everything. Appar-ently not seeing anything, according to most people round me. My wife will tell me, you see nothing, you notice nothing. And I know in my heart that I notice everything, or at least the essential things. I must! Because, damn it, these two who were talking: Jessie Kesson, she's written about three or four novels: Alasdair Gray is now thinking of packing it in after three. Now I'm going to tell you this without boasting: I could have written fifty novels! It's sheer laziness; I just can't be bothered doing any more than I'm doing. I can think up situations, I can think up characters. That being the case, I must as a child have built up a vast reservoir, because I agree with Aldous Huxley and those who say that you never learn anything about human nature after the age of, well, twelve. You may, as you get older, find instances to back up your instinctive knowledge, but your instinctive knowledge is all there, and it's built up when you're two, three, four, five and so on.

IM The one small thing in that rather disappointing interview with Jessie Kesson and Alasdair Gray was the nice point when Gray said that his sister had the same childhood as he did, and then stopped himself and said, Oh no, of course she didn't: she was two years different, *and* she was a girl. Perhaps it's not surprising that your family remember the childhood differently from the way you do. Because your own point of view is always part of it, isn't it?

RJ Yes, well to tell the truth I couldn't really tell you how my sisters – one of them is older than me and the other is younger – how they would see me as a child. I'm not terribly sure. (L) It's something that's not discussed very often.

IM I believe you lost your mother when you were quite young?

RJ This has got around: it's quite wrong. It's my father I lost when I was very young. My mother lived till she was over eighty. Died down in London, where she was living with my sister. But my father died when I was about seven. So I have the very faintest recollection of him, and he had no influence whatsoever on me.

IM He didn't die in the War, did he?

RJ No, he died soon after the War. When he came back it was 1919. He wasn't a very strong person, I understand, and when he came back he took rheumatic fever and died.

IM I see. Well, sorry about getting that wrong, but that's the sort of simple thing that we can clear up so easily.

RJ My wife had pointed that out. That somebody once said this, but I'm afraid that I just don't bother correcting these things.

IM So, after Hamilton Academy you went straight to Glasgow University. Did you choose that, or did it seem automatic: was it just that everybody expected it?

RJ Well, I had to get a job. The job was teaching. And I'm not terribly sure – ah yes, I think I would have to say yes, I had intended even then, before I went, to be a writer. I had won a prize in some lifeboat competition writing an essay. Writing essays is something I can't really do too well, but I did write this. I did have a great fascination with words, and I used to write paragraphs in imitation of famous writers, even Sir Thomas Browne, believe it or not, and Robert Louis Stevenson and all the great stylists, but I didn't know I was going to be a novelist, it was just that I had a fascination with words.

IM Were you a particularly voracious reader?

RJ I couldn't have been really, because I wasn't brought up in a

household where there were a great number of books, and I had
nobody to guide my taste; and I think that I would read a lot of what
I would now call rubbish. And yet I can remember some of these
books with great feeling – Zane Grey's *Riders of the Purple Sage*
[*1912*]. Many years afterwards in Kabul, Afghanistan, there was what
was called the Library, and it was also our Staff Room. I can tell you
a more miserable-looking room was never made! It was a bare brick
floor; the roof was leaking in a hundred places because there was snow
on the roof; and it was leaking through, and it was bitterly cold. There
wasn't any heating whatsoever, except your scarf, your karakul hat,
your overcoat. And all these rows of books sent by the British
Council, which would have been very suitable in Aberdeen University. One of the things I recommended when I went there was that
they should send out a bundle of *Beano* comics, and I meant it in all
seriousness. They thought it was a joke, but it was the sort of thing
my students could have appreciated. Anyway, this morning I was
waiting before it was my turn to take a lesson – and here was Zane
Grey, *Riders of the Purple Sage* – oh, and I took it. (L) I'm sorry to
say it was a terrible letdown. Because to me there was magic in my
memories of it, but when I came across it again in its reality, all the
magic vanished. Particularly in that background!

IM Did you find yourself reading comics when you were a boy?

RJ No, I wasn't a great comic reader. Except maybe *The Magnet* and
Greyfriars School, and so forth. These, I think, and the *Boys' Own
Paper*. I went through a spell of the *Boys' Own Paper*.

BT What about teachers? Were there any teachers whose particular
enthusiasms helped you, pointed you in the direction of certain kinds
of reading?

RJ Absolutely none! The very opposite! My experience of teachers was
discouragement upon discouragement. I really mean that. I have a
loyalty to the profession; I belonged to it for a long time, and I, as
a teacher myself, met many teachers I liked: but as a child I never
encountered a teacher who helped me one little bit! I found that their
attitudes were all stereotyped; they were all blasé about things. They
didn't understand that somebody who's going to look at the poem
that they've got notes on, – they're walking up and down the aisles
reciting these notes, which they've recited dozens and dozens of times
– they didn't realise that this was a magical thing to the child. Oh,
I've had that experience! Indeed, in History I remember rebelling,

and saying to the teacher that I would much prefer not to take his notes. It caused quite a stramash: I would rather sit in the corner and make my own notes. I was regarded as a bit of an eccentric, and well, all right, they allowed me to do that for two or three weeks, and then it began to get too much for him and I had to come in and take his notes. And it was the same with *Adonais*: I had to take the teacher's notes. That was school for me.

It was the same when I went to university. I have said that before, that I must have hundreds of characters in my books, but never once have I sent anyone to a university. [*He forgets Andrew Niven, the student son in* A Very Scotch Affair, *1968: but he is an unsympathetic character! Inevitably, there are some graduates in the non-Scottish novels: eg Harold Moffatt, Abdul Wahab and Laura Johnstone in* Dust on the Paw, *1961*] It had a bad effect on me. I detested my university days. Disliked them tremendously!

It was the same at Teacher Training College. I detested that too. I know you were connected to a Teachers' training college [*Bob spent some years at Aberdeen College of Education*], but I can remember this wee man Haddo. Now, God help us! He wrote a wee book on how to teach poetry. It's pathetic, it's childish! Our first introduction to him was his walking in and saying, 'My name's Mr Haddo. Mark my words! I can make or mar you!' Now that is true. 'I can make or mar you. If you don't do what I say, you're going to get a poor mark, and never a job. If you do what I say, you're going to get a good mark.' I thought, to Hell with this! And at Hillhead High School, I taught a poem with great enthusiasm based on John Keats and his relationship with Fanny Brawne, and at the end we discussed it with the class. Then Haddo came in and said his wee bit, and then he said, 'By the way, you didn't say who wrote it.' I said, 'It was me.' And instead of saying well, that was marvellous, he was furious. I had deceived him in some way. I had deceived him! (L)

BT Up to that moment he had been quite impressed?

RJ He spoke about it with the same seriousness that he would have spoken about something written by Shelley or Keats, but as soon as he discovered it was written by a crumby student, it wasn't worth tuppence!

BT As if you'd perpetrated a forgery on him.

RJ That's right! I had played a trick on him. Well, to some extent he was right, because I *had* played a trick on him. (L)

IM   I was going to ask whether you had ever written poetry? Did you even just go through the adolescent bit?

RJ   I did, I did write poetry, and I can remember the editor of the *GUM* – that's the *Glasgow University Magazine* – when I had written a poem, he said, 'That's not for a student magazine, you should send it to-' And he named one or two learned journals. (L) I was being far too serious as a poet. I discovered afterwards I really was not a poet, though I hope I can diverge now and again. [*The death of his wife May in 1988 prompted Jenkins to begin to write poetry again. See* The Scotsman, *'Now that May has gone', August 6 1988*]

IM   As much as you like!

RJ   I find that I have a more fastidious attitude towards words than many poets; and I could name one or two poets, but I won't name them, whose prose to me is as slack and flat and lifeless as can be. Now I would cut my throat rather than write a lifeless sentence. Yet poets are the ones who, as was said in this interview with Jessie and Alasdair, handle their prose with the deepest conscience and so forth. In my own case, I take a great deal of care with my prose.

IM   But you're not tempted nowadays to write poetry at all.

RJ   Never, never, largely because I have got into an attitude where I feel the words should not count; it is what the words do that should count. I know that there are a lot of arguments against that point of view, but for a novelist I think it is a mistake if there are a bundle of pyrotechnics on every page. That's why I can't take Dylan Thomas too much, for instance; in the end maybe it's my Scottish Calvinism, but in the end I see it as a showing off. Many a time I have, I thought, managed a beautiful metaphor, and I've scored it out because it just stood out, it was just shining in a page where it should not have shone.

IM   But you've confessed to an admiration for Evelyn Waugh, who I think can flash as many pyrotechnics as any.

RJ   Ah well, but his purple passages are painful, and they were painful to him too.

IM   I was thinking more of the funny ones. There's a sentence in *Officers and Gentlemen* about young Virginia's seduction, and it says something like: 'he had looked her up, looked her over, taken her out, taken her in, from her finishing school in Paris' [*1955, p 77*]. Very showy, but it says so much.

RJ   Well I suppose that if the author has created a situation where this kind of thing is going to work: but very often they don't create the situations, and it's just the fireworks you're getting all the time. That's a different matter.

BT   Could I go back to early influences? Most of the influences as regards school and so on would have put anyone off literature and writing by the sound of it; what about using local libraries, in Hamilton – there wouldn't be one in Flemington, I imagine.

RJ   No, the nearest one, and it wasn't much of a one, was in Cambuslang, which was over a mile away, and you know to a child a mile is a fair distance. But yes there were libraries there, penny libraries, you know, and I took books out of there, but I can't really say that I was going in for the classics at that time: though at school of course I would be reading Dickens and Scott and so forth.

BT   I'm just trying to find what fed your imagination: something must have given it some fuel.

RJ   Well I really do think everything under the sun has gone through my mind, (L) good things, rotten things and so forth. Now is a different story. I don't read very much what I would call rubbish these days: I don't read very much at all, to tell the honest truth.

IM   Who does it still give you pleasure to read?

RJ   I really don't think I read a great deal any more. I prefer to go for a walk, I prefer to play golf, I even prefer to watch television – but that's probably not true, because I do read a lot. In winter time I was in Spain for three months in my brother's apartment, and I took with me a whole bundle of books, Angus Wilson and this sort of thing, but I very quickly read them, and I was forced back to what was on the shelves. God help me, I was even reading Georgette Heyer before I was finished, and in the time I was there I read forty-five paperbacks, and in the end I kidded myself this was very useful for a novelist, who just had to see what was going on. I have picked up best sellers, or even books which were raved about by the *literati*, and found myself quite unable to read beyond ten pages: I've found that often.

IM   You mentioned Norman Mailer offtape a little while ago, and I was interested because he's the first American I've heard mentioned in your connection, and I was going to ask you if there were American writers whom you particularly admired.

RJ   I wouldn't put it that way. What I admire about American writers is the opportunity that they have; I can't say I think too many of them have made full use of that opportunity. Melville, to go back a wee bit, Melville I have a tremendous admiration for, a great liking for him. Hemingway: curiously enough, no, I don't much care for Hemingway. I won't care for anyone who will spend a whole book gushing love for a creature he's going to kill: that puts me off utterly, I just don't believe that. People like Updike I admire; I am always amazed at how elaborate their prose is, rather than short and curt and so forth, And Saul Bellow, yes, although I find him a bit too heavy for me, mind you. (L)

IM He has very similar concerns to yours in some of the novels, although I also find him very heavy. But I think it was in *Dangling Man* [*1944*] that he formulated the difficult question, How should a good man live? And that's much more your kind of question than the Who am I? kind of question, isn't it?

RJ Yes, but I hope after I have addressed myself to How should the good man live? I always end up with Who the Hell cares? I have to say that: an irreverence comes into me, and I have to poke fun at it, because I don't have a lot of time for human beings you know at the present moment. For instance, this sort of thing; I cut this out just for the sake of this interview. [*Takes out a newspaper cutting*] Evidently last night Gunther Grass and Salman Rushdie were discussing literature. Now here is the TV critic of the *Glasgow Herald* telling you what to expect: 'Gunther Grass and Salman Rushdie waffle and agonise endlessly over their roots as storytellers, and how they have looked for a means of expression adequate to this century's complexity'. Now what I find, I find out I'm in 100% agreement with this account of a conversation I didn't listen to. (L) And I immediately think, this century's complexity: what the Hell do they mean? The most important man in our century at this moment is a simpleton, Mr Ronald Reagan [*President of the USA 1981-89*]. How can we have a century of great complexity when this is the fellow who has the say as to how the century will go?

BT Or whether it will end.

RJ Or whether it will end. I would say myself that human beings are as complex now as they ever were. But I don't think our century is all that complex, to tell the truth. Human beings, yes. After all, Gunther Grass and Salman Rushdie have not produced a character as complex as Hamlet. So waffle and agonise are well chosen verbs to my mind. (L) That gives you an idea as to my view of this solemn philosophising about the novelist's art.

IM Perhaps I should hastily get back to some of the things we were talking about earlier on. I think perhaps one of the reasons why Bob asked if you had any nice teachers is, that you do actually portray one or two rather good ones: I think particularly of Limpy Calderwood in *Fergus Lamont* [*1979*], who obviously just seizes the children's imagination. This was more an idea of what you hoped teachers would do than what they did in your experience?

RJ As a teacher myself I met a number of admirable teachers, and I may have been taking it from them and putting them into my childhood. Because the only teacher I can remember vividly from my childhood was a man called Fletcher, and he was a drunk: he was a terrifying man. And even in the Qualifying class I realised then, and I am not boasting – any sensitive child would – that every day the people who couldn't do it were belted: the people who could do it got a pat on the head. Now luckily I got a pat on the head most of the time, except in one subject, and this must have made me understand the plight of the others. This was staff notation, which I couldn't understand to save my life. He would go right round the class, and you had to write doh, fah, me, ray and so forth, as quickly as could be. Now I could work it out all right, but if someone failed in between it upset me, and as soon as you were wrong you were out, bang. I was the star of his class. Hell, when I went to Hamilton Academy from his class to sit this bursary examination I think I was in the first three in the whole of Lanarkshire – and here's me getting the belt for this damn thing. I realised then what was happening in spelling, composition, arithmetic: all these other people were getting it every day. And that is what has given me this dislike of teachers in some way. Although my friend Brian Walpole, the headmaster of the school down here, I play golf with him frequently, and he would be horrified to think he was such a teacher.

IM I'm sure he's not, any more than you were yourself.

RJ No, I certainly wasn't that kind of teacher: I rather fancy I must have been quite a sympathetic teacher.

BT Did you enjoy it, teaching?

RJ Yes, I did enjoy it, but it was always a struggle, you always had in your class a number of characters who didn't want to be taught, and who had to be subdued in some way or other before we could get on with it. When I went to Borneo, and was teaching in Training College there I had as my students ninety per cent Chinese. The other ten per cent were Dusuns or Muruts, that's native people, and every single one dying to learn, every single one full of respect for the teacher. I didn't know what was going on! (L) Why shouldn't it be so here? Why should we have this, I don't know, bitter element in our society?

IM   Did you have to do outside subjects at university?

RJ   I took of course History, I took Latin, and Moral Philosophy. I have to tell you this wee story of Moral Philosophy. Reading Plato, I soon discovered, I thought, that Plato was making a logical blunder all the time, in as much as he was thinking that analogies in the spiritual world were equally true in the material world. I can remember saying this in an essay, and Professor Browning – I think he was quite famous in his field – read this with some dismay. And I got back my essay with written on it: 'Poor Plato: or is it poor Mr Jenkins?' – that's how they encouraged their students! Afterwards I discovered some famous philosopher saying exactly the same thing about Plato as I had been saying.

I'll tell you another reminiscence about university. The Professor of English Literature, his name was Peter Alexander. We had to read an essay to him, and I chose Charles Lamb, because I wanted to say certain things about Charles Lamb, whom I like, but certain aspects of Lamb I don't like. I remember he stopped, 'Mr Jenkins, do you know the meaning of self-opinionated?' I said well, I suppose it means having opinions, but I suppose that's what I'm supposed to be doing here, giving my opinions. Oh, and he started to show me how wrong I was about Charles Lamb. He must have failed, because I have the same views of Charles Lamb now as I had then. (L) A precious old maid, in many respects. I can enjoy Lamb, but I don't see why I shouldn't be allowed to criticise him. But there was the professor, striking dramatic attitudes!

BT   He was still doing it many years later: I attended lectures by Peter Alexander in his retiral year.

IM   Were there any compensations? Were the years at university fun because of the other students you met, and the way you grew yourself? Was there a good side to it?

RJ   There must have been. I would have liked to play cricket for the university, and I think I would have been able enough to do that, because you see I played them all when they were at school. But I then took to wearing glasses and I didn't fancy playing cricket with glasses. So

I took to cross country running, I was a member of the Hare and Hounds. On one occasion the Hares, damn them, – this was in the depth of winter – decided to cross the Kelvin: up to here in bitter cold, and the hounds, myself among them, yelping on the bank, and we all joined hands and crossed the Kelvin. (L) The most outstanding memory of my university days.

IM (L) And that was an enjoyable memory?

RJ Yes, because you cursed and swore and you laughed, and you got back to the clubhouse, and you had your bath. Yes, I enjoyed that.

BT You haven't mentioned Association Football, and coming from Lanarkshire I might have expected you to mention that, quite apart from the connection with the later book *The Thistle and the Grail*. You weren't as keen on that evidently as cricket, were you?

RJ Oh yes! I never got a chance to play cricket at home, because the boys I played with never played cricket. It's quite funny that I became a schoolboy star at cricket, to tell the truth: I never played at home. I played football ten times more often; very, very keen football player I can tell you I was, and went to see Cambuslang Rangers every Saturday they were playing down at Cambuslang, which of course gave rise to *The Thistle and the Grail* [*1954*]. It was Cambuslang Rangers I was thinking about all the time.

IM But I believe you set it in a sense in Rutherglen.

RJ Because I thought Rutherglen had more of an identity than Cambuslang, which is a sort of nondescript place.

IM You went to Teacher Training College at Jordanhill, Glasgow, and then started teaching. Do you remember your first reactions to teaching practice, and to being left alone in charge in the classroom?

RJ I was taking two sets of training, primary and secondary. You had to do that in those days, because you were not going to get a secondary job right away. You had to go into primary. My primary work was done at Centre Street. Now, Centre Street is down in the Anderston district, and it was I think at that time probably the toughest school in Glasgow: certainly there were few tougher. My secondary was at Hillhead High, and I was in two different worlds. (L) At Centre Street, the teacher whose class I sat in, well, his language was pretty lurid. He would curse and swear, not altogether in front of the kids, but about them, and I thought this was not the done thing! And then damnit he was off ill for two or three weeks and I got his class to run on my own: that was some experience, I can tell you! And it's that

that makes me furious when I read letters, say in the *Daily Telegraph*, trying to show what a teacher's hours are, compared to what clerical hours are. Hell's bells, an hour with that class – I would have done twenty hours sitting at a desk rather than that. Then I went to Hillhead High School: well, you were in Heaven, from Hell to Heaven, it really was.

Tape 2

IM We were talking about the beginning of your teaching career, and you described very succinctly the difference between the two worlds that you found. In a sense that's been quite a big feature of your fictional work, hasn't it?

RJ Yes.

IM Do you think this working in deprived Glasgow schools led you to that particular interest?

RJ Do you mean my having sympathy for the underdog?

IM And the way in which slum living can maim people so much; it's a very strong theme in some of the early books, with Tom Curdie, for example, [The Changeling, *1958*] or with Sam Gourlay [Happy For the Child, *1953*].

BT There is also the great difficulty that some people experience getting out of that, even given the opportunity.

RJ Oh yes, I think though that my sympathies with these people were with me when I was a child too. As I've told you, I watched children in the same classroom getting belted when I realised they were quite innocent, and couldn't do any better than they were doing. And no, I didn't think all this out: I was feeling it, and afterwards I started to have a look at my feelings, to think about them, and I think it was that has given me the sympathy for them.

IM So the early teaching was just a very obvious example of the favoured and the unfavoured in our community, our country, all the rest of it, something that you were going to go back to quite a lot.

RJ Yes.

IM So you graduated in 1936 and started teaching in 1937. And you were teaching in Glasgow then?

RJ In a school called Strathclyde Primary.

IM What happened when the war came along? Were you reserved, or –

RJ Oh no, I was a CO. And I went into Forestry.

IM   I could have guessed that!

RJ   You could have guessed that, yes. One member of senior staff once
     at a school camp in Pirnmill, where I used to go with Riverside Senior
     Secondary School, said to me in a friendly way – I got on well with
     them all – 'John, your being at Forestry was a great thing for you.
     Look how you've used it in the books.' (We had just been listening
     to George Blake's review of *The Cone-Gatherers* [*1955*] on the radio).
     And I said look, if I had been at the war, it would have been a damn
     sight better thing for me. If I had managed to remain alive, I could
     have made a lot more of the war than of Forestry. Do you not think
     so?

IM   Well indeed, but on the other hand you've got a lot of mileage out
     of both the Forestry and the conscientious objection, and sometimes
     the combination of the two. In *So Gaily Sings the Lark*, in *The Cone-
     Gatherers*, in *Love is a Fervent Fire*, in *A Would-Be Saint*. . . .

RJ   *A Would-Be Saint*, I think, is probably the book that sums up a great
     part of me, I must say [*1978*]. Because in that book I deliberately
     didn't make myself the hero; I was the sort of realist, slightly cynical
     realist on the side, but I did meet someone like Gavin.

IM   Did you like him?

RJ   It wasn't a matter of liking him: you had to respect him. You had to
     realise that here was somebody making an effort to stem a tide that
     was terrifically strong. And indeed still trying to stem that tide. I
     mean, I keep reading now about how this was a good war; about how
     this was a war to destroy evil. Now I wasn't concerned about object-
     ing to this war or that war; I was objecting to war: I'm still objecting
     to war. And they've now got the danger of a greater war than ever,
     it's simply a lack of trust. And nobody, nobody anywhere, is trying
     to build up trust. But I'm quite interested in you saying, did you like
     him, because somebody in the *Times Literary Supplement* said of
     Gavin that he was the most obnoxious hero she had read in modern
     fiction. Which I couldn't understand, because others had disagreed;
     in America he was regarded as a genuine eccentric. I didn't intend
     him to be a genuine eccentric at all: I meant him to be a would-be
     saint. (L) But that is a book that's quite close to my heart, I must say,
     and it should be said that Gollancz just pushed it through as if they
     were trying to hide it under a carpet.

IM   Yes, I was reviewing for the *Financial Times* at the time, and I never
     saw it, I never heard about it. Of course when you're actually review-

ing, if you don't get a book to review you don't have time to look for it, but I wasn't aware it had come out at all.

RJ I didn't see many reviews about it. But I'm listening one day to the radio and it was certain people giving their book of the year. To my great astonishment Douglas Gifford, whom you may have heard of, took as his book of the year *A Would-Be Saint*, and I was quite certain that he was talking about a book that very few of them had ever heard of. However, he thought he saw Hardyesque elements in it, and I said hmm, hmm. Later on in Calgary, at the university there, one of the lecturers said to me, 'You're nothing like Hardy.' I said no, and I realised he was talking about Douglas Gifford. And I said, I couldn't possibly be like Hardy, because I like Hardy very much; I've read all his books at least twice, but I still don't think he plays the game by his characters. I mean if you're a novelist, you realise that you have a great responsibility towards these characters, and you can quite easily, a wee bit viciousness, do them down, or a wee bit kindness, raise them up: you really have that responsibility. And he sometimes in a rather nasty way does them down, and I would have liked to have an argument with Hardy over that. (L)

BT Do you want to pick up about whether you like Gavin Hamilton now or later? I think one reason that Isobel raised the question is because we've been discussing this, and I don't think the question, do you like this man? is necessarily appropriate. But he is disconcerting, and we learn from various accounts of different kinds of sanctity that people who are saintly can be extremely disconcerting. And another reason for it is that other characters who do good things or who have benign influences in your work are often people whose impulses are to go towards people rather than to turn away from people.

IM They get stuck in.

BT Yes, they're liable to get committed to doing something and can get head over heels in situations which can be too much for them, but at any rate they get committed. And Gavin Hamilton seems to get committed to something which takes him further and further away from the human race. I don't find this as off-putting as perhaps Isobel does, and I'll tell you why. Because two very different philosophers strike me –

IM You have to admit you're a philosopher.

BT Yes, I should admit I'm a philosopher. And for all his well known sociability throughout his lifetime, Jean-Jacques Rousseau was noted for sometimes turning away from the world entirely, the better to see it, and acquiring another reputation among some French circles of being a kind of misanthrope. And so the terrific love of humanity which was quite evident in one part of his personality could appear to turn in a mysterious way to some people's eyes into misanthropy. And another one who's rather a different philosopher but has similar impulses in this century is Ludwig Wittgenstein, who in order to save himself from torment at what he saw as the cruelties and madnesses created in society would leave everything, and do almost exactly what your Gavin Hamilton does. And so I find this quite understandable in terms of philosophers who are trying to find a way of coping with what they regard as absolute principles of goodness and honesty.

IM And my problem isn't that I don't understand it, it's that I don't find the turning away very sympathetic. You know, I can respect him. Interestingly, I said do you like him? and you immediately said you respect him. So do I; but precisely when Bob said that Rousseau was a misanthrope: sometimes Gavin seems to me to be a misanthrope.

RJ Let me put it this way. Do you like an airman who goes out and drops bombs and kills thousands of people? Do you like him? Or would you say you respect him for doing his duty? There is the difficulty. He's doing something, and the problem of liking and respect comes up. Gavin is doing the opposite, and the same problem of liking and respect comes up. I would be on the side of Gavin Hamilton, every time. I'm forgiving nobody for things like Dresden, Hiroshima and the concentration camps: I forgive nobody for these things.

IM Surely, surely. But one interesting thing about Gavin, it seems to me, is this: I understand the point at which he opts out of the society he's in, but I can't really understand where he's going. We meet him towards the end of the book, years after he first went to the forest, and he's by now living entirely on his own; he won't even share a house with the other conscientious objectors. Is it McMillan, the character that you were saying was roughly you, who worries about him at the end that he's going to walk out into the hills one night? I don't understand that too well. (L)

RJ Well, you know, that is an impulse in me. Walking out into the hills and leaving the whole damned shooting match behind me. I get sometimes such a heavy weight of despair. I don't look like it, I play golf, etc, but I can get such a weight of despair and disgust that I feel the only thing to do is to walk out into the hills and say to Hell with you all.

IM   I would be quite happy with that, but I would find it odd if you thought that was particularly good or saintly behaviour.

RJ   Well, a would-be saint; I didn't say he was a saint.

IM   I know.

RJ   Then we would have to look very closely at the word 'saintly', I must say. I think he believed in God, which I don't, and therefore it's a wee bit difficult for me just to see what the fellow was after. But if you do believe in God, certain things follow. And I don't think it always follows that you must love your fellow man if you believe in God: I don't think that at all. God has shown great signs to me that he doesn't give one damn about fellow man. If you're going to exasperate me, you'll bring forward some instance where God has involved people in some dreadful predicament, and then has released them from it. I immediately say, who the hell put them into it in the first place? Therefore I think God has got nothing whatsoever to do with love of humanity, and we are on our own as regards that, and we have to look at humanity's manifold crimes, which are far greater, as far as I can see, than its manifold kindnesses, and are far more dangerous. We are now in a situation where we can and I do think that we will destroy ourselves. I do think that deeply. Not next year, not ten years, not fifty years; but you see – a hundred years is a short time in mankind's life, and I think we cannot keep ourselves going all that time. So what is a man like Gavin Hamilton to do?

IM   Well, you've already pointed out the difference, that he does believe in God and you don't, which gives him all kinds of belief and security, however real or unreal. And it's a Christian God he believes in, who says not only love God, but love your neighbour. But even woven into your own story, it seems to me there is a difficulty because again, the canny way you operate point of view, it's only what one person or another thinks, but several times there is a finger put on Gavin possibly having a terrible amount of pride.

RJ   Oh yes, oh indeed, I would think a tremendous amount. I think St Teresa had a tremendous amount of pride. I don't think you could be a saint without a tremendous amount of pride. No use saying to me, a saint is full of humility, not true! You cannot stand up against the whole of mankind and say, God loves me, without having tremendous pride. It would be a very meek thing to say: I am humble in God's eyes: God doesn't love me any more than he loves anybody else, but these saints don't think that. If they thought that, nobody would pay them the slightest attention. A saint has got to have arrogance: I do feel that. I'm writing a novel at the present moment which will be entitled *Child's Play* [*Childish Things*, *2001*], and its theme is that in every human activity there is an element of childishness which we simply cannot eradicate. And I'm telling you I'd back that up. Only saints were truly adult. Now when I wrote that I thought about it and thought about it, and I think I do believe that is true. Only saints are truly adult; they have put away childish things, the rest of us have not. And I would think that Gavin Hamilton would come to that, that he was not childish any more. The rest were all childish, with their this is right, this is wrong: he knew what was the right thing to do. After all I think I show him in one or two little things like his kindness to other people. He is kinder to other people than most of the others.

IM   But he does drop them off. Does he feel that God is calling him to give up his two longest standing friends, whose letters he does not answer?

RJ   Tell me, did Christ not have to go into the wilderness now and then? He turned his back on everybody several times, as far as I can remember.

BT   And called upon his disciples to leave that which they had, and those whom they had. . . .

IM   To go and teach to the poor: they weren't going into the desert. They were going *towards* people, to preach.

BT   There's a difference.

RJ   In Gavin's circumstances he couldn't very well preach, and indeed he is putting up a bigger challenge to his time, shall we say, than Christ, who accepted his times. He is not accepting his times.

IM   Well, that was a very interesting huge divergence from 'What did you do in the war, Daddy?' (L). You too were a conscientious objector, and you too were in Forestry – did you have trouble being believed and accepted by that tribunal? Because you weren't giving the religious account which in some ways was more acceptable, wasn't it?

RJ   No, there were two tribunals. One in Glasgow with say a sheriff and a trade-union leader and so forth, and they, to my great indignation, gave me exemption on condition I joined something like the Pioneer Corps. My objection had not one word of God in it, mind, no religion, and I can remember the sheriff saying to me, surely, Mr Jenkins, there is such a thing as a war for good against evil. And I said, could you give me an example, please; and he gave me the American Civil War. I said, that war was fought simply for the unity of America – it had nothing to do with slavery. He just thought I was talking rubbish. But it's true! Lincoln at one time offered to let the Confederate states continue to have slaves if they wished, provided they weren't going to break away. Well, they gave me this, and I was indignant because I was not going to be a lackey-soldier – I had my pride too. So I went to Edinburgh where it was Lord Elphinstone, and I remember (L) quoting *King Lear* and one or two other things, and Lord Elphinstone must have been fairly impressed, because he had no hesitation in giving me conditional exemption, if I took up forestry or agriculture or something or other. Which was fair enough. And I think I mentioned in *A Would-Be Saint* Gavin's gratitude to people for allowing him this concession. They didn't have to do it. And most people I spoke to at that time were a bit bewildered, but none of them showed outright hostility.

Although, as I think I mentioned in *A Would-Be Saint*, at first when we cycled into Tarbert (we were about eight to ten miles out of Tarbert) to the cinema, you would come out and find that your tyres were let down and the valve had gone. That sort of thing; you'd to walk your ten miles home [*p 123*]. But that wore away, and in the end we were playing Tarbert at football!

IM   I think that's very cheering, really. I don't know how I thought conscientious objectors were treated, but I didn't think it was as civilised as that! Were your family and friends particularly hurt, shocked or upset, or did they just accept it as well?

RJ   Oh, they all expected it of course! I didn't just discover my views then: I'd always had those views.

IM   Had you tried to convert others?

RJ   Well, I was in the ILP, before the war, and the ILP must be the purest political party that ever existed. So pure that they just were blown away in the end by this wicked world! (L) We thought that we could show men a better way! (L) But we found not.

IM   Were you in any sense an activist in the ILP?

RJ   In the ILP? Not really: I was the Secretary of the branch and things like that, but I never went out to do any public speaking. I never thought of myself as a public speaker – still don't!

BT Coming back to Gavin Hamilton, where do you think he goes? In the
end. Is there a way in which he can remain in touch with the world?
He is evidently tempted to walk into the wilderness, but the ambi-
guity at the end of the novel is very evident: he might have resisted
this temptation but it *is* difficult, and I imagine for the novelist it's
difficult to place him thereafter.

RJ Well no! I left an avenue for Gavin. You remember the minister's
sister? The minister has a sister, and I had thought. . . .

IM She's forty or fifty. . . .

RJ I had thought that I could write one day a sequel to *A Would-Be Saint*
where he marries this woman. Because I always like to think of stories
with such a background. I like that kind of thing! It seems to inspire
me. And to bring Gavin back into the fold – to see if he *could* come
into the fold, with her help. Not so much her help but through
helping *her*. To see what would happen to his views, but I was always
afraid that he would water his views down too much, and I wouldn't
want that. I don't want to make too many concessions to that world
out there, you know. I don't think it deserves concessions to be made
to it. [*Note: the 'preparation' for this possibility seems very limited in
the novel: it is glancing, and her age and lack of attractiveness are
emphasised: see pages 202, 206. Jenkins' words seem to apply more directly to* So Gaily Sings the Lark, *1950, which is close in many ways
to the plot of* A Would-Be Saint, *where the minister's sister Isobel Kinross
would be a more credible link to the world for the hero David Sutherland
if he is abandoned by his Kirstie.*]

IM The forestry itself; did you enjoy the job?

RJ Well, I think so. It was pretty hard work, but you see I had always
liked that kind of life. I was a great hill-walker: I must have climbed
hundreds of hills in my day. In my university days, I used to go with
a tent into the Scottish hills, into the Lairig Ghru, and spend days.
Therefore that kind of thing was all right for me. So I would say yes,
and we, of course were, let me say straight away, slightly more intelli-
gent, more enlightened than the average forestry worker. Who at first
looked upon us with some suspicion, but in the end realised that we
were a great asset to them, because we immediately, through messages from other forests, discovered what conditions obtained there.
And we insisted that these conditions, if they were better, (L) were
going to obtain where we were, and we got many, many concessions like that. So much so that at first they were standoffish, but in

the end they were up at our bothy taking part in sing-songs and so forth!

IM   And indeed, in your books, that kind of job becomes almost an image for a really healthy life, a life in touch with nature and all the rest of it – the life of the cone-gatherers, for example, as well as of the conscientious objectors who'll be brought in if they go away; and I think the image of the cone-gatherers in the trees on the Runcie-Campbell estate with the war going on in the background is a very powerful kind of picture, isn't it?

RJ   Yes, I've been in the trees gathering cones and watching a warship going down the loch. Oh, yes indeed, I've seen that! And they kept us out quite a long time, you know, a full year more than we needed to, I thought a bit vindictive; but in the end I came back and went into Riverside Senior Secondary School.

IM   That's Glasgow again?

RJ   That's right, yes.

IM   And then you were in teaching for some time, but one of the things I just *don't* have clear in my head is when you went on these various visits abroad.

RJ   I started off 1956, I went to Afghanistan, so I couldn't have been teaching so very long in Riverside. I was in Riverside when *So Gaily Sings the Lark* came out [*1950*], *Happy for the Child* came out [*1953*], *The Thistle and the Grail* [*1954*], *The Cone-Gatherers* [*1955*], and I had a totey, wee reputation building up. (L) I suppose if I had stayed in Glasgow, and Glasgow being the kind of place it is, Labour oriented, I could have stayed there and done quite well in the teaching profession. Because I can assure you I had people visiting me on the strength of, say, *The Thistle and the Grail*, high heid-yins in the Education and so forth. But I decided to everybody's surprise that I would come down to Dunoon and teach a humble assistant's job, because I wanted a place that had a beautiful background where I could get on with my writing. I was only here two years when I went off to Afghanistan. Yes, which was quite an adventure really – ask my wife about that! (L)

IM   Did you feel consciously restless before that particular opportunity came up, or had you always wanted to travel a bit?

RJ   I think I'd always wanted to travel, yes. Still is my great pleasure to find myself in a strange city; I don't know the language, I've never been there before – that's a thing I love!

IM So, how long was the visit to Afghanistan? It was a very important move for the books.

RJ Two years. Two years, yes. Oh heavens, my wife would never have stuck it any longer than two years. (L) I liked it! I did a fair amount of travelling in Afghanistan. You see, I was at Ghazni College, I was a teacher, I was a harmless character, whereas at the Embassy the Military Attache was a character looked upon with great suspicion. And I can remember I was going to Mazar-i-Sharif, which is up near the Russian border, and when I got permission to go – and this is true – he said, if you see any tanks, John, try to get their numbers! (L) True! Picture me standing in the middle of the road.

BT Of all people!

RJ And I said, what possible good would the number do? Oh yes, our intelligence people could work out quite a lot from that. Well, needless to say, I gave him no numbers of any tanks. Afghanistan was a fascinating place. Inspired me, I think, easily more than any other place I've been to. And I could have stayed there for some time, but as I say, my wife wasn't very keen. It's quite an experience. I was the only Briton, shall we say; this happened fairly often when my colleagues were away, in this college with two thousand Afghans, with Mullahs running around: they were the top persons who ran it. I knew all about the intrigues that were going on: I met the Minister of Education; it's that kind of country. And was that kind of city, and I thoroughly enjoyed it, but oh dear, you should have heard, not her indoors, but her upstairs!

IM And was there a 'them' indoors or upstairs? Did you have any children around at this time?

RJ Oh yes. Colin was there, and Anne was there. Helen was at Jordanhill Training College, and she visited us. She did two years at Jordanhill; she visited us during her break, and instead of us waving her goodbye, she waved us goodbye, because she married somebody in the Embassy! So we left her there. I was in the Victorian situation of having them come down one day and say, John, we want to get married. Well, she should go and finish her training at Jordanhill, but needless to say they didn't listen. He's an Englishman! I'm being slightly facetious, but this I will say in all seriousness, I could live happily and write happily in any country in the world except England. There's something in me, when I walk through London, I say, oh yes, all very well, a foreign country, a foreign capital, that's how I feel. Very deeply.

IM   More than a foreign country, because you're very happy in other foreign countries.

RJ   Yes, that's true. Very much so.

IM   A threatening foreign country.

RJ   A foreign country that I feel has done my own country a lot of harm.

BT   One of the striking things about *Dust on the Paw* [*1961*] to me is that – the way in which the characters from the UK are Brits, and you treat the English really quite sympathetically, if I may say so there. Is that because at that distance when they are forced into each other's immediate proximity, people from different backgrounds do coalesce rather than collide?

RJ   No. I find the English are fine in England. It's when I think of the influence that they've had in Scotland . . . If that is removed, then of course I like the English, but I'll tell you this: I don't feel happy portraying the English. I feel that no novelist is happy portraying anybody except his own people. I mean people that he was born and brought up amongst, say till about the age of about twelve or four-teen. This may seem a big statement, but I bet you it's true. I know English novelists, who if they put an American into a book, always hand the dialogue over to an American friend to check it, because, damn it, we must all have seen a thousand American films, but we're still not very sure if the dialogue on the page is American.

BT   The discomfort you speak of in depicting English or Americans doesn't show, I think, in *Dust on the Paw*. Not in the dialogue. Did you get it checked by someone for inflection?

RJ   No. I remember addressing some company in Glasgow, and William McIlvanney was there too, and that was my theme for the night; the novelist should only write about the people he knows best. And he afterwards said I was contradicting myself: my own practice contra-dicted what I had said. But I didn't really think that was so, because, I don't know about *Dust on the Paw*, but my current novel is set in California, and I'm having to be very careful, very cautious; every time there's an American speaking, I've to look over the dialogue, I've to speak it to myself, whereas when I'm writing about a Scot down it goes, I'm one hundred per cent sure! [*The novel Jenkins refers to here on p 19 as* Child's Play, *and here as set in California is probably an early version of* Childish Things, *finally published in 2001.*]

IM   To me, one of the really interesting things about all you've been saying there, is that surely Willie was right up to a point: one of the things that you've been both very daring and I think very successful in doing is getting inside the characters of Afghans and Chinese and others.

RJ I hope you're referring to 'Bonny Chung'? [In A Far Cry From Bowmore, *1973*]

IM I am, among others.

RJ I've a soft spot for 'Bonny Chung', because you see he was based on a young fellow who taught at the college. He was a teacher of English. You're not going to believe this, but his real name was Jolly Koh, and was I terribly sorry that I couldn't use that! So I had to change it to Bonny Chung. But Jolly Koh was marvellous. He and I visited Malaysia, Singapore, where his people were, and he was a real comic. It was easy for me really to write 'Bonny Chung' after being in his company, because he was a real rebel. Cursed and swore about being a second-class citizen, and also his old grandfather who had owned mines in Malaysia, and who had spent the whole damn lot and had left Jolly with nothing. (L) So he was the one that I based it on.

IM There are lots of other characters. Even in *A Far Cry from Bowmore* [*1973*] there are lots of characters, the Indians who are relentlessly pursuing that other teacher out of Christian principles, and 'Siddiq', which I think is a very strong picture. I think you must have met a lot of these young men who were very perplexed by British attitudes to –

RJ Oh well yes, my God, you see, in the college, Ghazni College, I was meeting these young Afghans all the time, yes and Siddiq I think would be based on this young fella who helped my to get my telephone in Kabul. There, I told you, the story is in that, that's exactly what happened. I had no telephone and I said I needed a telephone, and I went up to the company and they said, oh yes, you know the Afghan would not turn you down, yes, yes. So I waited for weeks, and no telephone turned up, and then Siddiq came and told me what I had to do. (L) I had to get these poles erected, about fifty poles to the nearest junction box, and wires, and a whole bundle of naffirs they called them – coolies – so I left the British Council own- ing quite a number of poles and wires and so forth! (L)

IM But it is interesting, isn't it, that you don't have the *same* self-consciousness going inside those characters as you do about say an English one or even possibly an American one?

RJ Well, perhaps I have more of a feeling for them than for . . . ?

BT   That's I think what we're driving at!

RJ   Well, probably I have a feeling about the English. Yet my grand-
     daughters, both of them, are half-English, and indeed, if you asked
     them what they were they would say English, because their mother
     now speaks with an English accent. And my other daughter is in
     Virginia, and she maybe doesn't speak with an American accent, but
     she speaks with an American vocabulary, and my granddaughter
     there speaks with an American accent, and I've been in America
     several times, so I really should have a feeling for them, but I think
     I blame Americans for all the troubles in the world, and I blame the
     English for Scotland being the wee dump that it is.

IM   But we'll not put it down to an inability to get into characters that
     don't come from Scotland, because I think very clearly that is just
     not true.

BT   Yes. I think I'm quite glad that Isobel pressed that point, because I
     don't think it does prevent you, at least in some contexts, registering
     English characters very subtly.

IM   When were the other visits abroad? Can I sort that out?

RJ   Well, when I came back from Afghanistan, I thought I had severed
     my connection with the British Council, but no. I was offered what
     I discovered afterwards was a plum, Barcelona, where I would be
     Cultural Officer. I also had a class at the Institute, and one at the Uni-
     versity. Now that seems good, and it would have been good, if I
     hadn't been a writer! I was finding I had no time whatever to write.
     I would come in, any cultural event that was on in Barcelona I had
     to turn up, and I was crawling home at 11 o'clock at night, night after
     night, and before I went out I would be teaching a class English
     Literature, so when my two years were up I astonished them all –
     I must say they *were* astonished – when I said no, I've had enough.
     It was a delightful city; I got on marvellously with the Catalans, who
     were all coming up to my wife saying, Mrs Jenkins, is it you wants
     to go away? Are you taking him away? But a writer gets desperate
     if he doesn't get an opportunity to write – at least I do!
         So that was another two years, and then I came back and thought
     I would like to see the Far East, and I got this offer of a job in Borneo,
     and that appealed to me immensely, Borneo! So I was there for five
     years, and during that time I visited Indonesia, Malaysia, Hong
     Kong, Philippines, and all over the place. I thoroughly enjoyed that!

IM   And still had time to write?

RJ   Well, I don't know whether I was writing a great deal then or not:
      I decided to enjoy myself, but of course I did write *A Figure of Fun*
      [*1974*], *The Expatriates* [*1971*].

IM   Did the books about these countries and experiences tend to be
      written later, rather than when you were there?

RJ   Later, yes. I really don't think I could ever write a book about a place
      while I was actually in that place. My Disruption book was written
      in Canada. [The Awakening of George Darroch, *1985*] Three years
      ago I was the Scottish writer in residence at Glendon College, and
      there I was. Now, I said, what can I do here? Because there were no
      duties attached to the job. None at all! If anybody came to me and
      said, we're doing the Scots ballads: would you like to come and read
      some, I said, delighted! So I had plenty of time, they lent me an elec-
      tric typewriter, and I wrote the Disruption novel.

Tape 3

IM   I wanted to ask Robin Jenkins very briefly about his attitude to being
      a public person because he's a writer, and indeed about I think his
      considerable reluctance to be that kind of a public person.

RJ   I think a writer must be prepared to spend an awful lot of time by
      himself or herself, and if you go out and become a public figure, I
      think you would be associated with other public figures, other
      writers, and I think you would begin to spend far too much of your
      time doing that. I would far rather go and talk to a group of people,
      not talk *to* them talk *with* them, people who don't bother that I'm a
      writer, just as I don't bother that the fellow's an architect, or another
      was a forestry worker, just a human being. I think a novelist must
      get to know people, not as a public figure gets to know people, but
      as someone who is amidst them. Most people here know me; some
      don't even know I write: those who *do* know I write might make a
      very brief reference to it, but that's all.

Tape 4

IM   Perhaps we'd better talk just a little more systematically this morning
      about the books themselves, and the obvious place to start is *So Gaily
      Sings the Lark* [*1950*]. Was it in fact the first book you wrote?

RJ   Yes, I think so. The first complete book I wrote.

IM And it was one of the books which does use a certain amount of autobiographical experience. The place where it happens is based on where you worked in the forestry during the war?

RJ Yes, but no character in it is based on myself, or. . . .

IM Oh, I wasn't suggesting that!

RJ Very often in autobiographical novels that is what happens. You have a character there that really and truly is the author.

BT Very often in first novels that is what happens, so it is worth emphasising that it did *not* happen in this case.

IM It's not really a Robin Jenkins thing, is it, to have a Robin Jenkins character?

RJ No, that's right! I don't think I ever put myself into a book, no. Perhaps it's a part of my caginess – hiding my true character. (L) You may see me in a book – bits of me – as various characters, I suppose, but I don't think in all my books you could say there's a self-portrait.

IM No. And yet, even in this first novel there are some really quite strong characters. I think particularly the women. Both Kirstie, with whom the hero falls in love, and the minister's sister Isobel Kinross are really quite memorable characters.

RJ The Kirstie woman there was based on a farmer's sister in the district. She had quite a reputation! And was a strong character herself and I think she certainly did influence me. But of course I've always really preferred women characters in my books to the men. I'm not quite sure why that is so. If my wife was here she would laugh at this, but I really do think that women are more admirable creatures than men. I do think so. And it just comes into my books for that reason. When I think of my favourite characters in my books they're usually women, not men.

IM You also have a way of making out certain kinds of sadness or lack of fulfilment in women, even right back here in *So Gaily Sings the Lark*. The minister's sister Isobel is very tantalising; you want to know what's wrong, why she is ever so slightly souring all the time.

RJ In real life that's often the case too. You meet people who have this sadness, and they might find it difficult themselves to explain just why they have this sadness. It's a feeling of inadequacy, which we all have, but some people more than others.

IM The first book that most people are likely to come across –because even if publishers haven't exactly done well by you, libraries have insisted on its reprint a few times – was *Happy for the Child* [*1953*].

RJ   I was quite unfortunate with *Happy for the Child*. It was published by John Lehmann, who had started his own publishing firm, and he was very enthusiastic about it, and it was given some great reviews, and I thought my star had appeared in the sky – but I got a sad letter from John Lehmann while the book was going through the process of appearing, that he was being taken over. He was in debt, and Macdonald and Co stepped in and said they would take over my book. If I agreed, well, of course I had to agree, and therefore it was put out by John Lehmann, but thereafter I was with MacDonald. Now they didn't have anything like the prestige that Lehmann had, and if my subsequent books had come out under Lehmann's imprint, they would have far better notice down in London. [*John Lehmann was one of the twentieth century's great literary talent-spotters, most famously for editing Penguin New Writting, 1940-1950. Jenkins is right that he was unfortunately disadvantaged here.*]

IM Yes, I think that's very true.

RJ   Perhaps, of course, *The Thistle and the Grail* was the sort of book that would baffle southern critics like J D Scott. As George Blake said, he had a good laugh at the London literary world who just couldn't make head nor tail of a book like *The Thistle and the Grail*.

IM Yes. The only book of Scott's which I've read in living memory was about the kind of Big House and Scottish upper middle class people, so he may well have found *The Thistle and the Grail* a bit daunting.

RJ   The very fact that it was about football, a plebeian sport, you see, that would put him off. It would put quite a lot of people off. Although Pamela Hansford Johnson gave it a great review: I simply couldn't believe that it was her who had written it. She said she hadn't seen a football match in her life.

IM I think that's important, because I'm by no means football daft, and I think if I'd been reviewing the book, one of the main points I would have had to make is that you didn't have to be into football to appreciate the book. I've seen people put off when I've simply said you must read the football book.

RJ   Well that's why I was surprised by her enthusiasm. I could quite understand her enthusiasm for *The Cone-Gatherers*, where she saw some resemblance to Dostoevsky (L). I tell you I have been compared to some odd novelists, among them Mauriac. (L)

IM We should get back to *Happy for the Child*. John Stirling had some of the situation that you yourself remembered. How did you know so well, though, about someone like Sam Gourlay?

RJ Because I would play with people like Sam Gourlay. There was a boy whose name was Flanagan, and he was Sam Gourlay without any doubt, except of course I put in elements of sadness into Gourlay, and I don't think they would be in Flanagan. Perhaps I'm doing him an injustice, but novelists are apt to make their characters a wee bit more sensitive than perhaps they are in real life, in order to make them more interesting, and to enable the novelist to try to make discoveries. One doesn't like to be snooty about this, but ordinary people *are* ordinary. This is one of the reasons why I sometimes smile when some reviewer talks about a novelist having a good ear for dialogue, which is so realistic. Realistic dialogue would be the dullest thing under the sun! And maybe realistic people too! (L) They have to be touched up by the imagination in some way, not falsified. Very often the novelist is just finding things that are there, but perhaps the person himself is never able to express them. So perhaps Flanagan in his way did have the same sadness that Gourlay did. For instance, I wouldn't know Flanagan's home life. Of course, I knew Gourlay's home life as I created it (L), but yes, I would say that I played with these boys.

IM One of the things that makes the book so resonant is that as early as that in your novels you were writing particularly with a moral slant, and one of the frightening things about these children was that they could be wicked. They were quite often wicked. Whether it was John wilfully letting his mother suffer – indeed, *making* his mother suffer, or somebody – was it Charlie Dean? Who used to go out with Gourlay, because Gourlay's inadequacies made him feel better, and they all enjoyed being cruel to each other. I found this very chilling.

RJ Would you not also find it very true?

IM Oh, yes!

RJ This problem of cruelty is something that does worry me a great deal, because we can all be very cruel. I can remember in the Staff Room at Riverside having a discussion about concentration camps, and one fellow – I think he was naïve more than anything else – said well, you couldn't get anybody in this country to staff a concentration camp. And there was one great roar from the rest: who are you kidding? You could get them easily! They said, you could get them in this school.

IM That book is full of children with as it were an adult capacity for evil, what we usually think of as an adult capacity for evil, only occasionally lightened by the fact that there are one or two boys who are just not like that. In particular John's friend Tull, who has in some ways a worse situation than John as regards poverty and all the rest of it, but who openly loves his father instead of being ashamed of him, and doesn't seem to mind the school uniform and so on. He's an attractive character. In a lot of ways I think several of your books *are* essentially comic, but *Happy For the Child* is a very stark book, really, isn't it?

RJ   I certainly wouldn't claim that I was trying to make people laugh in *Happy For the Child*, no.

BT   I was thinking about the Tulls, the McIntyres and the Smouts of this world again. When you think about them going off to do things like die for their country, what kind of view do you take of that? As you rightly say, it takes nothing from their heroism, their ability to sacrifice themselves, but on the other hand they are also the backbone of precisely those armies. They *are* the decent citizens – the decent soldiers who will commit atrocities, and you're known for pretty strong views about people who commit atrocities: you're not given to excusing them very lightly.

RJ   No. This is me trying very hard, you see, to admit that the vast majority have got a different view from myself. And I have to realise that what I would call an atrocity they don't think are atrocities! Obviously the soldiers in their many thousands who go and kill other many thousands, they really and truly do believe they're doing this for a good purpose, and that prevents it from being an atrocity. I can remember up in the golf club some friends who were talking about terrorists, saying a terrorist would throw a bomb into a pub not knowing who was there and killing them, and I said, what's the difference between that and an airman dropping bombs on a city not knowing who is down there, and they immediately said, Oh, but it's your country that orders you to do that! I said, well that's where you're different from me. What is a country? It's a collection of people, how many millions? It's not really a collection of people like that, it's just a government, but how many people have to be there so that it becomes morally right? Well, I didn't convince them, and they represent a majority view; so unless I was writing some book on philosophy I would just have to accept that they have a better chance of being regarded as right than myself, although, in my heart, I certainly think *I* am right, and I try to show in my novels that I am right.

BT So the Smouts of this world have a different view. You can understand that they have a different view, but you can't see it as being justified. Now, what about the causes. In *A Would-Be Saint*, there's a line that wars are caused by fear, envy, greed, I think, and hate. Would you say that rather sums up what you think causes this, in your view, distorted perspective?

RJ Yes. It's a great astonishment to me, though it doesn't seem to be an astonishment to other people, that even before the last war was finished the Germans had become our allies. They were *waiting* to become our allies. Now, how does it happen that there is such a terrific hatred that you will try to destroy each other's cities and so forth, and then next day, next year, you're buddies, you're friends! It's not any great deep thing that's causing this war, it's something that can be got over quickly, and trust seems to me – it's as easy to build up as distrust. But for some reason our leaders find it better for them to have the distrust.

BT But there doesn't seem to be much of the qualities that appear in general to cause wars. Fear, envy, hate and greed. Those characters, Smout, Tull, McIntyre, they don't seem to be too much infected by fear, or envy, or hate or greed. Yet they go off and commit atrocities. . . .

RJ Yes, I see what you mean. As a matter of fact they quite like the men that they're fighting!

BT There's another paradox.

RJ And given the chance could trust them. But you see they are being told all the time that there is a higher loyalty, and this higher loyalty discounts everything else.

BT So there's this further factor, a delusion or illusion created by some in the minds of other men?

RJ Oh yes, oh, absolutely! In the minds of millions of men. And the funny thing is that it's done in every country. Every government seems to be able to do it.

IM And it's something clearly that you've always distrusted. It's the reason, I think you said before, that when you decided to do a football satire you made it a small town junior cup team, so you wouldn't be able to get the big patriotic fervour. *The Thistle and the Grail* [1954] is a satirical book. It's also perhaps the first of your big books – it's got a huge cast of characters, hasn't it? Do you find that easy to handle?

RJ Yes, I think so. *Dust on the Paw* [*1961*] has got quite a large group of characters, and I was quite pleased with it. W L Webb of the *Guardian* talked about the sheer technique, the handling of the crowd scenes. I'm never aware of technique at work; I just do it. But yes, I don't really have much difficulty in keeping my eye on all the cast.

IM Some have said that your treatment of the football-following towns-people in *The Thistle and the Grail* is an updating of the talk and behaviour of the *House with the Green Shutters*-type characters, the town bodies. But that chorus that you get as it were through the book is a very important part of its success, I think.

RJ Yes. You're dealing with a small Scots town – you're bound to have this chorus, aren't you? These worthies are there, and they're pretty effective in expressing themselves too.

IM But with understanding. For example, you treat Rab Nuneaton, the chap who has his daughter buried early in the day so that he can get to the match, and then asks everybody whether he should go, and he does go. But you don't let us just feel angry or annoyed with him: you allow us, however briefly, to understand enough just what a Hell his life is.

RJ When you bring these things up I'm a little startled at the sympathy I seem to have been able to show for many people, because I regard myself as a person who's not very given readily to sympathise.

IM Never trust the teller . . .There is a fairly relentless moral view in your books, so we can be fairly sure whether somebody is right or wrong in what they're doing, but you have a very effective way of always just showing enough about the character's circumstances or life or what's happened to them so that the reader can't sit around making moral judgments.

RJ Now that I have reached maturity, I have the sympathy, but when I was young, writing a book like *The Thistle and the Grail*, I was a passionate young man, and I would think pretty severe in my views: and that's why I'm a little surprised when you bring this up, you see. I was finding it very hard at that time. I was working in Riverside School, a pretty tough school. Teaching was no picnic there at all – good grief, no, it was an ordeal every day, and yet I would go home and get stuck in at this writing. The book had appeared. I remember I didn't get any papers, or many papers that had reviews, and I went into Rutherglen Library on my way home from school. I had to walk up to Rutherglen and get the bus there, and it was pouring, and I was sodden, and I went in to see if there was a review in the *Glasgow Herald*. Oh, and there was, and it was a good one! So I went home cheerful. These things had to happen to me, because I was finding it quite difficult. I mean, teachers weren't paid all that much even then, and writing every night. I had two children then, and I must give myself some credit for sticking at it the way I did. I must have been enthusiastic about it, must have liked doing it. Yes.

IM   And, for all you say you're surprised I find your writing sympathetic, I think you've always shown characters with a degree of compassion, and none more so perhaps than the really enigmatic character of Andrew Rutherford at the centre of *The Thistle and the Grail* [1954].

RJ   Oh yes. Funnily enough, he was a character that I didn't think I saw too clearly. He worried me a wee bit. He worried me in the sense that I don't think I brought off what I was trying to do.

BT   So if an outsider calls him an enigma, that's the outsider's way of reflecting perhaps some ambiguities that you didn't resolve?

RJ   I would say that's true. But it's a long, long time since I read *The Thistle and the Grail*!

IM   Well, let's move on to *The Cone-Gatherers*, which you've gone on record at least for a time as saying was your favourite book, or perhaps your best book [1955]. Do you still think that?

RJ   I think perhaps I would say it is my favourite book. It's set in a place that I like very much, and I suppose it was an opportunity for me to show kind of a poetic side of my writing capabilities. And I was lucky enough I think to hit upon a collection of characters that I found it interesting to try to develop, particularly Duror, the sort of person I have great sympathy for. Yes, I think I would put it as my favourite.

IM   The one thing that people have said to qualify their admiration of that book at all was about Lady Runcie-Campbell. You were telling us that most people didn't notice at the time was that Lady Runcie-Campbell was not a born aristocrat. She's the daughter of a Law Lord.

RJ   Yes, I don't know anybody who ever noticed that, and I make it very clear. Her father is a Law Lord. She married above her. And I thought well, she has to work hard at keeping up her end and keeping up her husband's end while he's away, and therefore she makes mistakes.

IM And she has a bigger problem; she's more self conscious of the problem of putting her Christianity at ease with her aristocratic position. She's self conscious, and inevitably she's going to be wrong, because the way you present it the two things don't mesh, and her own son is constantly seeing flaws in her Christian position.

RJ Yes. Let me put it this way: he is more of an aristocrat than she is. I don't mean aristocrat as far as social rank is concerned.

IM One of Nature's gentlemen?

RJ Yes, that's right. He has got an instinctive sense of what's fair.

BT So he's a patrician.

RJ Yes. And I am not going to run down patricians!

BT I didn't think you would!

RJ I often feel that I would have loved to be one myself, and have my stately home, and act very benevolently to all my retainers.

BT That was a deliberately wicked and mischievous intervention by me, I may say!

RJ Yes.

IM There is a sense too in *The Cone-Gatherers*, for all that you personally find yourself opposing some aspects of religious belief, perhaps because of the moving quality of Calum, the deformed cone-gatherer, there is a way in which you endorse the teachings of the Sermon on the Mount very movingly in the book. Meekness, gentleness and love.

RJ Yes. I'm not too sure I contain these qualities myself, mind you. The doctor in *The Cone-Gatherers*, he's apt to express a philosophy of mine too. We just have to endure, have to put up with what must be put up with.

IM You'd have time for Mr Tulloch as well.

RJ The forester? Oh yes!

IM I think he's a marvellous character.

RJ We had a forester at West Loch Tarbert, MacKenzie, his name was, and he started off being antagonistic to us, but oh in the end that wasn't so. Some of the COs went back after the war and stayed with him and so forth. But I wouldn't say he was altogether like Tulloch. I've often thought of asking MacKenzie, did he see himself in any way in Tulloch. I may say some of the forestry workers that I worked beside did see themselves in *So Gaily Sings the Lark*, and were very pleased. (L)

Tape 5

IM   The next book that we come to is in contrast to *The Cone-Gatherers*, back to the big kind of canvas of *The Thistle and the Grail*, and that's *Guests of War* [1956]. I think you let slip yesterday that some of that was based on actual fact?

RJ   Well, I did go with Strathclyde Primary School kids to Moffatt, and quite a lot of the things that happen in the book did happen in real life. Pretty much as I describe it, too: it was hilarious!

IM   It is in some ways one of your most light-hearted books. Most of the big books have at least two themes – you've got football and the Andrew Rutherford thing in *The Thistle and the Grail*, and in this one you've got the whole evacuees comedy and the close-up on Bell McShelvie as well, but the comedy is really fall-about funny, isn't it?

RJ   Yes. I've been accused at times of going in for slapstick, and indeed why not?

IM   Quite! I think for example that this is a book in which you very much surpass the comedy that Waugh got out of the same situation [In Put Out More Flags, *1941*].

RJ   Yes; I've often felt a little peeved that his book was regarded as so true and so funny. I thought *Guests of War* was a better picture of evacuees than his. Far more sympathetic, anyway!

IM   And more realistic. One of the things one finds unfortunate in Waugh is that he lacks humanity whenever he discusses what he would call the lower classes.

RJ   Yes, decidedly he does!

IM   Yes, it's a shame. What about Bell McShelvie? To me, she's perhaps your most interesting female character.

RJ   I often wonder now about Bell McShelvie: did I ever see a woman like her there? Or was her thinking influenced by my grandmother? That's on my mother's side; a very formidable lady I can assure you, and her name was Bella Affleck. I must as a child have been much impressed by her – a big, strong-minded woman – and strong-bodied woman. Probably she was the beginning of Bell McShelvie, and then a few other women too, because where I was born and brought up there were a lot of poor people, and a lot of women putting up struggles like Bell McShelvie.

IM   One of the things about Bell is that she seems to contain and articulate very strongly an idea that comes up in all sorts of other places, particularly in your early work, of the terrible bad influence, the bad effect that for example living in the Glasgow slums has on people. She believes, a bit like Charlie Forbes in *The Changeling* [*1958*], that if she can get away from the city she can get back to a pastoral identity of her own. She can become a better person, and she's actually looking to refuel herself in the country so she can go back to the slums. Is that an attitude that is important to you? Living here as you do in such a beautiful place. . . .

RJ   Yes, very much so. Although I sometimes regret that I wasn't born and brought up in a big city, because it's very useful for a novelist. I was born and brought up in this small place, tiny village surrounded by fields and coal bings – extinct coal bings! But it means that I don't set my books in big cities because I do feel that my imagination was formed when I was a child, and that's why it's always a small town I want to set my things in.

IM   Yes, but I would suggest that your books are very remarkable for the number of times that a squalid working-class area is juxtaposed not with a small town with fields and coal bings, but with radiant nature. The number of times you come to say this part of the world [*Argyll*] or to islands that are particularly beautiful, with the feeling that that kind of surroundings can have a positive, as it were Wordsworthian, effect on us.

RJ   And of course I have to admit I don't really think that does happen, as you'll find an awful lot of smallmindedness in beautiful places. But I do hope there are congenial souls in the slums who do feel that they would flower a little better in more beautiful surroundings, and it does seem one hell of a pity to me that the earth is so beautiful and yet people have to spend their whole lives in squalid places.

IM   That seems to take us on to one of your more unusual books, *The Missionaries* [*1957*]. It's not unusual in that it has people going to an island; that often happens in your work: but it's the kind of people and what they are going for that makes it unusual.

RJ   In *The Missionaries* I set myself a challenge, to describe an island where you might believe miracles could take place. It was an atmosphere I was trying to achieve, and I don't know whether I brought it off or not, but May will tell you that when the children were young I took them all to the islands of the Hebrides, including Eriskay. We spent the whole of the summer holidays in Eriskay, and I think these islands have an effect on me: I can almost believe that miracles could take place there, in spite of the fact that I don't believe in miracles! And therefore in *The Missionaries* I was going to create an island which had this atmosphere and which was inhabited by people who also believed in miracles. It's a funny, funny, silly book isn't it, because . . .yes, because the characters have such funny names ands so forth.

I think the weak bit in the book would be Andrew. Now it's a long time since I read it myself, but I still remember this book for some reason – love affairs. I wasn't any good at describing love affairs. To hark back to *Guests of War*, the love affair there between the hero and his girl is so perfunctorily done, my heart was never in it. I would do better I think now. In fact my son-in-law, a diplomat, accused me of never being able to describe love in my books. He probably meant love with sexuality in it, thought I was too much of a Calvinist. I've often wondered if that is the case, because I don't see why I should be a Calvinist. None of my family, – I'm talking about my grandfather and so forth – were ever churchy people. I don't remember any of them going to church; in fact they were pagans, not Calvinists. Pagans.

IM   But you were Protestant pagans.

RJ   Oh yes, we were Protestants! And I'm telling you they would have fought bitterly to get Protestant in front of that word pagan, which is astonishing.

BT   Can I just come in again about Nature and the strange, almost miraculous power it has? Again we come across ambivalences in the surroundings. They can be magical, and they can bring out the best in people, but at the same time they are ambivalent companions. I remember for example in *A Love of Innocence*, the birds which at times seemed to be threatening and other times reassuring. Always Nature is to be read in all sorts of different ways – not just as a wonderful cradle to bring children up in. Would you agree with that reading?

RJ   Yes I think so. You are analysing me and my attitude to Nature in a way I haven't done myself, you see. I'm inclined not to search into my mind to see just what I believe in, or indeed what I'm trying to do: I leave a good part of it to instinct. I feel if I sat down deliberately to think something out it would become pretty turgid: I have to just let myself go, and this is why I have sometimes said boastfully that yes, I think I really am a novelist. I have this facility to create characters and to put them into interesting situations, and I really have never worked out how it comes about that I have this facility, or where it comes from. Just, I was a very sensitive child, and I was building up a great reservoir of recollections: I just use them.

IM   The next book is *The Changeling* [*1958*], and the first sentence sets up a puzzle: I'll quote it: 'Though no one would belittle the benevolence of the Good Samaritan, in one respect he was lucky: he was alone with his conscience and his neighbour in trouble.' The puzzle is that Charlie Forbes sets out to be the Good Samaritan, and he finds that life just isn't that simple. He's another character, surely, about whom you have mixed feelings, or you force your reader to have mixed feelings.

RJ   He's a bit of an ass, is Charlie. I quite like asses who start doing things that they're not really capable of doing, but they think they should be done. I suppose in my own way I've tried that many times, although I really don't think I have really enjoyed life as much as I should have. I have lived my life in other people. These characters – I sit for hours and hours not having any life at all! That's how it seems to me at times – it seems to May – you go nowhere, you meet nobody, and I have to admit that's true, and then I say well, where do all these books come from? Where do all these characters come from? I've never understood it, you see.

IM   Charlie Forbes is particularly interesting. I wonder how many of the novels could be entitled – or subtitled – *A Figure of Fun* or *A Man of Principle*? There is a sense in which Charlie is both. Is Charlie your first central humbug?

RJ   Indeed, I think so! I'm not sure whether I myself am a bit of a humbug. When I accuse Mrs Thatcher and all the wealthy Tories of holding all the goods of the earth to themselves, I could be accused too. I'm sure I must have written this somewhere: nobody is so poor that there isn't someone poorer to whom you could give your little bit, and we don't do it. I do feel that every one of us is in a sense a bit of a humbug, inasmuch as we are forced to adopt attitudes that we cannot really back up with actions. We are creatures of our time, creatures of our society, and also creatures with human nature, which is limited. That is one of my themes, the limitations of human nature.

IM   Certainly you make it clear that Charlie Forbes doesn't know what he's taking on in the first place when he wants to take Tom Curdie on holiday. He doesn't understand that what he was trying to do was always impossible, and yet he is so good-hearted, I think the reader has to warm to him. [*In passing, RJ confirmed he intended no reference to George MacDonald's Curdie*] The end of *The Changeling* is very shocking: did that go down with the reviewers at the time?

RJ   It was so shocking that they made a film out of *The Changeling* for TV, and changed the ending! So it must have shocked a number of people – I had no control over that, of course, but I wasn't pleased.

IM   Don't tell me they gave it a happy ending?

RJ   I think they tried to give it the kind of ending that you could assume it was going to be reasonably happy.

IM   One other character I'd like to mention, impressive and again female, is the daughter, who starts off being very antagonistic to Tom Curdie, and thinking he's laughing at them, but she's the one who comes to sense some of the incredible problems Charlie Forbes has forced on Tom.

RJ   Well I really can't make any comment: she's there because that's how I would see her, and this is quite enlightening to me, because you are showing me to be a much more sympathetic person than I had thought myself.

BT   You start off being pretty hard on this little girl – she's a bit nasty, but in fact she proves to have more psychological insight than any of the adults. Another character who is adolescent – female pubertal at any rate, and she has a gift of insight denied to older people.

RJ   Well, I've always been quite happy portraying children. I think I can do it quite well, and I'm not surprised that people like the children in my books because as I say I delight in them.

IM   Your time in Afghanistan produced *Some Kind of Grace* [*1960*], which you've described as an adventure story with undercurrents. More importantly, it produced the largescale novel about race and racism, *Dust on the Paw* [*1961*].

RJ   In *Dust on the Paw* I was being very wilful – you will have noticed there's not a Scot in the whole book –

IM   Laura Johnston has Scottish grandparents. . . .

RJ   Is that right? Did I mention that? I've often said to people, now here is a book that has sixty characters in it, and there is not a single Scot. I am a Scot, and I defy you to find any other book in the world written by a writer who has got sixty characters and not one of them a countryman of his. I was wilful: I could have made Moffatt a Scotsman, but I didn't choose to do it. Not a single reviewer noticed it, because reading a book like *Dust on the Paw* they wouldn't think of me as a Scotsman at all: they would think I was an Englishman or something.

IM   Yes. You could pick up *Dust on the Paw* and think about *A Passage to India* [*1924*], because in some ways they invite comparison.

RJ   It has been compared with E M Forster, or described as one of its offspring. I'm not quite sure that's true. I liked *A Passage to India* [*1924*]: it's one of my favourite books, but I don't think I was thinking about it very much.

BT   Another thing that struck me about the prose in *Dust on the Paw* which might explain why English readers or readers in general didn't notice that you're a Scot: it moves into a range of Anglo-Scots educated modalities. Just a little more self-regarding mockery; a little quizzicality, a little more whimsy in the prose. Would you agree?

RJ   Well, very often the characters in the book shape the prose that you are using. If I've got a whole load of Scots characters I've got a lot of Scottish flavour in my writing, that's certain.

IM   I think the way in which you dissect these embassy people is tremendous. A chapter of the lady ambassador at the sewing afternoon to which coloured ladies are not invited, and then you have the ambassador in the next chapter with his henchmen – I think there's a lot of comedy, really quite loving though.

RJ   Yes, yes, well thanks, I seem to be a nicer person than I had thought. I enjoyed writing that book. I did, because it recalled Afghanistan to me.

IM   And your central character, Wahab. He's one of those that you weren't frightened to take on; this very different person, and I think he's very endearing; he has all these absurdities and contradictions, and yet the good heart as well.

RJ   I don't know whether I mentioned this in the book or not, but he's based on the Headmaster of Ghazni College. Now he should never have been the Headmaster of Ghazni College. This is the real man I'm talking about – his wife was the daughter of an Afghan general, and that's why he got this job as headmaster of this big prodigious college; lots of high-ranking ministers sent their children there – the boys. Now he was inadequate as a headmaster but loveable as a person. You would invite him to a party and at the end of it he would go round gathering all the wine bottles that still had a little wine in them, asking could he have it. Well, before I left Afghanistan, I arranged for him to get a scholarship. Some kind of bursary which enabled him to visit Britain, and I said now be sure to look me up in Dunoon. Oh, I didn't reckon he would ever reach Dunoon, but damn it he reached Dunoon! And he wanted me to take him out to a Scottish pub, which is dead against his religion, etc, etc. I can picture him now: he had a hard time with the Mullahs – they were the real power – in the college. He was somebody that I liked and I hope I portrayed him as likeable in the book.

IM   Yes. Like Bonny Chung [A Far Cry From Bowmore, *1973*].

RJ   Yes, that's right. Although I feel I never had much of a life, I have met quite a number of interesting people too.

IM   Would you agree if I said that *Dust on the Paw* and *A Far Cry From Bowmore* are the most successful of the books about foreign parts? Well, about the East anyway?

RJ   Oh I think so, yes, I think so. You see, Afghanistan was quite a challenge, Borneo was not. Borneo was Shangri-La; you could just lie on the beach there, and walk into the sea, and walk back out again, and you had servants, and life was just too easy. Borneo did not catch my imagination the way Afghanistan did.

IM   I think among your very best books is *A Love of Innocence* [*1963*].

RJ   Yes, I have a soft spot for *A Love of Innocence* myself.

IM   One of the things I like about it is a basic sense in which it's an optimistic book. There's a very general sense in *The Changeling* in which the good intentions fail, and Tom Curdie dies, but you get the feeling that there's almost the reverse of that in *A Love of Innocence*. By the end these two kids who were so wounded by their father murdering their mother are going to be to some extent healed by these people on the island.

BT   And not least by Angus, the rogue who turns out somewhat magical.

IM   He's certainly a mixed blessing. But he's like what we were saying about *The Thistle and the Grail* or about *Guests of War*. One of the strengths is that you're putting together the one major theme, the children, the nestlings, the orphans, and also a study of this complex man, just as you've got Bell McShelvie in the one and Andrew Rutherford in the other, so that there are always different kinds of themes playing off in the books.

RJ   Yes. The one thing a novelist is afraid of is having his story too thin. You have to thicken it, and as naturally as possible.

IM   Galloping on, Bob Tait didn't much like Mungo Niven in *A Very*

Scotch Affair [*1968*]. If I didn't like Angus in *A Love of Innocence*, Mungo who is just desperate to get away from his background, and who doesn't even have the goodness to love the woman he uses to get away. . . .

RJ   I wouldn't expect anyone to approve of Mungo Niven, mind you.

BT   And even then you're not quite as outright condemnatory as I think you see yourself. I mean you're not as censorious a person towards your characters. (L) Because there are reasons why you could understand the chap being so desperate to get away he'd take almost any doubtful dubious path he could. But he's certainly to my mind humanly speaking your least attractive central character.

RJ   What do you think of the book itself? It was a book I think the critics didn't like very much.

IM   I think it's a good book. It's not as attractive as some of the others, because the subject matter is rather unpleasant, but he seems to me to be in a line with the later characters. In the later novels you lead up to Fergus Lamont through the very different Gavin Hamilton, also Gavin Campbell in *A Figure of Fun* [*1974*].

RJ   I'm not very keen on my Borneo books. I feel I didn't put as much into them as I should.

IM   I suppose what I was liking was the neatness with which you show this man's humbuggery, if you see what I mean.

RJ   Someone said how neatly I set traps for them.

IM   He's always just failing to understand what he's being told, and from that point of view I think he is leading on to Fergus Lamont, for whom I have enormous affection.

RJ   I see what you mean; they're all bits of rogues and humbugs, that's right. Humbugs in as much as they would pretend to be better than they really are. Mind you, I do think that we are all humbugs in that sense.

IM   Yes.

RJ   But I think, yes, that it's quite interesting of you to say that it's leading up to Fergus, who was the kind of combination of all this sort of thing. (L) And I would accept that, because after all he does start as a boy in a poor area and take on the world. I've often been accused of not handling the aristocracy very well, usually in a paper like the *Daily Telegraph*. As if I could! I don't know the aristocracy at all. And I doubt whether I've seen an aristocratic lady at a distance of fifty yards, so I'm guessing, and I take it an astute reader will see that I'm guessing. (L) I don't feel too comfortable dealing with such people, and therefore to get away with it, you put on a gallus air, you exaggerate, you don't give a damn, and hope you get away with it.

Books mentioned in the Interviews, with dates

So Gaily Sings the Lark, 1950
Happy For the Child, 1953
The Thistle and the Grail, 1954
The Cone-Gatherers, 1955
Guests of War, 1956
The Missionaries, 1957
The Changeling, 1958
Love Is a Fervent Fire, 1959
Some Kind of Grace, 1960
Dust on the Paw, 1961
A Love of Innocence, 1963
A Very Scotch Affair, 1968
The Expatriates, 1971
A Far Cry From Bowmore, 1973
A Figure of Fun, 1974
A Would-Be Saint, 1978
Fergus Lamont, 1979
The Awakening of George Darroch, 1985
Just Duffy, 1988
Childish Things, 2001

JOAN LINGARD

I HAD MET Joan Lingard only occasionally and briefly, before she came
to Aberdeen in May 2001, to take part in the children's sections of Word
2001, a writers' festival run by Aberdeen University. We had already
arranged the interviews by letter, but her visit to Aberdeen meant we got
to know each other a little, and I was fascinated to see her sure handling
of an audience of school children and their questions. At the end of June
2001 I interviewed her for two consecutive days in her home, a very
beautiful flat in the Edinburgh New Town. I had read almost all her
books, both those for adults and those for children, but I had had to
consult the National Library for scarce copies of some of the former.

IM   I'd like you, if you would, Joan, to tell me a little bit about your life.
It says on all the blurbs that you were born in Edinburgh, and you
went to Belfast when you were two.

JL   First of all I can tell you I was born in a taxicab in the Royal Mile,
in the Canongate of Edinburgh: it says so on my birth certificate. And
then when I was two we went to live in Belfast. My father had been
in the Navy: he'd joined the Navy as an able-seaman when he was
a boy of fourteen. He was actually English, but this side of me doesn't
seem to come up very much. He was the eldest of eleven children,
and his mother kept a pub in Stoke Newington, The Monarch, which
is still there, in Green Lane, because I've been to it. He left home
because it would be much more peaceful in the Navy. But it must
have been a horrendous life in the Navy then, way back at the
beginning of the twentieth century. He retired early, and then he was
in the RNVR, and he went to a ship in Belfast harbour called HMS
Caroline. My mother was from Edinburgh: in fact she grew up in
Bryson Road, which is in Fountainbridge, off Dundee Street.
Neither of my parents came from a particularly educated background, but my mother was a great reader. I think the Scottish tradition has always encouraged the library. I always feel indebted to
libraries, I have to say. Also, she had gone to evening classes, which

is another thing that Scotland has been particularly good at encouraging. Certainly back then.

IM Did she have a job before she got married?

JL Yes, she was working I think in the Co-op, as some kind of clerk. I'm not exactly sure what she did. I have an older sister, so I suppose she was married reasonably young. They met because my father was torpedoed in the First World War off the Scottish coast, and they came into Edinburgh for rehab.

IM It's a very dramatic story, so far!

JL My mother was very shy; a very nice woman, and probably suffered all those years in Belfast from being lonely, away from her family. Obviously communications weren't what they are now: nobody flew anywhere, it was overnight in the boat to Broomielaw, which we used to do when we were going back to Edinburgh on a visit. So from my age two to eighteen we lived in Belfast. My mother was not a Christian Scientist, so to say I was brought up as one is not exactly true. There was a family round the corner from us who were also from Scotland, and therefore my mother got friendly with them. And they were Christian Scientists, and they went to the church. So when I was four or five they took me with them to the Sunday School, with their daughter Lillian: she and I were friends. So I went to the Christian Science Sunday School until I left Belfast, because they went on at Sunday School until about twenty. My mother used to go to the church occasionally, but never joined: but I was much more ardent than that. When I was twelve I joined the mother-church, the First Church of Christ, Scientist in Boston, Massachusetts, run by Mary Baker Eddy, who I suppose was dead by that point [*1821-1910*].

IM When was this?

JL During the war – or just after. I was really very ardent. The main tenet of Christian Science is the belief that man is made in the image of God, and therefore as God is perfect man is perfect, and that there is no sin, disease or death. This was one of the main things, that they were all an illusion. If there is disease, it's because of wrong thinking. And of course they believed in spiritual healing. And they believed in the force of mind over matter, which in those days other people would have sneered at. Not so much now, because we know there's a strong connection between mind and body. I suppose this is one of the things I've always known, going back to my childhood. I was very happy in this Sunday School, because it was a very happy place:

it was so totally different from, say, Scottish Presbyterianism. It was a white church, in University Avenue, and it had a blue ceiling and a green carpet, and it was very tranquil. The people were not like fundamentalists, not rabid or anything, and there was a lot of kindness. I had very good friends. But it's not a very good preparation for life ultimately, in that you find it's quite a shock once you come to the age of adolescence, and realise that some things can happen that in your childhood you never thought could happen – that there is quite a lot of sin, disease and death around, and you don't know how to cope with it.

IM For quite a few of your characters, for example, a parent falls ill, and the other parent won't let a doctor in the house. [*eg in* The Lord On Our Side *1970 A, and* Sisters By Rite *1984 A*]

JL That didn't happen in my case, because my father didn't go to the church at all. But when I was fourteen my mother had an operation for breast cancer, and it was at that point that I began to challenge all the ideas that I had accepted without question before. But I still believed with part of me that she would be healed. She did have medical attention, and they have Christian Science practitioners who work for people, and she did have someone who was 'knowing the truth' about her. However it didn't work, of course. I was very close to my mother. My only sister was eleven years older. So when I was six and she was seventeen she left to go to work in London. And my father was not a family man. I never, ever in my life went on holiday with my father and mother: I always just went somewhere with my mother, in a twosome. He didn't come to anything, when I look back, say prize-giving, when I was getting a lot of prizes. He didn't come if I was in a school play. When I was in the Girl Guides and went to camp, my mother came to visit me, but he didn't.

IM Was it because he wasn't fond of you, or . . .

JL No: I really do think he was fond of me, and I was fond of him, ultimately – not nearly as much as my mother, of course. Perhaps I would put it down to selfishness. That he just lived his own life. And my mother was left to get on with hers.

IM Would you say theirs was a reasonably happy marriage?

JL I would say not on her side, probably.

IM Again, this is something that comes up a great deal in your writing in different ways.

JL I would say she wasn't happy, because she was left alone with me. We were very close because of that – we went to the pictures together, and things like that. My sister told me that my mother was always short of money. Sometimes my sister from London would send her a ten shilling note in a letter, because I think he didn't give her very much money. He went out a lot and I'm almost certain he had other women in his life. I suppose that she maybe knew that too. You always wonder if something like cancer starts from unhappiness. So those were very difficult times for me, my mother being ill, and then she died.

IM   Were you just living at home with your father at this stage? Or these people round the corner?

JL   They were a big support.

IM   You must have been so lonely.

JL   Yes. We had another friend who was also Scottish, from Fife, but she didn't live near us. In fact she was probably the main support for my mother in a way. She had four children and she was younger, but she used to come over when she could. I think my father *was* very fond of my mother – he was probably afflicted with conscience too. She died, and ten days after that I had to sit my Senior Certificate. So you can see that the months leading up to that were absolutely – I went in and did it, because everyone said, that's what your mother would have wanted. I *did* become closer to my father after her death: I suppose in a way he needed me too. For the first time in my life I went for walks with him, and he said to me things like, 'people maybe say I didn't love your mother, but I did'. And I'm sure his conscience on that did afflict him. I suppose I was closer, but not close: I don't think we had enough in common to be close, my father and I. He wasn't a generous man – my sister and I have often talked about that. Every Christmas and birthday he gave us two pounds, but it was like a payment. As I say, I suspect he was just selfish.

    I was only sixteen: I was too young to go to university.

IM   But you had passed the exams?

JL   Yes.

IM   That's amazing. But presumably you didn't do as well – maybe they didn't tell you?

JL   They did. I got distinctions in English, Latin and Maths, and I got credits in French and History and Chemistry. But I was capable of distinctions in French and History. But I didn't revise. My mother was ill and she died at home: it wasn't in hospital. I could have done even better: I was always at the top of my class at school.

IM   Was it a girls-only school?

JL   Yes. I got a scholarship at eleven. I went to the ordinary public elementary school until I was eleven, and then I got a scholarship into this girls' school. If you've read *The File on Fraulein Berg*, you get a picture. It was that kind of school. [*1980 C*]

IM   A touch of Enid Blyton's Malory Towers?

JL   Yes. It has gone on now: it's one of the top schools in Northern Ireland, because it has developed and grown. It was run by two batty women, the Miss Walkers. Miss Walker was the headmistress, and Miss Barbara Walker was the deputy head. But in a way it was quite a good school for a writer, because it was eccentric (L). It wasn't straight down the line. I always feel all these different things feed you as a writer.

But nobody ever in my career talked to me about going to university. And my father wouldn't suggest it, because it wouldn't occur to him. And so when I was sixteen, one option was to go back to school and repeat my final year. They didn't have a sixth year, post-exams: I would have to have gone back and redone the whole of my senior year, because you had to redo the whole of it in those days: you couldn't do odd subjects, or a different subject.

A friend of mine whose mother died when she was thirteen; her father had then sent her to boarding-school. She also was young, and she was going to go to the Methodist College for a year. Methody is probably still the biggest school. It's not actually Methodist, but I suppose it was founded by them. It's a very well known school in Ireland, a big school, co-educational. She was going to go there for a year, because they had a Scholarship year. So I went there with her. But I couldn't settle to it at all: I suppose I was too disturbed emotionally. Suddenly thrust into this enormous school, I just didn't settle down at all.

At that time, teachers were very short in Belfast. (L) I could be a teacher straight away.

IM   Yes: several people do this – Josie does. [*The Lord On Our Side, 1970 A. Also Cora in* Sisters By Rite, *1984 A*]

JL   And somebody else I knew was doing it, with only Senior Certificate as a qualification. So I applied, and I was sent to this slum school in East Belfast: it was in Short Strand. Condemned building;

Dickensian. I had fifty-four children aged six. But the infant mistress had seventy in her class. That book is all very autobiographical. It was in the most appalling building: it had been condemned pre-War, but post-War nobody was getting round to all these things. The post-War situation lingered on longer than people realise: it wasn't cleared up by 1950,or anything like that. One room in this building had no desks, and the kids were on benches, and they had to change rooms every half hour, so that everyone got a shot of the benches. (L)

IM And as in the book, was there one room where they weren't allowed to sing?

JL Yes. And twice a week the infant mistress taught sewing to the older girls, and I had to take her class. So I had 124 in the Hall for Recitation! (L) To recite poetry. These poor kids who all came from really poor homes, and a dragon of a headmistress, who used to come in swishing a cane, and tell a child of five, 'Get up and recite the poem'. A nightmare! And here's me at sixteen, with no training. I stuck that for eight months, and thought, there's no way I can go on with this.

The other great thing that girls of my age were doing was working in the bank, because it was well paid. The Irish banks had been on strike, and conditions and pay were very good. So I joined the Ulster Bank, and worked there for eight months as a clerk, which also comes into *The Lord On Our Side* [*1970 A. Also* Sisters By Rite, *1984 A*]

IM How economical you are (L)!

JL Yes. I enjoyed part of it. I used to go once a day with this guy to the Bank of Ireland to exchange notes – it seemed like such a waste to take our notes to the Bank and swop them, and have a cup of coffee on the way back. Then they trained me on the ledger machines, which I hated. But before that what happened was my father left Belfast. He sold the house and returned to Edinburgh, which he preferred.

IM Just leaving you to it?

JL Yes. So this Christian Science friend of mine, Lily, her mother took me in, as it were, and I lived with them for I suppose nine months. And then I decided I would go over to Edinburgh and join my father, well, sort of join my father. It was a displacement in my life – I've written a lot about displacement. Also I was coming out of Christian Science, which meant losing friendships, because they weren't tenable afterwards. But I had very strong friendships from my school-days, and still have. Eight of us were very friendly, and still are.

IM   I knew there had to be some of that somewhere, it's so strong in the
     books.

JL   Very strong. Three are still in Northern Ireland, and three in Canada,
     and one in France and one in Stratford. Some links are stronger than
     others, but we're all still in touch. We had a very strong friendship
     from school. Anyway, I came over to Edinburgh and my father got
     me a job working in the Edinburgh Savings Bank, which I did for
     a day (L) and I just knew that it was so utterly boring that I just didn't
     wish to do that, so I said at the end of the day to the manager 'I'm
     sorry but I'm not coming back' because I just knew – because it was
     quite different from the Ulster Bank – it seemed more intelligent –
     (L) maybe it was just the manager, or whatever. I was living in digs,
     because my father was living with an aunt, my mother's sister and
     her husband in Marchmont. I was living in digs in Murrayfield
     Avenue, because they were run by people who were Christian
     Scientists: that was how the connection had happened: someone in
     Belfast had known someone.

     So I decided I'd like to work in the library, because of course I was
     so young (L) so I joined the Edinburgh Public Library at this point.
     But of course it was much more boring than I had anticipated,
     because as a junior you're just shelving books and things like that. I
     worked for a little while in the children's library, and then they sent
     me to Corstorphine Public Library, and I worked there for probably
     about another eight months – everything happens in units of eight
     months – but you had to work there – I think I'm right here – for
     about two years before you could take the library exams. I'd had
     visions of taking the exams and rising up the system. But I realised –

IM   It was going to take a very long time. . . .

JL   If at all. I think I realised this wasn't the way on. So I had to think
     again what I was going to do. At this point I was eighteen. I suppose
     by then I'd had three major jobs for people who were just leaving
     school . . . (L) This sounds mad, but I knew someone who was
     working as a nursery nurse, and I was fond of young children: I
     thought well maybe this would be something for me to do, so I
     applied to do a nursery nurse course. I went along and had an
     interview at the City Chambers, and they said to me, it would be
     ridiculous to do nursery nursing: you're far too highly qualified and
     experienced to do that. Why don't you do teaching? We're terribly
     short of Primary teachers. In a way I suppose I hadn't known how

to go about doing it. They said, take this form and go down the street to Moray House. So I went down, and I felt Fate was here (L) – I'd been born in the Canongate, and after eighteen years I'd returned to the portals of Moray House. So I filled in the application form, and went to Moray House for three years – three of the most stultifying years of my life.

IM   Yes, I gathered that – for Rose for example in *The Headmaster*, which I read yesterday. [*In the National Library. None of Lingard's characters much enjoys Moray House, but see especially Rose Sinclair, who does three years there as a slightly older student in* The Headmaster, 1967, A]

JL   Oh gosh, I can't think what that must be like.

IM   It certainly gives the impression that three years at Moray House. . . . (L)

JL   Dreadful. I should have at that point gone to university, but I couldn't know, and how to go about it. My father, and getting grants and so on. I got a grant to go to Moray House, which my father got: in those days they paid it to the parent, for keeping you, not to the student. So he bought a flat then in Marchmont and I lived with him during those years. But I suppose again no experience is wasted: at the end of the day I came out as a teacher, and I have that experience of teaching, so when I started to write children's books or when I give talks in schools, all of it adds to your general background.

IM   It also comes out again and again in various books – the classroom experience, a knowledge of how awful it can be, and a knowledge of how bad and inadequate a teacher can feel, like that poor man in *The Headmaster* . . . [*See the early teaching career of Malcolm MacGregor, in* The Headmaster, *1967A*]

JL   I know. I can't even remember that book – it's so far back. But it's just as well I can't (L). I had no guidance from anyone anywhere, like floundering along on your own, but I always knew I wanted to write, since I started to write when I was eleven.

IM   You said from about fifteen to twenty-two you never finished anything.

JL   Yes. You come to the self conscious years. . . . I suppose also you're doing other things.

IM   So was Moray House totally stultifying – what about the people you met there? Did you make any new good friends?

JL   No, not that I've actually remained in touch with: I did for a while.

I found even most of the lecturers dreadful. There was one good one called Maxwell, and he taught Psychology, and I got on really well with him, and in fact used to go and have tea in Crawford's with him, as somebody to talk to. He'll be long dead now, I'm sure. But I was able to talk to him on a different level to any of the others. But I found some of it so footling, and I have to say in the third year I hardly went, (L) and yet I came out – what they didn't like was I was often top in a subject, when I hadn't been to their classes, which I suppose is galling, isn't it. (L) But you didn't need to go, to be honest. So I came out with a top distinction. But nothing is wholly wasted. I was twenty-one when I came out. I think also I found in the first year most of the other girls had come straight from school: I found them terribly young – well, I suppose I had lived elsewhere.

IM   You'd lived far too much for your age!

JL   My mother's illness and death, and also the crisis over my religion; leaving Belfast, all sorts of things. Three different jobs, teaching, the library and the Bank, so I had been through a tremendous amount, compared with some of these girls. It didn't stimulate me. But I do remember reading a lot of Scottish writing. We had to do that, or maybe you got a list and you could do it if you wanted. I hadn't of course come across this in Ireland. Poetry, and –

IM   Did you feel at that stage more or less exclusively Irish?

JL   Yes, probably, because I had one lecturer – I think he taught Geography – He used to call me 'Belfast' – 'Oh you're here this morning, Belfast?' (L) He addressed me as Belfast – Yes I did. I'd only made occasional visits to Scotland in a way, because with the war and everything you couldn't get there, and it was expensive. I felt almost exclusively Northern Irish– but then I've always not quite fitted in any environment, because when I was in Belfast I didn't totally belong there.

IM   No. You were what Jessie Kesson called an ootlin.

     I've heard you telling about how even playful kinds of sectarian brainwashing of children got you interested in writing about the Protestant/Catholic thing, but when you yourself were young had the Christian Science kept you out of that thing, or were you always very conscious of it?

JL   Well, you couldn't not be conscious.

IM   Did you go on the Twelfth of July marches?

JL   I didn't go on them, but I remember going up to the end of the street and watching them going past. And we lived in East Belfast, which was predominantly Protestant, and my street was called Holland Gardens – you couldn't really get much more Orange.

IM   So, would you have been horrified at that age to go into a Catholic Church?

JL   No, I wouldn't have been, but I never did go in. There were two Catholic families lived in our street –

IM   And everybody knew that?

JL   Of course. And one family a few doors down, my mother was friendly with the woman, because my mother didn't come from that background.

IM   As in *Sisters by Rite* [*1984 A*]. That's how the three girls become good friends.

JL   Exactly. I envisaged her coming from that family down the road, and it was that kind of street. And in fact when my mother died we gave her clothes to this Catholic woman.

IM   Before I realised how much Christian Science had been at the centre of your actual upbringing, I was wondering how you had remained so very even-handed about the other things. I know you were being deliberately even-handed in the children's books.

JL   Yes, but I think that that informed it. My mother certainly wouldn't subscribe to sectarian attitudes, – or my father, for that matter.

IM   Your father didn't really have a religion.

JL   No, he didn't have any religion whatsoever. But on the way I went up to school, there was a mural of King Billy on a gable end, and I passed that every day, it was part of the whole thing, and of course loads of Orange all around. There was a Catholic Church just up on the main road too, and I can remember a friend of mine from school saying, 'Don't look! Don't look!' The nuns would get you (L), or if a priest came anywhere near you on the bus, it was like, horror, because of course it was a religion of black nuns and black cassocks, so I was very aware of all that. As a writer you absorb all sorts of things. I have gone back into my background so much, steeping myself into thinking about how it was when I was ten, nine, whatever age, walking up the street, remembering the kerb – you know, you can do that: some friends in Belfast have said, 'How do you remember so many things?' Because I have deliberately put my mind back, whereas most people don't, so in a way as a writer nothing is lost: you take all the strands on with you, and hopefully at times weave them together into a piece of tapestry that might make some sort of cohesive order and sense.

IM   And you've got a slightly different angle from anyone else, really, both for adults and for children, on posing problems and describing conflicts, because you have this interesting oblique approach to it.

JL   I think that's probably why my books on Northern Ireland have been so successful, because that Kevin and Sadie quintet has been immensely successful.

IM   You can use your imagination for how they all felt, but you can also see it from outside, which none of them could, really.

JL   And the books are immensely successful in Ireland itself, north and south, and with Catholics and Protestants. When I went to Portadown recently I was speaking to teenagers from two Protestant schools and one Catholic one, Drumcree High School, all together. And I think teaching in that school in Short Strand. It was a Protestant school – I wouldn't have – you'd need to have been a Catholic to have been teaching in a Catholic school.

IM   But you didn't have to be a Protestant to teach in a Protestant school? Nobody cared? Or was it called a Protestant school or a State school?

JL   It was just Ravenhill Road Junior School. It was a state school. But automatically Protestant.

IM   And was the Protestant Church of Ireland?

JL   No: Presbyterian. In Northern Ireland the kind of top dogs are Presbyterian, then there's Church of Ireland, next is Methodist, then below all that there are the oddballs (L) like Christian Scientists. I was very self conscious about being a Christian Scientist, and didn't tell my friends that I went to the Christian Science church – I was just vague about where I went to church. I went to the Brownies that were attached to the Church of Ireland, and the Guides that were Methodists, (L) so even in religion I got round. And as I say we were friendly with a Catholic family down the road – I don't know what everyone else in the street thought of that. We weren't regular anyway.

IM   Right. And that's the great advantage, really. Okay, we've got you now twenty-one or twenty-two?

JL   Twenty-one when I came out of Moray House.

IM   Are you going to teach?

JL   I did teach. I taught for a year in Preston Street, East Preston Street School. And then got married, and went to live in Temple village, and lived there for eleven years, and had three children while we lived there, all girls, three sisters, and I taught in the village school before I had the first child, and that I really enjoyed: it was quite different. I wrote one children's book, *Hands off our School*. [*1992 C*] It was while I was there that my first book was accepted for publication. *Liam's Daughter*, in 1963. I must have finished it in 1960 or 61, I think.

IM   Did you have difficulty getting it published?

JL   Not enormously, really. I had never, ever met a writer in my life. I didn't know any. But I got the *Writer's and Artist's Yearbook*, and I looked through that. And I more or less stuck a pin in an agent, and I sent it to the agent. I suppose all of this takes a bit of time, but he read it, and decided he would like to take it on. He tried two or three publishers, maybe a couple; one was something like Hutchinson's New Writing and he sent it to Hodder, and my eldest daughter was six weeks old when I got the acceptance, because it was November, and it was raining outside, and I was a little depressed by the baby blues, sitting by the Rayburn trying to keep warm. (L) And I hadn't heard from this agent for ages and I heard the post come, and I went through to the hall carrying her on my shoulder. Picked up this letter with a London postmark and I opened it and it said, 'I am delighted to tell you that Hodder & Stoughton would like to publish *Liam's Daughter*.' Then the editor I had came up to see me, because there was no way I could go to London –

IM   I don't think they'd do that these days!

JL   No they wouldn't, specially for a first novel. She came up to see me, and she remained my editor for my first six books with Hodder. We'd a good friend called John Currie living in Temple – he was a bachelor – and he was a very close friend of Robin Jenkins, and I met my first writer, and it was Robin Jenkins.

IM   Isn't that interesting, because I've often thought you had things in common with Robin. (I've done one of these interviews with him). There were even things in that early novel *The Headmaster* that Robin early in his career might have written.

JL   Robin and John Currie had been conscientious objectors together in the war, *The Cone-Gatherers* time. I had read all of Jenkins and admired his work. So he was the very first writer I met.

IM   Isn't that interesting? The whole business of conscientious objection; it links on to that poster – it was you that was responsible, was it not, for that poster, 'Scottish Writers Against the Bomb', which Bob and

I both signed, and when I interviewed George Mackay Brown he said, 'Oh, I've got it in my kitchen'.

JL   Yes, I was the instigator of the 'Scottish Writers Against the Bomb' poster. When my second novel came out, *The Prevailing Wind* [*1964 A*], Hodder had a reception for me in Edinburgh, and to that reception came Mary Stewart, whose writing is not my thing exactly, and Nigel Tranter, who's not either, but one thing Nigel said to me I must join International PEN and the Society of Authors. So through him I joined, and I then got to know other writers –

IM   Which must have been really quite important.

JL   It was, because I felt a kind of isolation. I had three children very quickly.

IM   Even a young mum who doesn't want to be a writer is liable to feel kind of isolated.

JL   I'd had three children in three years. And I was living also in Temple, where there was no public transport, and my first husband had the car to go to work. So I was isolated. Of course I read whenever I could: I had the library van that used to come round on a Thursday morning, and I always plied them with numerous requests. So as I say the library has been a great support. So through the sixties I published these six novels, writing them I would say when I look back now, under tremendous pressure and difficulty.

IM   Even if you had been single, and doing a very undemanding part time job, you were producing novels at a great rate, let alone with three demanding children.

JL   I remember someone saying to me, do you not think you should put it aside for a few years, and I said no, because I couldn't. I feel that in a way because I had to – I would hate to read them now.

IM   (They're actually better than she thinks they are).

JL   I don't know about that. I think that I didn't have enough time to be reflective about them, and I know more now, even about the skills, than I did then.

IM   But there is a kind of youthful quality: I do think most writers tend to undervalue their early stuff because they've learned so much since.

JL   Yes, it makes you cringe to think of reading them. But I think parts of *The Prevailing Wind* – I still have a kind of fondness for it: I can still envisage her in the place. [*1964 A*]

IM   That's the one with the woman who comes back to Edinburgh with a small child that everyone thinks is illegitimate.

JL And she lives in a basement.

IM And she has a strange Indian friend.

JL And I did have a strange Indian friend, in Edinburgh when I was a student.

IM And she also has one man she falls in love with, and another much more suitable man who wants to marry her.

JL And she marries him. I think I said to you I wouldn't write it with that ending now. (L) Although it was meant to suggest in a sense a not very happy thing, like people compromising. But I probably wouldn't: I would have some other way out at the end.

IM Why did you call it *The Prevailing Wind?* Because she didn't seem to me to be bending to what I would have thought it.

JL Well she did in the end, by marrying George. But the prevailing wind, I feel it was the whole attitudes of Edinburgh, which were more marked in those days, of course. I think it's probably a bit dated now, because that was Edinburgh of the early sixties, which was quite a different place.

IM I know – I was there! (L) I was a research student in Edinburgh at that stage.

JL But it has changed; it's opened out so much more. Even people like the Indian – people thought what an odd little man, whereas now people are much more accepting.

IM Or do you think you know the more accepting people?

JL Well it's possible, of course, no I'm sure you're right.

IM I don't think some of these things change too quickly.

JL No. One tends to know the people who you'd in inverted commas call liberal. (L)

IM You wouldn't really have much time for the sort of people who live next door to the girl in *The Prevailing Wind*, and who may still do that.

JL Yes, the wind is maybe still prevailing in that way, when you get right down to it.

IM So: there you are at Temple, for the whole of the sixties.

JL No: we left in 67. We went to live in the Grange.

IM I thought you had to live there some time! [*Like eg the family home of the eponymous Headmaster, 1967*] Did you also live in Portobello?

JL No. Somebody I knew did. (L) The Grange. We moved back into town. And then 1970 was another major turning-point for me, because my marriage broke up, and I also started to write for television, and I started to write for children. I suppose you could say I started to write for television out of economic necessity, because I wasn't going to live very well off the fortunes of the adult novel. I had the opportunity to write for STV, and it was soap opera, a series called *High Living*, which meant flats, you see, high flats, and I was asked by someone would I be interested, and I wrote two as a trial and I was taken on as part of the team. Jack Gerson, Cliff Hanley – one or two other people. It was like Consequences – you wrote two episodes and you passed it over. Now I think they give you the story line, but then you made up your own, which meant at least you had more freedom and it was amazing because in those days they made the television programme as if it was theatre, no breaks and no re-takes, it was shot right through as a piece. It needed a lot of discipline!

IM   It must have been an amazing learning experience.

JL   Yes. But I have to say I did it for the money. I went on to write quite a lot for television. I wrote some plays as well, like Play for Today, which they used to have in those days, seventy-five minutes. And several half hour plays. And also there was a series called 'Square Mile of Murder', about four major Scottish cases. I did Madeleine Smith and Jessie McLachlan, the two women. [*Madeleine Smith 1835-1928, Glasgow woman accused of poisoning a former lover in a sensational murder trial, 1857: not proven. Jessie McLachlan 1834-?1899, Glasgow woman spent fifteen years in prison for murder, but her innocence was widely protested.*]

     I also did some schools programmes.

IM   You did *Maggie* for schools, didn't you?

JL   It wasn't for schools. That went out on BBC 2 early evening. It wasn't school: it was in fact done by a London production team. Other things for schools – I did one thing which was interesting with Alasdair Gray, Stephen Mulrine and myself, and we did a thing, I think it was called 'The Group', and it was about two girls and two boys, and their life things, and the other two wrote the two boys, and I did the two girls. But they all knew each other, so they wrote my girls into their scripts and vice versa.

IM   That's fascinating.

JL   Yes, and I don't know where it is now, or whether I ever got it back. That's how I first met Alasdair Gray.

IM   That's something that somebody should look out. When I say that I know it's very hard to find stuff in the BBC archives.

JL   I don't even know if they're scripts or what.

IM   Well, they may or may not survive, to be honest. It was accident
     which of Kesson's survived, and which didn't. It would be very
     interesting to dig that out.

JL   I don't think I kept them – I threw out a whole lot of television scripts
     – I had so many, and also *Maggie* was in eighteen parts – I don't know
     if I kept all those – it was silly not to. But I also then in 1970 pub-
     lished *The Twelfth Day of July*, my first children's book. You know
     why I wrote that, because this friend came, and that's what trig-
     gered it.

IM   This was the Protestant friend-by-marriage who was found half-
     jokingly teaching Joan's children about sectarianism (L).

JL   He said, 'Who is the good man?' And they said, 'King Billy'. And
     he said, 'What does King Billy ride?' And they said, 'A white horse.'
     'Where's the white horse kept?' 'In the Orange Hall'. 'Where's the
     Orange Hall?' 'Up Sandy Row.' Then he lowered his voice and said,
     'Who's the bad man?' They shouted, 'The Pope!' [Cf. eg. The Lord
     On Our Side, *1970 A*, The Twelfth Day Of July, *1970 C*, Sisters
     By Rite, *1984 A*]

IM   This is Joan's children being told a bedtime story, but at this point
     the former Christian Scientist couldn't cope!

JL   And he said of course it's only a joke, don't take on. So that really
     started me off, and I wrote *The Twelfth Day of July*, though interest-
     ingly enough I sent it to him to vet, to make sure that I didn't have
     anything wrong about the Orange Order (L). He has since left the
     Orange Order. But it's still there. They're the ones who live in France
     now. But it's still there: he's still got the things up on the wall, King
     Billy and all that, the Lodge. It's quite deeply engrained.

IM   So at the same time you were getting a bit fed up with the demands
     of television, which wasn't exactly what you wanted to do, and the
     first of the Kevin and Sadie books paid quite well. . . .

JL   I must have written Kevin and Sadie in '69, which was the beginning
     of the Troubles. It came out in '70, so I must have done. In '70 I
     started to write for television and I wrote for television right through
     the seventies.

IM   I didn't realise that went on so long.

JL   In fact the *Maggie* ones were the early 80s. So I suppose I wrote for
     nearly fifteen years for television.

IM   But you didn't enjoy it all that much, especially as it got more

professional, and there were more retakes and rewrites, other people
interfering with your script.

JL   Now I wouldn't like it at all, because it's got even worse. But it did
allow me to make money to support myself, and I didn't resent doing
it, because writers have to find some way of financing themselves:
they can teach, or they can edit, or write reviews or whatever. For
me it was an extension of my writing, but it seemed on one side of
it – I always was more interested really in the novel. But also my
children's books took off very well, so gradually of course they were
making more money for me, and Kevin and Sadie have been my bread
and butter really for the last thirty years.

IM   And you also enjoyed writing them more than you enjoyed television?

JL   Oh yes, absolutely. So in fact I ceased on the soap opera front about
the mid-seventies: I didn't carry on with that as long, because then
I did some individual stuff. Like the Square Mile of Murder. Gerda
Stevenson played Madeleine Smith.

IM   Having learned the skills that could be an interesting thing.

JL   Yes, I did things that interested me more, and because I was working
so much for children and television, the adult novel got put to one
side. I had a long gap. I can't even remember how long the gap was.

IM   Well, *The Lord on Our Side* was 1970, and *The Second Flowering of
Emily Mountjoy* was 79.

JL   Yes, so there was a nine year gap there, in which I was writing – well,
a lot of television, and a lot of children's books. I feel that because
I have written a lot for children I haven't had the chance to develop
my adult novels as much as perhaps I might have liked to have done.
But on the other hand I have enjoyed writing the children's books.

IM   And you have done I think an awful lot for children's writing, and
helped to change the whole subject matter, the fact that real subject
matter features . . .

JL   Yes: when I was writing *The Twelfth Day of July,* which was '69, my
then agent advised me, oh drop that idea at once, because no
publisher of children's books is going to publish a book about politics
and religion in Northern Ireland. Honor Arundel was a friend of
mine, and she was published by Hamish Hamilton, with an editor
called Julia MacRae, who's very well known in the children's world,
and she said, write to Julia MacRae and tell her what you're doing,
because I'm sure she'd be interested. I had a letter immediately saying
please write this book: I want it. It was on the cusp of change, because

I was speaking around 1970 at the East Lothian Literary Society in Haddington, and I was introduced by this woman who was a teacher, and she said I didn't know Joan Lingard wrote children's books, but I got my book box this morning and I opened it up and I took out this one called *The Twelfth Day of July* but I have to tell you when I saw what it was about I put it back in the book box. I had a few things to say about that when I got up! But that attitude about what was suitable for children – there was a change with those books definitely. They opened up a whole lot of aspects of children's writing and now of course you can write about anything. But before that it was much more what is suitable for children, never mind that children are involved in all sorts of issues and problems, let's pretend. I always remember speaking somewhere, and Mollie Hunter was in the audience – Mollie was quite a firebrand – I like her – We do not want to rub our children's noses in the dirt: we want to show them the bright shining star (L). What is writing supposed to be about? Exploring bright shining stars all the way? They can see stars in the middle of all the other things. She wrote about quite difficult things at times herself. I was very absorbed in those books, because in the seventies I wrote the four *Maggie* books and the five Kevin and Sadies.

So in 1972 we left Edinburgh to go and live in Cheshire, because Martin was teaching architecture at Liverpool University. We stayed in Cheshire for about twenty months, where I was not very happy, I have to say, that was another displacement for me, with three children and I was at home writing but I couldn't associate with the place or people or anything particularly, but I did use the background in the fourth book of Kevin and Sadie [*A Proper Place*, 1975] and also in *Hostages to Fortune* [*1976 C*] – we often went over into North Wales. Also Honor Arundel's family had an estate across there, which I do actually write about in part, so the background gave me something for my books as well. Of course Kevin and Sadie are displaced as well, from Belfast, into that area, and Liverpool as well.

IM And it's quite important that they have to be displaced.

JL They have to be displaced, because they couldn't remain in Northern Ireland. It had always been my intention to write a sixth and final book in which they came back to Belfast, but it's never been possible. They had to stay in exile, because that was their fate in the end. To have brought them back – nothing would have been any different: neither family could have coped with it.

IM (L) Maybe one of their children might come back.

JL Yes, well when it came to *Dark Shadows* [*1998 C*] I wrote about a
couple who married in a similar way across the divisions and he
became a Catholic, but they didn't leave, so I explored a couple who
didn't leave, and why they were able to survive was because they
became middle class and lived in a nice house in Holywood, looking
over the sea.

IM But they didn't escape the conflict.

JL No. Because the family was totally split, and the family then had
nothing to do with them after that. So Kevin and Sadie were
displaced, and I was displaced in a minor way.

IM And of course in his own time and place Martin was displaced. [*Joan's
second husband, Martin Birkhaus. His family's story, outlined here, is
fictionalised in* Tug of War, *1989 C, and* Between Two Worlds, *1991
C*]

JL He has suffered the ultimate displacement, because he grew up in
Latvia, born and bred there, and they had to leave in 1944 because
of the war. The Russians were coming into Latvia, and they posed
a very strong threat to his father's life because he was listed as an
enemy of the people because he had been chief city architect of Riga
before the war. So they had to leave everything: they suffered what
really is the ultimate displacement, and I think it is one of the major
themes of the twentieth century, the displacement of people through
wars and conflicts and sectarian divides. It's still going on: we see it
in the Balkans and everywhere. They had to leave everything and
everyone: the grandmother was left behind, all their possessions –
you could only take out what you could carry.

IM And one of the most shattering things you said in the Belmont was
that at the end of the war there were ten million displaced persons
in Germany. [*JL had been speaking to an audience in the Belmont
Cinema, Aberdeen, as part of the 2001 Word Festival.*] And that was
just in Germany.

JL And the Allies had no concept of what it was like, because people had
come in from everywhere, and been shuttled about in trains, as they
had: they were in numerous camps before they finally ended up in
Leipzig, waiting for the end of the war, and his father used to listen
to the BBC, and in Germany you could be imprisoned or put to death
for listening to the BBC. But they were listening to see who would
come in first, the Russians or the Americans. I had to do a lot of

research for this book, and I must say I do enjoy the research – about conditions in Hamburg and Germany. Both armies were advancing on the Elbe, and the Americans came in first. The first American Martin saw – the kids were out playing, and the tanks rolled in and the hatch was opened up and a black American (L) put his head out – the first time they'd ever seen a black man, and he proceeded to clean his very white teeth, spat over the side of the tank and disappeared, and the hatch was battened down again. But then shortly afterwards the Allies divided up Germany and they found they were going to be in East Germany, so they had another trek in coal carts through to West Germany, where then they lived as refugees until '49 or the end of '48, when they went to Canada. So for four years they were displaced people.

IM   And I think this is one of the things that makes your books, both the children's and the adult ones, so totally appropriate to the twentieth century, because it was a century of displacement and as you've been describing it this morning, your life has been such a series of displacements that you were ready, open to these themes.

JL   It is one of the major themes of my work. You don't set out to do this – I don't start writing thinking I'm going to write about displacement, but it comes out through the stories that you tell. And also about the resettling. In the country we have numerous immigrants who have to resettle, and they start not knowing the language, having no homes, knowing no one, so I think those two things, of being an emigrant and an immigrant, so many people have had to cope with that.

IM   And we're still very bad at doing it, asylum seekers being badly treated everywhere they go.

JL   Certainly after doing all the research and talking it over with Martin's family I was terribly impressed by their fortitude and endurance, particularly of course of the parents, bringing four children out. It must have required immense strength – and a lot didn't make it. Martin's father was quite a remarkable man.

IM   They must have been remarkable people – and lucky.

JL   He wrote two thousand letters to Canada and got two back. He didn't want to go as an official immigrant with that status, who could be sent anywhere to do anything. He wanted them to go in an independent way, because the person he worked for then I think paid for their passage.

IM So there were just these two people prepared to give them a start.

JL The amazing thing too about them is they went – the children couldn't speak much English – yet all of them went on to university. They had no money: his brother worked as a labourer: his sister in a dry-cleaners at the age of fourteen.

IM And they were building the house by hand (L)

JL Metaphorically: that was the bit that I created. They lived in a small house: the two girls slept in the sittingroom, and yet they all went to university. And that was of course because Martin's family had that in their concept. Here was me you'd think would have more chance -

IM Oh, you had every chance, if you'd had anybody to help and guide you.

JL Just even one person to say, why don't you go? I also think in North America it was easier to think in terms of going to university – it was more open. Martin was twelve when he went there and couldn't speak English, but at eighteen he went to the University of Toronto to do architecture.

IM So: he was at the University of Liverpool, and you weren't terribly happy in that area, so what moved you on?

JL Well we wanted to come back to Scotland: he did too. A job came up at Dundee University in Architecture which he took.

IM He was preferring being an academic architect to being an architect's architect?

JL Well, he had worked as an architect in Canada, but he came over to Britain to do postgraduate work at Cambridge, and then I met him, and he didn't go back.

IM He was already on the academic path.

JL I didn't go to Dundee. Martin went to Dundee, and we stayed in Cheshire for a bit. We moved up at Easter because we had bought a flat in Scotland Street – we'd just rented the house down in Cheshire. I stayed for the girls to finish school and moved back. Very soon after he started in Dundee a job came up in Edinburgh University, and he applied and got it. (L) So he did something like a term and a half in Dundee.

IM Who were no doubt very pleased with his antics (L)!

JL But we were delighted he got the job in Edinburgh, because we didn't plan to live in Dundee. So he worked then at Edinburgh University until he retired.

IM   And you must have felt, after moving back, that if you had roots, this is where they are.

JL   Oh they are. It was the nearest thing to home. I definitely now feel more Scottish than anything else. With a foot across the Irish Sea in Ireland. And maybe half a foot in Latvia. When you write a book set in other places you feel as if you've lived there. And then I wrote *Dreams of Love and Modest Glory* [*1995 A*], which gave me the opportunity to expand it much more, and I became interested in the relationship between Latvia and Russia, and the three northern ports of Aberdeen, St Petersburg and Riga.

IM   And for all the displacement, these books also emphasise the connections. That made me realise how near Aberdeen was to Riga and St Petersburg.

JL   Aberdeen and Dundee and Leith were constantly trading there, strong links across the Baltic, and a lot of Scots working in Russia.

IM   If when you were twenty-two or twenty-three you'd gone to University, what do you think you would have studied? It would have been English, and not History, for example?

JL   History's another subject that would interest me.

IM   English was the school favourite, but History has come up as well?

JL   Yes, English at school, followed by History – and French – I was also very keen on French.

IM   So when you start the next novel, if you haven't already started one, will it be something you need to do research for, partly because you just enjoy the research?

JL   (L) Well you could say, open to the idea of a topic. I have an idea for a children's book that will allow me to research in Spain, because we go there every winter anyway.

IM   So that's one of the reasons why you wrote that book about the father who steals his children back.

JL   *A Secret Place.* The white village which is the secret place. [*1998, C*]

IM   So there might be another one set in Spain.

JL   Yes. I'm going to set it, I think, just post the Spanish Civil War, about 1939. My language is coming on. I'm going to the Institute for Applied Languages at the University. I've just done four years.

IM   So you would do your research in English or in Spanish?

JL   A lot of it will be in English, because what I want to read are a lot of books by people who actually went out to serve in the Spanish Civil War. I'm thinking of a boy who goes after the Spanish Civil War to

look for his father, who went to fight in the war. A journey into it.
It would look at the conditions. I've already started to read quite a
lot. What I plan to do with that is to try and write a draft over the
winter and then when we go to Spain I know what I need to research.
[*The children's book,* Tell the Moon to Come Out *was published by
Puffin in 2003.*] When I wrote *After Colette* I went to Burgundy before
I started, and I know Paris pretty well, but it was only after I wrote
the book that I knew specific details that I needed to go and get. You
have to go back at that point.

IM   Well I think I've pestered you long enough for this morning, because
as I warned you it's quite tiring. So I'll stop it now.

Joan Lingard, Tape 2: Wednesday 27 June 2001

IM   Again we're in Joan Lingard's house, which I think you moved to,
Joan, in 1978?

JL   Yes, after four years in Scotland Street. We've been 23 years here
and 4 in Scotland Street – 27 years in Edinburgh New Town.

IM   That makes you sound very permanent and almost staid, but I think
there have been a lot of other places too.

JL   We've got a house in Inverness-shire, in Glen Feshie, which we've
had for sixteen years. This came about through my Maggie books,
going back a bit before that, we were up on holiday in Easter Ross one
year and staying there for a couple of weeks with the children in a
cottage and we went to Croick and Strathcarron and so forth. And I
became very interested in that whole area. And the church, with the
engravings on it, and therefore I began to explore the Clearances. [*See
eg* Maggie I: The Clearance, *1974, where Mr Fraser tells Maggie how
the 'cleared' Rosses of Glencalvie 'scratched their names and messages on
the windows of the church' before they were lost to history (p 44).*] This
house we now have, I knew the previous owners, and we used to rent
it from them and one year when we went up with the children many
years before, there had been a cottage across the road in which an old
forester's widow lived – she was in her eighties –

IM   Maggie's Granny?

JL   Maggie's Granny. She wore men's laced up boots. But the Granny
that I had in England who lived in a small-holding in Hertfordshire
wore men's laced up boots and wrap-around overalls, so somewhere
maybe the two are crossed (L). And she used to lean on her gate and

look at the hills. And one year when we came up and turned the corner, her house wasn't there: it had been burned down during the winter. So that was a Clearance taking place, a form of Clearance. And I began to think of the different forms of Clearance. So out of this was bred Maggie, because that was Maggie's Granny, and I had her coming up from Glasgow and hating the countryside but gradually being seduced, and in the house across the road lived the family from Edinburgh, and that is now ours. I wrote then four Maggie books, on the whole theme of displacement, because Maggie's family in Glasgow are being cleared because of a road clearance scheme in Glasgow at the time, a lot of which was going on at that point, in the early seventies, and I linked it back to the Clearance in Greenyards [*1981 A*] So I had three Clearances going in my mind, *the* Clearances, the clearance by fire and clearance by changing inner city. So I wrote four books on that. [Maggie I Clearance, *1974 C;* II Resettling, *1975 C;* III Pilgrimage, *1976 C;* IV Reunion, *1977 C.]* And then after it was made into the television series, – it was shot up by Tomatin – with the money that I got from the television series I put down half the money to buy the house, (L) so that was how we came to acquire this house.

IM Has it got a name?

JL The Old School House. As we said before, when you do research you do far more than you need, and you become sidetracked; and I was so interested in the whole thing at Greenyards that I wanted to write a full length novel about it.

IM And this is very interesting, because it's the only time that you've attempted a conventional historical novel.

JL It was, a pure historical novel – I don't view the ones that go back to, say, 1913 as historical in the same way, because I'm weaving it in and out of contemporary. I don't think I am basically a historical novelist. I think I have a surer instinct for the contemporary thing. But when I think about the Russian Revolution, somehow or other I get in there very easily (L). The other thing, in *Greenyards [1981 A]* I used this house here in Edinburgh as the Edinburgh house, so I could imagine the whole house, going out to the back lane and all. My agent must have talked to Puttnam – I can't even remember how all this happened, but they commissioned me in the end to write this book, and in fact paid me a bigger advance than I've had for any other. But it was the first and last time I wrote a book like that. I never take a contract for a book in advance.

IM Did that put you off the book?

JL Well, what it meant was they felt they had more right to interfere, and at one point an editor rang up and had cut out three pages, but I had a row and they did reinstate them, but you can do without all this going on. I feel that they influenced me in a certain way, just even the discussions with the editors and so forth. Again I haven't reread that since it was published. I daresay there are parts in it that are OK, and other parts I probably wouldn't support – it wasn't a particularly enjoyable thing for me to do in the end, not because of the material, which I enjoyed – I talked to people all over Strathcarron, Greenyards, talking to old men – it's amazing you could find people with memories going back, and tales of the whole thing, and the factor Gillanders, and so on. I did thoroughly enjoy all the work on it. But since then I have never had a contract for a book in advance. Television is something else, of course. *Greenyards* was published first in the States with a dreadful cover – it was so bad I took all the covers off! (L) And then it was published by Hamish Hamilton.

IM Maybe it was the commissioning and all the interfering that put you off: is it inconceivable that next week you might say to yourself, I've been fascinated by this or that historical situation: I might like to try another historical novel?

JL I think it's unlikely, because I'd have to find a way into it, as with *Natasha's Will* [2000 C], where I did it through a will which enabled me to go back to her life.

IM This whole business of moving backwards, and forwards in time, which is more recent in your work and is very evident, for example, in *Dreams of Love and Modest Glory* but also in *After Colette*, this approach is very effective, and it's neither simply historical novel nor contemporary.

JL *After Colette* went back to her birth in 1873. I enjoyed doing that: you see it was a challenge: I didn't want to write a straight-through kind of book: I needed to have something else going on which would interest me, and I didn't feel there was any other way I could have written that. I had to involve the present-day person. If I'd started in 1873 and gone straight through it wouldn't have any meaning. I wasn't writing a book about Colette: I was writing the book about the woman who was a one-woman artist, about Nancy Cole, that was the trigger that I came in on with the disappearance of Nancy Cole. [*Nancy Cole performed a one-woman show in many parts of the world, and on the Edinburgh Festival Fringe for many years, usually portraying Gertrude Stein. Lingard became a friend in the late sixties. Cole mysteriously vanished for ever at the end of August 1987 when leaving Austin, Texas for New Orleans. Lingard wrote an article in search of her in* The Scotsman, *13/8/88.*]

IM Did you know Nancy Cole well?

JL Yes. And every time she came to Edinburgh she always came here. I did know her well, and we were in touch, and I saw her in Paris as well. Iseabail Macleod was another friend, and when she disappeared Iseabail and I became concerned because she had set off for the States. I'll not go into her whole life thing here: I wrote a whole article on this for *The Scotsman*, which was published under the title 'Last Seen in Austin, Texas'. She left Paris because it was becoming so difficult. In a way it was writing the article that started me thinking about writing the book. Now she had been living in Paris in the seventh *arondissement* in a kind of cold-water flat. She was one of these women who really engaged my imagination because she lived on the edge, without security. She never owned anything.

IM Was that because she didn't want to, or was impractical and couldn't cope?

JL I would say probably both. She came from a wealthy family in the States, and had fallen out with them. Her father had been a very wealthy lawyer in Chicago, and she'd fallen out with the family and it's extremely difficult to work out whose fault it would be. When she was thirteen and her sister was nine, her father went to New York on business and never came back: he died of a heart attack. The mother went to New York, leaving the two girls in the care of some relative, and she came back after a year, married to another man. The mother sounded mad, I must say, so Nancy really from the age of thirteen detested her mother.

As Nancy was getting on, I think she was doing less of the one-woman show thing – she used to go to Australia and Holland, and always to the Edinburgh Festival wearing her black hat with cherries on it and she had two suitcases, and all her worldly goods were in these two suitcases. Life in Paris was getting rather difficult: she used to do some typing to help make up the money, and I suppose that went out of vogue with modern machines. She decided to go to Austin, Texas, because the son of a friend was there and he worked at the university. She hoped to get work typing students' theses. But

when she went out there, the American universities were at the point
of shutting down for the summer. It was very hot in Austin, Texas.
And she could only afford a flat without air-conditioning. Well,
things weren't working out, and she decided she would move to New
Orleans: I presume she thought it would be more sympathetic with
the French connection, and Gertrude Stein and so forth. So on the
first of September – it must have been 1988 or 89, she set out for
New Orleans. And she always travelled by bus, so she went to the
bus station, and was never seen or heard of again.

After we hadn't heard from her for about six weeks, Iseabail and
I were getting a bit worried. Iseabail wrote to this guy: he didn't reply.
She didn't write at Christmas. She had connections all over the
world, but not many friends, and it must have been March by the
time I said to Iseabail, I'm going to ring him up and ask. I talked to
him, and he sounded fine: it was all a kind of mystery. What he said
was he had been out of town when she left, and she had left a note
for him. He had lent her bed-linen and stuff, and she'd left a note
in this box. But when he went round to collect it there'd been a break-
in, and the box had been taken, plus the note. But the landlady's
daughter purported to have read the note, which said she was leaving
for New Orleans. So he then did nothing. And her mail was coming
to him. In March Iseabail and I phoned Nancy's bank in London,
and nothing had been drawn from the bank. At this point I decided
to write this article. Magnus Linklater [*then the Editor*] had asked me
if I'd like to do any feature thing for *The Scotsman*, and I said yes,
because my idea was to get information. I hadn't heard back from this
guy. I think Magnus put it out at the Festival. I rang up Nancy's
friend and got his answering machine and I said I'd be very grateful
if you could ring me back, because I'm writing this article about
Nancy's disappearance for *The Scotsman* newspaper. He rang me that
night, because he would be worried about that. He was a lawyer, and
he'd done nothing at all. When I rang in March I'd asked him to
enquire at the bus station, because she was very distinctive. He'd said
the police wouldn't help initially because she'd gone of her own free
will. I suggested the police in New Orleans. He said he'd had no luck,
whatever he had been doing.

We were going to New York in September, Martin and I. Nancy's
sister lived in New York and she was a painter, and someone remembered her husband's name and profession, and found him on the list

of psychiatrists. I wrote to her, sending a copy of my article, but it didn't arrive. When we arrived in New York I rang up. The sister hadn't seen her for twenty-five years, but she asked us to come and we spent an evening with them. The family were then able to instigate a police search, but nothing was found: it was a year later by now. There was no sign of her ever.

That was how I came to write *After Colette*. I had always had a deep interest in Colette and her writing, but I had never known quite what to do with that. This gave me the opportunity to go into her life and go everywhere she'd lived in Burgundy and Paris, and to connect the two together as a theme. For me it was a very enjoyable book. I'm not sure about how successful the ending is: I had to find some means of finishing the story.

IM   We were also going to mention your connection in Spain.

JL   This is just something that has grown up gradually. France has always been the country I've felt most at home in outside of Scotland or Ireland.

IM   But you don't have a home of any kind in France?

JL   No. And in Spain we rent the same apartment each time we go. I had an aversion to going to Spain because of Franco but when it gradually changed I began to be more and more interested in it, and particularly in the South. It is an amazing, fascinating country, with so many diversities of language and terrain. It's Andalucia, on the coast: it's on the Costa del Sol, which sounds awful but it's not, because you don't go west to Marbella, you go east and it's Nerja, which is about the only resort on the Costa del Sol which is at all reasonable – more Spaniards around than other people. We rent an apartment about three or four kilometers outside, looking over the sea and the beach, and you look back and you see the Sierras. We had been several times there on shorter holidays, and then one year when we were in Ronda we met this Canadian couple who go to a white village up in the hinterland. It's not exactly the one in *A Secret Place*: this one is more remote. But there are many, many white villages in Andalucia. That was how we got the idea that when Martin retired we might as well go for part of the winter. And I've got more and more interested in Spain itself, and learning Spanish, and as I said yesterday, delving into the history of the Civil War. *A Secret Place* is contemporary: I came back one year thinking of white villages, and next day opened *The Scotsman* and somebody had abducted their child to somewhere

else. I think often it happens that you have two ideas. One has come
in and is kind of waiting in the wings for you to find a way of dealing
with it – I felt that with *Colette*. I'd been thinking of Colette for years.
It happened with *Natasha's Will* as well. After I wrote *Dreams of Love
and Modest Glory*, a friend who is a Russian expert and read both
books for me and has been very helpful – she said to me at the time
you should write a book for children about the Russian Revolution,
but my editor said children don't like historical books; so I put that
on one side, till I had this sudden thought about bringing it into the
present day and having a will, which is more intriguing, for children.

IM   I think that is a neat way to do it. Before we leave *A Secret Place*, that
was a subject you had to handle with enormous care, because even
for you, who go into the biggest bogey fears of children's lives in some
ways, a tug of love situation could be just so frightening for your
readership.

JL   Yes, there is a responsibility. I think I showed that both parents were
reasonable people, whereas I'm sure sometimes in such a situation
one person is not. But they both loved their children, and came in
the end to a reasonable decision about it. It had to be resolved amic-
ably. So many children are involved in broken marriages and new
marriages, so I think in a way it's a topic that quite a few children
could relate to to a certain extent.

IM   We've been talking places: I was fascinated by one of your reasonably
recent adult novels, *The Women's House*, which was published in
1989, because I couldn't tell where it was actually set.

JL   In this case I decided I wasn't going to specify the place, partly
because of usually being very specifically Scotland or Northern Ireland or Canada. It was just the street and the house that mattered.
Yes, it's one of the few that I haven't located – mostly I do.

IM   All I could work out in *The Woman's House* was that it was a city,
a biggish place, and it wasn't a million miles from London, but it
wasn't London.

JL   No, if it was anywhere it was around the whole Manchester/Leeds
belt. I have one daughter lives in Bradford, who was living in Manchester at the time: she went to Manchester University. It was meant
to be one of those big old houses that you see down there, that's had
former glories, and people haven't been able to keep them up.

IM   I found it a fascinating book, with particularly interesting treatment of something you're in any case unusually good at, which is

relationships between women, and relationships between women of different generations. You deal with women of different generations much more than a lot of writers do.

JL I hadn't consciously thought that.

IM Older women have almost disappeared from fiction (L). And the mature woman in this one somehow to me related to the *After Colette* thing. I know it happened in a book written before *After Colette*, but with this Anna, who is a mime artist, and who does the kind of travelling that Nancy Cole did, and who eventually takes young Holly with her, and embarks on a new career, I felt you had an interest in this kind of performing art.

JL Yes, I think that's right. That was probably because of Nancy. Then when I wrote *After Colette* it was expanded more. Women who live completely independently and without security have always interested me.

IM Yes: that's again something notable and very healthy in your books, both adult and children's, the interesting heroine-type woman is never just looking for a husband and a family.

JL No. Maggie! (L) [*Maggie is of working-class origin, but very independent, determined from the start to go to university, and to have her own career, and avoid early marriage, and specifically and significantly to be an anthropologist.*]

IM Not just Maggie: it's a very prevalent thing in your books, that this is a different world now, and women are to develop their own lives.

JL I have been very consciously creating heroines like that, definitely. In the children's books particularly I like someone with a very strong independent spirit, feisty: I'm not writing mini Mills & Boon for teenagers! (L)

IM Would you object to the label feminist? Apart from objecting to labels in general!

JL No. I don't like labels, but yes, I would say that I am. I feel I've lived my life that way. I've always worked, earned my living, I've kept my own name, Lingard, – I only use Martin's name at the doctor's, because it's easier. Yes, I would say so. I'm not a crusading feminist obviously, in any militant way .

IM No: but there is a sense in which you've crusaded quite a bit, especially in the children's books.

JL Yes, because I do put the idea to female readers, definitely. And even when there is what they call a love interest or relationship, as there is with Sadie and Kevin, I had to be true to their backgrounds. Sadie is not going to go to university and light up, because I know her background: but she had an independent spirit of her own. And particularly when I wrote Maggie, very definitely she was independent: she was a chip off the grandmother, who even at her age was also an independent spirit. And there's a relationship there. I think I myself have always had friendships: when I was younger, quite a few of them have been with women who were quite a bit older, and I'm now having friendships with some who are younger. I had a good friendship with this old lady who was Russian, who died about two or three years ago. She was very interesting, and in fact an inspiration for me when writing *Dreams of Love* because her family had to leave St Petersburg in 1917 because of the Revolution, and they fled down through Estonia into Riga, where they settled .

IM A bit of a coincidence!

JL Yes. Her father was a professor of Medicine. Then she married a Latvian, and eventually ended up in Edinburgh . She was well into her eighties, but she and I connected very strongly, and her daughter said her mother didn't usually take to new people that easily. Yes, I've always had friendships, and I think it's very good to have friendships with different age groups: you don't want to be in a ghetto, where everyone's the same age. And as a writer it isn't interesting to deal only with your immediate peers (L).

IM But you would have described your own home background as?

JL I suppose lower middle. My mother came from working class Edinburgh: her father was a blacksmith. My father came from a background that's difficult to classify, in that his mother had this pub that her father owned. He owned several pubs, and had been a farmer in Lincolnshire. Yet my father just joined the Navy as an able seaman at fourteen, which is a very working class thing to do. The background was sort of working class in a sense, because a pub in Stoke Newington. . . . And my grandfather was a jeweller. I suppose we were rising up into the middle class. I went to the local elementary school and then got the scholarship into the girls' school, which elevated me into the middle class. But our family had had no one professional in it, ever. It's a feature of our century, that surge into the middle class.

IM Can we come back then to politics?

JL My children, when they were at school in their teens, were very politically minded, as young people were in the seventies, and are not now, so much. Also it was an era which was much less commercially minded: they hadn't got their sights fixed on working in the city – and it was at the time of banning the bomb, Greenham Common, all that. Jenny in particular, my youngest daughter, was very involved in all that, and she would go on marches and protests, and it seemed to be that if there were twenty thousand there and three were arrested, she'd be one of them (L), so we got phonecalls from various police stations around the place. And then she went to Greenham Common, not to live (L), but for a long weekend, and was one of the people who lay down in the road in front of the lorries bringing in the missiles, and so was arrested. Her case came up for trial in New-bury, and she did not intend to plead guilty, and she did not intend to pay any fines: so Martin went with her and another of her friends – a very noble and wonderful father he is to the girls, really. He went with them on the overnight train sitting up to London, feeling sick the whole way down. We employed a solicitor and she didn't want Martin to go to Newbury so he stayed in London. She went on to Newbury. If you plead guilty, you're not allowed to speak, for one thing. She wished to speak. So she got up and said, basically, I do not believe that I am the guilty party: the guilty parties are the people who are forcing these missiles and instruments of death etc on us. She made quite a dramatic speech at the end of which she was fined £60, and she said, I don't intend to pay the fine, so she went to prison in London, Holloway. She was taken in a police car, and a police-woman said, I think you're right: I would do the same. So she spent a week in Holloway. Martin sent in £25 worth of flowers, (L) and this was quite a long time ago, so that was a *lot* of flowers; they were drowning her cell. Lots of other people did too: eventually they were turning away flowers: they couldn't cope with all of them. She'd a sore throat before she went off, and I rang up the warden to say she had a sore throat (L): they probably hadn't many calls from parents. That week in Holloway she shared a cell with a girl who was a prostitute. She learned a lot, and I subsequently wrote a book. [The Guilty Party, *1987 C. The friendly policewoman and the flowers survive into the novel.*] In the end I think they were glad to release her early because she was probably causing a diversion in the place, and when they were out in the yard for exercise they would just hang about, but she had them doing leapfrog. Bridget was a student in London at the time. She went and camped outside the prison with other people and quite a few friends kept up this vigil outside, surrounded with television cameras. And people came round giving them soup and drinks, and then one morning the gates opened and out she comes at six in the morning, when they were still sleeping under their plastic. She rang me, and I said, are you all right, and she said I'm fine Mum, but the women in there are not. Some of the stories – in for not paying a television licence and held on remand for things for months on end. I decided then that I ought to do something more than just paying my subscription to CND and going on a couple of marches, so I decided to found this Scottish Writers Against The Bomb. We decided we needed to do something physical and we got the poster, and got as many Scottish writers to sign as possible and distribute them, which we did. I do feel still that the force of public opinion must have some effect at some point. If you don't speak out then you are going to be steamrollered over. It was a way of focusing people's minds. It all took a lot of time – I didn't write for about three or four months – even the letter-writing, and some writers like Willie McIlvanney never reply to letters! (L) But it's quite a good representation of the writers at that time. Hardly anyone refused to sign that I did make contact with. People said I should write a book about Jenny's experiences, and she didn't want to do it, so two years later she was happy for me to write *The Guilty Party*.

IM   Does it concentrate on the bomb thing, or does it go into the women's prison issue?

JL   It goes into the women's prison as well. And it's actually a protest about a nuclear power station, rather than the bomb.

IM   Did you have any trouble getting it published?

JL   No: Hamish Hamilton published it, and Puffin. It was in print for quite a long time. It's gone out of print now, because I suppose the issue seems to have gone away, although it hasn't. The specifics have changed.

IM   Would you perhaps go back to the theme?

JL   No: probably not. I tried with the Kevin and Sadie books to be even handed, but I find it very difficult on these subjects to be even handed (L). I did it partly by having her involved with a boy whose father is a manager at the power station, but I did have him more or less converted by the end! (L)

IM   Would you say you were politically speaking a one-issue person?

JL   No, I wouldn't say so. One issue that I have campaigned for, maybe.
     But I am or have been concerned about many issues, like women's
     rights or everything to do with equality. Human rights, of course.

IM   You said you were a member of Scottish PEN, or International PEN.

JL   Yes, and also writers in prison: that's another issue. I think all writers
     should be concerned about writers in prison. And censorship, obvi-
     ously. I remember years ago taking part in an anti-censorship debate
     with John Calder. He and I were anti, and two people whom I can't
     remember were on the other side. It was a PEN occasion. I suppose
     I'm not as politically active now in the sense of going out on marches
     and walks, but I daresay if there was something really pressing
     enough, I would.

IM   Is your daughter still strongly anti-bomb?

JL   She's still anti-bomb, but she's not still out marching (L). She
     became a homeopath and she's living in Argyll with two children. All
     my daughters were active in it, and they were active when they were
     at school, and this is where I think young people now are not as
     politically aware or active about things. It was definitely an era when
     many young people both at school and university were actually trying
     to do something .

IM   It's odd though how little it features in books on the whole.

JL   Yes, that's probably true: I'm trying to think where else it has
     featured. You put yourself in a difficult position if you treat it,
     because you are accused of writing messages, it's fraught with prob-
     lems. *The Guilty Party* was something I felt I had to write, and it was
     actually short-listed for the Federation of Children's Books Prize,
     and that was chosen by children. It's more possible to do it for
     children than in an adult novel. I just don't know how you'd have
     written an adult novel: it wouldn't be a central theme, maybe, but
     it could come into an adult novel through characters' beliefs.

IM   Apart from the Nancy Cole thing, have you done any other big
     journalistic pieces?

JL   No: I'm not really into journalism. That was something that moved
     me so much I wanted to write about it.

IM   And you haven't written any plays, as opposed to television?

JL   No, and no poetry. The odd short story.

IM   So it's very definitely the two kinds of novels, the adult novel and
     the children's novel.

JL   Yes. I am a novelist. I always wanted to be a novelist, from the age of eleven. I didn't want to write poetry or short stories because for me the novel offers the opportunity in depth and breadth to go into other worlds and other skins and inhabit them. I like reading short stories, but it's like a short visit somewhere, and then you come out and close the door. For me I'd be left wondering about what was coming after that. I've written maybe a couple of children's short stories for anthologies. [*Eg 'Silver Linings' in Gordon Jarvie, ed, The Wild Ride and Other Scottish Stories, 1986*]

IM   I did threaten to ask you about happy endings. If we just looked at the last three, *The Women's House*, *After Colette* and *Dreams of Love*, *Women's House* ends on the one hand very seriously and tragically, because Evangeline slips home from the nursing home and is burned to a crisp, but you also have a new start with Anna and Holly touring the USA. Is that a deliberate contrast?

JL   Yes, it was.

IM   And that began with a death as well, as *Natasha's Will* does: it began with the funeral of Dorothea.

JL   I suppose my attitude to endings is that there isn't any way I could write the ending of any book, children's or adult, with roses round the door (L). The nearest I've got to that is *Natasha's Will*, but then my thing in *Natasha's Will* was that it's almost told in the form of a fairytale at times, like she pricks her finger, the sewing basket, and at her birth everybody giving her these presents.

IM   It's a wonderful mixture of genres.

JL   Yes. This is deliberate, and at the end it was really like 'And they danced under the moon and the stars, and were happy ever after.'

IM   There has to be a happy ending to that kind of story.

JL   It demanded a happy ending. And the villains were villains. Mr Hatton-Flitch – 'but they were never seen in those parts again'. It was very deliberate on my part to do that.

IM   But it's much more typical Lingard to have a compromise .

JL   It's like with Kevin and Sadie in each one: it isn't the conclusion of their lives or even, now they're settled: they're never settled: they're always in exile. And in *The Women's House* it is a compromise, but the two, the middle-aged one and the young one, go forth to do something different and new, and so there's hope – I do mostly I think end on a note of hope.

IM   For some. But I felt sorry at the end of *The Women's House* for the Italian father, Maximo. He had a horrible son, and the horrible son was a baddie, but Maximo wasn't a baddie, and he had to end un-happily. But there's a certain realism about this (L).

JL Well I felt there was a realism about it. But I really couldn't have him making a happy relationship with Anna. It is difficult for a serious novelist which I think I claim I am – I'm not writing genre fiction, or romantic things – you are really denied the possibility in most cases of having a happy ending. One of the novelists I know that has relatively happy endings is Carol Shields, and they work, so I suppose it is possible, but not there, I couldn't have.

IM And you are very clear about death, I think. Death is more likely to happen and be mentioned in your books than in many others.

JL It has been part of my life, with losing both parents, my mother at sixteen, my father when I was thirty-one.

IM But there's also the fact that a lot of people just prefer not to think about it and not to talk about it and pretend it's not there in a senti-mental watering down of the Christian Science doctrine that there is no death.

JL And I suppose in *After Colette* the thing is that she was found in a sense. Again it's a sort of compromise, but I come back to the vision of Colette at the end.

IM As soon as you do the kind of things you do with time in *After Colette* and *Dreams of Love and Modest Glory* there isn't a simple question of ending: it doesn't really matter, in a sense, at which point in past or present you actually finish the book, but it comes to some point of rest.

JL And I think probably the ending is much more difficult to determine: I didn't know exactly where it would finish – very often I do know, but I think with Colette I had vague notions but I had to work through an awful lot of stuff with that book, and I rewrote it in different ways. In the end I felt the structure was right for it. Going back, often just slipping back in memory to a trigger point that would take you in.

IM Or generations going back, as for example in *Dreams of Love and Modest Glory*. The whole centre of the story only comes out through much later generations physically going back and finding out what happened, and the tragic consequences of the initial – it's not even adultery, is it? (L).

JL No, it's not. And that's obviously a device. One uses devices. It's a literary device, as the twins were a device, so that one married an architect in Petersburg and one in Riga, and it's a very good way then to explore the differences that happen when you start from that: it's a literary device.

IM   Yes. And you use the twins in the *Tug of War* as well. Can I though finally maybe ask you. You were being very rude yesterday about your early adult novels, and I don't agree with most of what you said – or what you don't say, because you haven't read them for so long, but I did think there was a new kind of life and excitement coming in with *The Second Flowering of Emily Mountjoy*. [*1979, A*]

JL   Yes, probably, compared to the early ones.

IM   It's a very unusual book. In a way this is the one I'd love to teach on my course on post-war Scottish women's fiction, because it would make my nineteen and twenty-year-old students sit back altogether. Emily is let's say middle-aged and over-weight, – I can't remember her exact age, but she's old enough to have a grown up daughter, and she falls in love with this bizarre young actor – and so does her friend – it's so unexpected and –

JL   And leaves her comfortable, stuffy (L) husband –

IM   The George. She's really been married to the George character in *The Prevailing Wind* –

JL   That's right, she has, and whether subconsciously I was thinking at that point, all those years later (L). I don't know if I can say how I actually wrote the book: it's extraordinary, because apart from the fact of the setting, the flat which belonged to Alex McCrindle and Honor Arundel, also I've always had a certain fascination with dress-makers – because when I was young we didn't seem to buy many clothes, but my mother went to a dress-maker, and we went to this wee woman: she always had a small teapot on a sort of gas ring – obviously a woman who just existed in this room filled with fabrics, and this is in Belfast – who spent her whole day with inch-tapes and measuring other women's hips and fitting on things. I can remember when my sister who's eleven years older was getting married I was bridesmaid in this blue taffeta –(L) I can remember hating the feeling of this dress. I was thirteen. But it always seemed to be we didn't go to a shop: my mother bought material, and we went to this wee woman. So I think the dress-maker thing was a part of it.

IM   Just the fact of somebody of Emily's age and experience being woken up like that, however unlikely – my students will think it's very unlikely if I put it in front of them – but it's so vivid, because Emily wakes up, like the Sleeping Beauty.

JL   That's right. All these years she's been dormant. I suppose it was a book about what was happening right through the seventies in a way with women wakening up and suddenly – . . . But the unfortunate thing was that I'd published it with Paul Harris, and his books blew off the lorry, and I was involved in that, and we all went into remainder from the wreck, and I bought quite a lot of *Emily Mountjoy* at the time.

IM   I have great hope that *Emily Mountjoy* will come back to us before too long in a paperback, as a product not of 2001 but of 1979 and very well standing up to its own time.

Books mentioned in the interview

Adult

Liam's Daughter, 1963
The Prevailing Wind, 1964
The Headmaster 1967
The Lord On Our Side, 1970
The Second Flowering of Emily Mountjoy, 1979
Greenyards, 1981
Sisters By Rite, 1984
Reasonable Doubts, 1986
The Women's House, 1989
After Colette, 1993
Dreams Of Love and Modest Glory, 1995

Children's

The Kevin and Sadie quintet: *The Twelfth Day of July* 1970, *Across The Barricades* 1972, *Into Exile* 1973, *A Proper Place* 1975, *Hostages to Fortune* 1976
The Maggie quartet: *I Clearance* 1974, *II Resettling* 1975, *III Pilgrimage* 1976, *IV Reunion*, 1977
The File on Fraulein Berg, 1980
The Guilty Party, 1987
Tug Of War, 1989
Between Two Worlds, 1991
Hands Off Our School, 1992
A Secret Place, 1998
Dark Shadows, 1998
Natasha's Will, 2000
Tell the Moon to Come Out, 2003

ALI SMITH

AS BECOMES CLEAR in the interview, Ali Smith was born in Inverness in 1962, and was an undergraduate student of English at the University of Aberdeen from 1980-1984. It was during that time that we met, and she chose the Special Subject I was then offering, in modern Scottish fiction. She was also a leading member of the student-led Creative Writing Group, and a major contributor to its magazine *Scratchings*. Meeting our first Writer in Residence, William McIlvanney, was a major milestone and confidence-booster for her. Academically, in her final year she had over-modestly failed to apply for any postgraduate research grants, so she graduated with the top First of her year, and the Lucy Fellowship for Cambridge that went with it, but nearly a year's gap before she could take it up. In the end, she spent an exuberant and exciting year doing an MLitt on modern Scottish fiction, with me as her (often breathless) supervisor. This 'auld acquaintance' probably accounts for the robustness of tone sometimes affected here, and our willingness to interrupt each other, and argue, rather more than I have used with any other writer.

She lives in Cambridge, and visits to Scotland tend to be too far apart, and too crowded. Thus two projected sets of interviews failed to eventuate, and a visit to us in Aberdeen had to be cancelled. We finally managed to coincide for some time in Edinburgh, and thanks to Fiona Morrison and the Librarian of the National Library of Scotland, we met in the august office of the Librarian, which doubles as Board Room, and did our interviews on consecutive days at one corner of the vast table. I began, as usual, by asking about her background, and her parents.

Thursday 5 December 2002, in the Librarian's office at the National Library of Scotland. Present: Ali Smith, Isobel Murray

Tape One

AS My parents were both bright but totally disadvantaged as regards education. They both won scholarships and neither could take them up because of family poverty. My father had to leave school and work as soon as possible; his father died young after being gassed in the First World War. My mother came from a very large family of Irish Catholics: there were something like seven kids, plus two who died, in her family. She was at the tail end, again, of that family, herself the second youngest, and by that time there was no money at all; the husband died, my grandfather, so she had to work. So she had to leave school too.

IM   So what did she do?

AS   She came to the Highlands of Scotland from Limavady, where she was born.

IM   Where's that?

AS   At the very north tip of Northern Ireland.

IM   I can't be absolutely sure that the tape recorder can pick up your gestures. (L)

AS   (L) I was waving my hands; I was drawing a map of Ireland. There! That's where Limavady is, there! (L) Not far from Belfast. So she'd come from there to Inverness, where one of her sisters lived. And she lived with her and she worked on the buses as a bus conductress. That's when she was fifteen or something. And then her brother also came across, so when we were kids, there was this little network of people, Mum's sister and her brother, who lived across the field from us in one of the other houses, council houses on the other side of the field.

IM   All in council houses?

AS   Mmhm.

IM   Dad was making quite a good thing of it?

AS   It took him a long time to. He had an electrician's business. First of all he came up and worked on the dams and the hydro-electric schemes, and that's how he ended up in the Highlands, and he liked it. Then he met my Mum, and they started a small electrician's business, with a contractor's side and a shop. When I was a child, this was doing quite well, in the late or middle seventies. And then of course rates went up, Thatcher came in, small businesses went to the wall, and so did my father's. There was a time back there when we had, oh, a lot of presents at Christmas. Suddenly he'd done well, and he had lots of people working for him, something like thirty-five men on his books. That didn't last very long, but while it lasted it was pretty astonishing that he'd done that.

IM Your Mum was an Irish Catholic. The family was Catholic and you were born into it.

AS Yes, completely Catholic by that point: my father had just converted, I think, either just after I was born or just before. He did convert, because he wasn't Catholic before, and God knows how he did: he gave up smoking and converted I think at the same time. (L) I don't know how Mum pulled that off, but she did! We all had gone, and I went too, to the Catholic school in Inverness, which was a very small school, compared to the other primaries. And we were one of the four families I think in our long street who were Catholics. And that's how I remember it. We were definitely supposed to be different in some way, because we didn't go to the local school; because all the kids went to the local school, but we went off hiking into town to go to school. That's how I remember it.

IM But it wasn't a hostile situation, as it might have been in Glasgow, say?

AS It was just a bit strange, that was all. With it came a very tightly structured family, like I said, and a tightly structured notion of what was decent, according to my mother, and being a Catholic was definitely decent. It was a really interesting school now that I think about it, because there was the core class which was huge: there were forty-three kids in it in my year at one point – more, maybe, but there were always itinerant kids coming through, because the Catholic school was the only school that would take the kids of the travellers who came in and out of the Highlands. There were still quite a few then, so there were always kids who were there some years and not there the next year; or Spanish kids would turn up, or – it was small and tight, and a very safe place, because all the teachers knew who you were. It was very homely.

IM Okay, so then you went off to Inverness –

AS High School. Which was at that time I think about four years into being Comprehensive. There had been a big fuss about me going to the High School, because everybody else in the family went to the Academy.

IM What was the difference?

AS The Inverness Academy was the Grammar School, and the High School used to be the 'Techy' where the people who did not pass their eleven pluses went. But by the time I was going to secondary school, the Comprehensive system had come in, and I was supposed to go

to the High School. There was a great fuss about it at home, as to
whether or not my parents would move house, so that I could go to
the Academy like everybody else had gone, and get this decent
education that I was supposed to get at the grammar school. By the
time I got to the High School, the High School was staffed with extraordinarily enthusiastic, clever, open, playful teachers, and it was the
most fantastic school. Thank God I was there, because it was
brilliant. At one point there were so many societies in that school,
you had to have a society for societies; there was so much going on.
They made a sweat-shirt that was called High Society, and there were
something like seventy societies – I don't remember how many: it was
extraordinary really, the amount of energy that was happening just
at that point. I can perceive a difference between my education and
my brothers' and sisters' education, from that point of view. It just
was alive, and open, and possible. In my year, more kids went to university than we could imagine. All my friends went to university.
When my sister Anne had gone to university, hardly anyone went.
We all went! It was a general opening up.

IM   We're talking of course of a time when people would get grants.

AS   We're talking of when education was still practically free. There were
grants, and you would be means-tested to some extent for your grant,
but you could go to university, and your parents (or you) would not
have to be responsible. I can't believe what's happening now. The
point is that there's a real difference now between what is available
when it comes to education, and what isn't. I noticed it as soon as
I went to Cambridge actually, that education was really about money,
in a way in which I had never imagined education could ever be about
money. And I knew that the first week I was there.

IM   About money, and also perhaps about background?

AS   Definitely about where you came from, but where you came from was
about money! It was all money, in a way that would never even
impinge on anything that I had come through. Presumably different
from my brothers and sisters, who *had* been through a grammar
system, where people had been judged suitable or wanting.

IM   Okay. Going back to being a Catholic, for the time being. Your
mother was obviously keen on good behaviour as a Catholic: were you
a believing Catholic in a meaningful sense?

AS   Yes, I was definitely believing, in all sorts of meaningful senses. And
I still am, and I can't help it, and at the same time I'm not. I haven't

been a practising Catholic now for something like fifteen years. But they got me as a child (L) and it's hard not to be that thing, and at the same time, there's such a force of understanding of level of meaning, and how symbol relates to the real, and the real relates to meaning, and meaning relates back to symbol again, in clauses in which I know it's at the centre of everything I do.

IM   But some Catholics would say for example that the sacraments were at the centre of everything they do.

AS   That's what I'm talking about, sacraments.

IM   Let us specify. (L)

AS   Well, if we talk about our old friend the transfiguration of the commonplace [*See below, pp* 204-5], we talk about the transubstantiation, the idea that what's everyday, what's kind of taken for granted, and what's what you need for sustenance at its most basic level can become the most meaningful thing ever. . . .

IM   Yes but, the Catholicism that I suspect you learned connected all of that very directly to the Trinity, and the sacraments very directly to the body and blood of Jesus, and all the rest of it. In that sense, you don't believe any more? You don't miss them?

AS   Oh, I miss it all the time. Of course I do. I miss it all the time. And how can I not believe in it, but at the same time, . . . it must mean more. This is a Church which (L) doesn't allow for me, in all sorts of ways, doesn't allow for all sorts of things in my life, and also it's a Church which is a horrific religion. It's absolutely based on paying money, and how much you can get out of the masses, in both of those senses (L). When it comes to belief and when it comes to being alive, if you can relate those two things together then that's when it will work, and it's almost possible to make them relate to each other. Living, and a pure notion of what that religion is, a real notion of what that religion is – they don't meet.

IM   Most Scots that one talks to at length like this, who have a religious background, be it Calvinist or Catholic, have as some part of the result of that a well-developed sense of sin and guilt. You have never struck me as being madly guilt-ridden. How did you escape?

AS   I think because I had a very happy childhood. I think it's really that. I had a very sunny, happy one. When I think back on it, I felt very secure, was very loved, felt very safe in all sorts of structures. In all the right ways, I felt very provided for and loved. What would I feel guilty about? (L)

IM Sin! I was made very conscious as a young adult Catholic convert, of sexual sin, for example, from masturbation onwards, as being 'Mortal' sin.

AS I just never believed it. How could it be a sin? And also, my Catholicism is post-Sixties Catholicism, which is supposedly more open-minded. But when I *was* a bit worried, I met a great priest. Fr Bloggs. I went to see him at the Chaplaincy, because he'd given a sermon about St Paul's 'pure body', how you mustn't misuse the body, and I was *stricken*! I thought, all this time I've been misusing the body, and what am I doing? I was terribly depressed, in a terribly bad way, and I went to see him. And he simply said, that's all right: I am too, and it's fine, and why would it not be fine? He said, don't worry: off you go! (L) I came out of the place with my arms open, and walked out onto College Bounds. He'd let me off the hook, sexually, and I was lucky. But I feel like I've been lucky all along. He came to one of the readings I was doing about three years ago, and he was a man, not a priest; and he said, I am Joe Bloggs; do you remember me? I've come out, and I live in Edinburgh, and I'm not a priest any more. And it was so fantastic to see him, and he did me such a good turn that day, and God knows how many other kids he did a good turn to. [*IM has changed the name, although AS suspects her friend would not mind being named.*] I mean, it wasn't exactly easy: I was in love with a girl for a long time, and I felt very lost and hidden, and frightened about it, but because it was mine, if you like, and hers, there was something which also felt very pure about it. You know when something's pure and you know when something's not – you just know.

IM I think you're a natural Protestant, in a non-denominational sense.

AS I think I'm a natural non-denominational person who believes in God, but in a much wider notion of what God is, really, than is given by any of the religions in Scotland, for sure, and probably any religions in the world, really.

IM Okay. So you went on to become a writer: when did that start?

AS I always did write when I was very small; I just could do it. And was good at it. And wanted to do it. Those things are all important, but the last one is the most important: you have to want to do it. And I wanted to do it; it wasn't what I played at: it was what I wanted to do. It's what I was serious about; it's what I found I was serious about.

IM   Did the family indulge this?

AS   No. I was odd and bookish, and especially as I became adolescent I
     was really odd and bookish. Why wasn't I like a normal girl, who
     would be out doing stuff, or helping to do the dishes, or wanting to
     talk about make-up? I was reading H G Wells: that was odd and
     bookish. But in a way that gave me space as well.

IM   Did you show your writing to people? Do you remember who you
     showed it to, say when you were at school?

AS   I was good at English anyway: I just was, in that Jean Brodie way,
     I was good at it. And so English teachers were always very lovely to
     me, and I was lucky again with them, I had some great English
     teachers. Brian Denoon at the High School got me involved with the
     magazine. The newspaper came out every month, and the magazine
     came out every year. And then I had a wonderful teacher after him
     as well, called Mrs Moodie, who then became Anne McKay, who is
     still my friend. And Alan McKay. Alan is her husband: they met next
     door to each other, in rooms 49 and 50, Geography and English, and
     she was a great teacher: she taught us Eliot and Browning, and *A Man
     for All Seasons*, and the Brontes. They were great teachers to have.
     I wrote poems, terrible poems, and they published them in these
     magazines. And I wrote some plays, and Anne McKay helped us put
     the plays on: she said, if you write a play, we'll put it on. And so I
     did write a play, and we did put it on.

IM   Has it survived?

AS   Somewhere, yeah. It was called *Peanuts*. In brackets (*Unsalted*) after
     it. It was to do with the election of a female Prime Minister. These
     men in the government can't find a Prime Minister, so they elect a
     girl who comes to collect stuff at the door, and so they make her Prime
     Minister, and they do a make-over, and she becomes Prime Minister,
     and then she gets fed up with politics and PR, and she refuses to do
     any more, and then someone comes in and rips up the script, and
     there's a kind of power struggle: it's basically about what's happening
     in '78 and '9. (L)

IM   That's when you wrote it?

AS   Yes. We put it on in '79–'80.

IM   That would come probably as quite a surprise to people who only
     know you from your fiction, because that's a very political sort of sub-
     ject, and from the small amount I've read of your plays, the political
     interest tends to come in there more obviously than in the fiction.

AS That's interesting: I never thought of that. But I think my fiction is political.

IM Oh, I wouldn't say it isn't, but overtness – you know, I'm thinking of *Trace of Arc*, for example, which is dedicated to Dounreay and Thurso.

AS I'm sure this comes from the impact of 7.84. [*The late John McGrath was writer and Director of 7.84 (Scotland) for some years after the play which revolutionised Scottish drama,* The Cheviot, The Stag, and The Black, Black Oil, *1971. Other plays mentioned here were all by McGrath.*] And when I was fourteen the Eden Court Theatre opened in Inverness. And we started to get proper drama – we hadn't had drama for a long time, because the Empire had been there, and it had been a wee theatre and it had shut in between me being a child and being an adolescent. And suddenly we had plays and films, so I spent a lot of time there. But I remember 7.84, and I remember the excitement of *The Cheviot* on TV, which I never saw in a theatre. And I remember them coming round with – oh, I can't remember the name of the play, the one about the Highlands, the one about the Clearances –

IM *Boom?*

AS No. It's got three words. *Blood Red Roses?* No. *Little Red Hen!* [*1975-6*] Anyway, I remember seeing that, and just thinking that was the most fantastic thing I'd ever seen. And knowing you could do anything on stage, and you could absolutely take the piss out of what was happening right round the corner at the HIDB [*Highlands and Islands Development Board*]. You could say the thing, and if you had an audience there they would probably want you to, and they'd want to be able to say back what they thought.

IM So did you always have strong political opinions?

AS I was just always a socialist, and I think I always knew that I was more left wing than my parents were. They voted for Russell Johnston [*local Liberal*] because he was a good MP – and he *was* a good MP, but before that they were Tories, because they were small business holders, and they wanted to buy their council house, and to be able to move on.

IM Let's hear a bit more about how the drama developed. None of it of course has been published, but I've got a very slight sense of it from having read *Trace of Arc*, and one you wrote called *Fifteen Minutes*, and a throwaway remark in a piece about 2001, that you'd spent two months writing a play – [*I was wrong:* Trace of Arc, *which I had read in typescript, is available in a collection edited by Lizbeth Goodman called* Mythic Women: Real Women *(Faber, 2000), and has had several productions in the UK, the USA and Australia*]

AS Oh, it was maddening, and that play's still not anywhere, and it just makes me sad. It was absolutely of the moment, as well. At the beginning of last year, the Highland Theatre Festival said to me, would I write them a play, and they would pay me – I can't remember now – quite a lot of money, £6000 or something. I said yes, sure, I'd like to do that. They were going to put it on in May, at the Highland Festival. So I did: I spent two months – it must be the end of 2000. It's called *The Seer*, and it's my first two act, my first big play, and it's all right, I think; it's hard to tell when you write something yourself. But they couldn't get the money for it, and they wanted to put on something that was 'more Highland' or something. So I never found out why; they never got the grant they needed. It's about this posh couple living a kind of Lifestyle life in Edinburgh, in an Edinburgh flat with their walls painted deep red, and the anarchic sister of one of the couple comes to stay, and she's a complete liar; she's just anarchic; she tells them all kinds of lies; she's not even her sister. She's just a person who has come (L) from if you like another dimension. She's come through from the audience and found herself on the stage, and more people come up from the audience and find themselves on the stage: and what it's really about is whether or not you can have difference, or notions of difference, in people who have different lives or kinds of life in Lifestyle Scotland. It really rose out of all that stuff with Brian Souter and Clause 28. [*Brian Souter of the Stagecoach group funded a private referendum in opposition to the Scottish Executive's move to repeal the anti-homosexual Clause 28 of Margaret Thatcher's 1985 local government act. This did reveal a degree of popular opinion opposed to the Executive's liberal instincts, but much less than expected. The Executive pressed the repeal through.*] And it's basically a paradigm for that, about the idea of what happens if you let something which seems anarchic into your world; and whether or not (L) it's worth actually opening your world out into wider worlds or different forms or different notions, or whether there's anything beyond the wall you think that's in front of you, which is basically the audience.

IM Do you think the Brian Souter thing was obvious?

AS   How do you mean? In the play? Yes and no.

IM   Would it have been part of any reason why they couldn't find money?

AS   Who knows? That's the thing, whenever you write drama. That's
     why when I was at Cambridge – I was there for five years and we
     put on our own plays, and we just did, because we could get money
     there, because there was lots and lots of money rolling about Cam-
     bridge: there's lots of talent; there's really talented people, and that's
     where I met Sarah, my partner, and we put on plays, and we did
     it off our own bat, and with our own work, and that way we knew
     we didn't have to depend on anyone else. Because doing anything
     in drama or film is a nightmare, because it has to be collaborative in
     a way that means you have to go to someone and ask for money.
     You're not going to do anything, not just in a way that means you
     can sit down in a room and do something really brilliant with
     someone, but in this awful way of having to beg for more, and beg
     for more; which is just a waste of time, if you can just go on and
     do it.

IM   This is something I've heard a lot of writers say, they can't afford
     to write a play unless they were asked to. So – why write them? When
     they have so little chance of going on, so little chance of a decent sized
     audience, so little chance of an impact, and so little impact once
     they're written down and published?

AS   We wrote them then in Cambridge in the late Eighties, because there
     was an audience, and because there was money, and because we knew
     we could take them to the Fringe, or put them on in small places in
     London or Cambridge, and people would come, and there was still
     some notion of a political open-mindedness that meant people were
     still interested in going to see things which weren't going to be just
     funny stand-up like it is now at the Fringe. For years we came to the
     Fringe in Edinburgh. The Fringe changed palpably from year to
     year. The first year we came, we were in a little place right at the
     top of the Mile there and there was a group called Able Bodies, and
     they were running it, and they were very politically correct. They
     were called Able Bodies because they had people who were not Able
     Bodies, if you like, who had different abilities, in that group. We put
     on a little one-person play there, a monologue play called *The Dance*.
     The second year we came back we were at the Canongate with *Trace
     of Arc*, and that is as you say definitely a political play, absolutely
     about the poll tax and about nuclear empire, and small town and large

corporation. We put it on at the Canongate, but there was a girl, who chose which plays went on that they thought would make money, and they thought our play would make money, because it was funny, so we did the play there and it went really well. The third year we came back we were up the Mile again in that little place at St Columba's by the Castle. But now in 1990 it was run by this guy with a baseball cap on, come up from London, taken the whole site on for a basic rent, and he was making an absolute fucking fortune out of packing it every night. And the only reason we got a slot at all was because we were doing the Footlights, the Cambridge Footlights, which of course sold out like that. Sarah and I were directing it, and we had written half the show. It was a political Footlights; it was the women-only Footlights: it was the first year that there was a women only Footlights ever in the whole of history, and the reason there was one was because the year before there had been no women at all in the Footlights, which was uncannily like in Edwardian times (L) when there were also no women in the Footlights. But that's how we got in there, the only reason we could do a play, which was called *Comic*, a little two-hander, in that venue, was because we would sell out on the Footlights. But by that point audiences also didn't want anything very different; they really wanted stand-up, and they wanted things to be funny, and dribs and drabs of people were coming to drama, whereas two years before, the drama crowds had been very different: it was very interesting to see that die off.

IM Would you want to suggest a cause?

AS It's just the change in how money is spent, and what people want for their money, and how people want to think, and what entertainment is. What the Fringe was about as well, because by that point then and definitely now the Fringe is about big-style entertainment. Actually the Fringe wasn't about entertainment at all; it was about agit-prop: it was about sideline, it was about margins: it was about all the things you couldn't say in the mainstream. But that was the death of the Fringe: we saw it: we were there. In fact the very first year I ever came to the Fringe was my first year in Cambridge, 1986, with a group called Trouble and Strife. They were undergraduates, and they were feminist, and they were a girls' group and the play we did was also a take off of Thatcherism: it was called *Stalemate*. That was uproari-ously applauded and attended, and those things have changed, in a very short time. All the rhetoric is changed – you couldn't call a group

Trouble and Strife now, without people thinking they wouldn't be interested in it, because it might be feminist.

IM You said it was hard to tell how good a play was: is it harder to tell with a play which hasn't been produced, than with a novel or a story?

AS I always think everything is rubbish.

IM Haven't you got a shit-detector, as Bernard MacLaverty says of his wife Madeline?

AS Well, yes, I'm very lucky: I've got Sarah; and Sarah and I have great talks and arguments, and thank God, because then I know what I want to do, or I know that something is or isn't working, or could work differently or better. So we have a really good discursive thing: we work well together; that's why we did plays together, and I help her with things she's doing, scripts for films.

IM Do you rewrite much?

AS The plays take the least rewriting. The plays are the easiest to do. They just bowl along: it's because there's dialogue – if someone says something, someone will probably say something back, and they need an edit and that's it. (L) And then, that would be the point where it would go on to people on the stage and you would find out whether it would work or not.

IM So, would you like to write for television, film?

AS I just would hate it. Radio I've enjoyed writing for. I've written two plays for radio, both of which I really loved writing, and they were again really easy to write, and they seemed to work fine. Radio's so for voice. As it says in your Jessie book, where she knows it's about voice, and she's a person who's all about voice, and radio takes away everything else, all the distractions. [*'Next to the printed word I love radio and I'll tell you why. Because words mean so much to radio and words and the sound and the meaning of them is* my *thing. I love radio'*: Jessie Kesson, quoted in Jessie Kesson: Writing Her Life *by Isobel Murray, Edinburgh 2000, p 13.*] The whole world comes out of that voice: I love that. And you can do all sorts of playful things with voice as well; you can suggest all sorts of possibilities or places – I love it.

IM Would you say it's fading as much as the small theatre thing did? I was very despondent about it by the time I finished my book on Jessie, because there was a huge time when you could really write for radio, and it has dwindled so much.

AS It's just the same: just in my time of writing – I've only been writing really for a living for ten years – and just in that time what it's possible to do is getting smaller and smaller, in things like BBC, because BBC won't give you money to do things. They won't take chances on things. The producers get a book of guide-lines, and they look at what you're supposed to be doing at three fifteen or whatever it is in the afternoon, the kind of person who'll be listening to this. The idea that there's a kind of person listening to anything is a killer dead anyway, from the start, because there's no such thing as a kind of person, ever, anywhere in the world. The notion that the BBC think they can categorise us all down to this means that they think they can also categorise what can be written to be the right kind of thing for the slot. It can't be done! And if it is done then the thing is killed stone dead. And that's not what the BBC did when Kesson for instance was writing those fantastic things, and when they brought this country together basically, from individual voices.

IM So before we leave the question of your plays entirely, do you think you'll be writing more?

AS I don't know. I've got another one coming up for radio. David Jackson Young, who's based in Edinburgh, got me to write a play which we did last year or the year before, *State of the Art*, (L) which is also political – you're a smart lady! Anyone ever tell you're a smart lady? (L) I would never have thought about it, but it is true; they are overtly political, which is a relief, and very good to do. I did that with him, and it was lovely, and I did a wee play about Dusty Springfield for radio, and that was great fun. That was only fifteen minutes, but it was a real pleasure to do. And I've one more coming with David Jackson Young. [Big Bed *was broadcast on Radio 4 on 14/7/03, directed by David Jackson Young.*]

IM Tell me about Dusty Springfield. I've got her underlined in my notes.

AS Why?

IM Because you talk twice about her in that article about everything you did in 2001, and drew attention to the fact that you were going to talk about her further on.

AS She turns up in *Hotel World*, as one of the ghosts at the end. I felt that *Hotel World* was kind of blessed by the sense of her at the end of it, in this weird way which I can't even explain. She is an extraordinary figure to me actually now, particularly because I wrote this wee radio play about her and read up all about her, but I didn't know anything about her until about a year before she died, when I saw a thing on TV. I was watching this extraordinary performance: it was like at two in the morning, it was an old repeat of an Ed Sullivan show on, and there was this extraordinary, extraordinary person singing 'Son of a Preacher Man'. Do you know that song?

IM Not immediately; I might recognise it?

AS It's a song about how the only man who could ever reach her was the son of a preacher man; and she did this little thing, a curtsy with her hands clasped in a kind of praying way as she sang. It was one of the most extraordinary live performances I ever saw: it was so subtle, and so gentle and so strong. And I thought, that's fantastic: that's Dusty Springfield – I've never even thought to listen to her before. And when I did listen to her I realised that I'd listened to her all my life, and not really thought about it. I grew up with that sound of those Sixties singers, particularly Springfield, and it was a big part of my childhood, and also into my teens really. And it sounds like the changes of those decades, through Sixties into Seventies, the way her music changes.

Anyway, I read up about her, and she was a most extraordinary person: she was the first person to bring the Motown sound to Britain. She brought a Motown tour herself, to Britain. And she went to South Africa and she was one of the first singers to refuse to sing to an apartheid crowd. Even so, there was apartheid in the theatre, because the black people were on the one side and the white people were on the other, and in that apartheid-divided theatre, the police were stalking about the whole time, and after she'd played that concert she was arrested, and held in house arrest in this hotel in South Africa. And she was deported three days later. She came back to Britain in a storm, where people said she was rude and uncouth for having done this thing. That's what she was like: she was also a completely non-out gay woman, and she had this extraordinary life, being completely hidden and at the same time completely brash. Her songs are all shouting songs, and of course she's shouting but she can't say anything, so there's the most extraordinary force of being held back and at the same time speaking out, in all of her songs of the Sixties. You just have to listen to them to know that that was the force that was kind of coming out of girls at that point as well, because you could speak out loud, you could really shout, but what you were shouting about was that you couldn't shout! (L) Her songs are a real mixture of a kind of winsomeness and feminism, and both those things are kind of fighting, particularly in those early songs. And so I think she has just the most extraordinary sound.

   She's all strength and all vulnerability, and she's what basically reminds me of my sisters at that point, and also my Mum, and you get the sense of those people who were there, and coming through things, and things are changing, but they're not changing fast enough. And yet they're changing enough to see what's possible, but things are not yet possible. That's what that means to me. That's what pop music is: pop music's a great thing – it's the way that we hear our times. To me it's very important; it's the same as lyrical poetry, if you think about it. If you think about the First World War as coming through the War poets, if you think about the Georgian poets just before that, the sense of peace, and those little, lyric Edward Thomas poems of the moments before it, when it's all about to go: think of pop music as a kind of innocent moment, the kind of lyric moment for now, in a way that poetry isn't really allowed to be in lyric mode. I'm suggesting that for most people it forms some kind of outlet or backdrop to their lives.

IM   It's inevitable that at some stage I shall ask you about feminism, which is something that must have meant something very different for you, for your sisters, for your mother, from what it did back there for Naomi Mitchison.

AS   Exactly. For me, it meant positive discrimination, and it meant it always, and all the way along the line. It meant for me that there was possible positive discrimination, that we knew that there had to be space made, that we knew that we had to keep space open, because eventually (L) it would not be there, because space gets grown over as soon as you take your eye off it, when it comes to feminism. You grow through adolescence thinking no no, anyone can do anything; and then you realise as you get slightly older that no no, it's not possible for anyone to do anything. When I went to Cambridge I went to Newnham College. I thought – going to an all-women college: what a joke; why would I do that? Because I'd got that scholarship from Aberdeen, which is the Lucy scholarship. [*The Lucy Fellowship was founded in 1953 under the will of A A Jack, Regius Professor of English at Aberdeen 1915-37, in memory of his wife and her father. In Smith's time, it was to be held only at Peterhouse or Newnham College, Cambridge*]

IM   We've changed it now.

AS Have they changed it? You can go somewhere else?

IM You can stay in Aberdeen now.

AS You can stay in Aberdeen! Oh my God! Well I went to Newnham, and that was a real education again, because I shared a house with a metallurgist who had been taught by women, and who understood how important it was to be taught in a university where most of your staff are men, if you're a metallurgist.

IM This was a female metallurgist?

AS Yes, one of my housemates, Philippa Reed, who's now practically a professor in Metallurgy at the University of Southampton. She will be a professor, and too right she will, because she came through exactly that system, knowing how there were no spaces for girls. And that's what Newnham was about; that's what I found out. It's not quite the same in the Arts, because there are more women who teach the Arts, or seem to be allowed to teach the Arts. Meanwhile at Newnham I also met Helena Shire, who was retired but had been teaching at Robinson and at King's at one point, I think, after the Second World War; and she was one of the first Lucy Scholars, who had come at a time when you had to send your washing home in big trunks because nobody would do it for you. She had to send her washing up to Aberdeen, when she'd dirtied it all. (L)

IM There was nowhere she could have washed it herself?

AS You weren't allowed! You weren't supposed to touch it. Everyone sent their washing home: it was extraordinary. So she was a reminder of what it meant to be a Girl Student, in the days before girls were allowed to have degrees anyway at Cambridge, which didn't happen until about thirty years after she was there. 1948 I think, girls first got degrees at Cambridge. That was incredible, to meet her anyway, and also at Newnham there was another ex-Lucy Scholarship holder, who was Isabel Henderson, who was the graduate tutor there, and she was a Lucy Scholar in a very different time, in the Fifties and Sixties – she was a contemporary of Sylvia Plath at Newnham. That meant another echelon of what it had meant; what was possible in education at various times. Feminism starts to begin to mean all of those things, and you begin to understand, and I did then, begin to understand the whole notion of what it took to achieve any space at all, and to keep any space at all, and to keep the Borders back. And I still feel that. And then I was teaching for a college called Homerton at Cambridge, where the girls who were coming to be taught by us,

aged about eighteen or nineteen, were coming to the house for tutor-
ials, and they thought feminism was just a waste of time: in fact, it
was embarassing; in fact, it was really scary lesbianism and you
shouldn't go near it, and politically it was very giggly and unsound,
and nobody would touch it with a barge-pole. And that was a very
interesting time. That must have been in the early Nineties. And now
I don't know what people think feminism means any more: in fact
I think they think it's completely unnecessary again.

IM   People just talk about Post Feminism.

AS   Yes, Post Feminism. I suppose this is Post Feminism; but never
mind, because feminism will have to come round in its cycle again:
it just does, (L) because has been it has been going round in this
endless cycle, called different things, which all stand for terms of
equality –

IM   It's got a heck of a long way still to go.

AS   I know: I know it has.

IM   Did you ever feel that the discipline that we both engaged on was
male-defined and male-structured, and therefore a particularly difficult thing for women to enter?

AS   Always, always. If you were allowed to enter into it in any way, you
were that one maverick who would be accepted by the boys. And I
still think that's true: I still think that female academia, and Arts
academia, is a boys' club. Female academia always has to fight the
boys' club to be accepted, always. In fact, it's almost the same in terms
of literature. You look at Winterson, or . . . I'm trying to think of
writers who've actually challenged the status quo in some way, and
who are the big writers? It's Amis and MacEwan that everyone talks
about. It's a massive boys' club. It's a matter of just knowing that and
slipping past the door, really.

IM   So did you feel you were trying to learn like a man, and write like
a man, because you were going to be examined like a man?

AS   No: I never for a minute thought I would be examined: it's why in
the end I never passed my PhD: because in the end I didn't do what
they wanted me to do after it was referred. Because why would I
change it? I'd done it! (L)

IM   Also, they'd made you change it such a lot before they even let you
submit it.

AS   Extraordinary, really.

IM   I remember, not in detail, but I've looked again at things; how it grew out of what you were doing in Aberdeen: perhaps you should tell us a little about that. We can't expect everybody to go and read your thesis in Aberdeen University Library!

AS Oh don't! My God, what a bore that would be for everybody! (L) When I finished my degree at Aberdeen, I had been too shy to think I would do well, I think. And I did do well, and that was quite a surprise, because I hadn't applied for any money for the next year. And then my parents were in a kind of electric shock mode about this – why had I not applied? I would never get money now: I was going to miss out. And then you, and 'fellows' like you, (L) kindly found a space for me at Aberdeen, and I did that MLitt on the modern Scottish novel, which was a continuation of our class, your class, which was the modern Scottish literature class, and something I would have written as a dissertation then. It was an idea which actually came into my head on the spur of the moment in your class, and I'd nothing else in my head, and you said, what was I going to do? And I said the thing, which was so obvious, which was Sandy Stranger's Transfiguration of the Commonplace, her thesis. [*In Muriel Spark's* The Prime of Miss Jean Brodie, *one ex-pupil, Sandy Stranger, becomes an enclosed nun, and writes a peculiarly successful psychological treatise with this title. Smith borrowed it for her Aberdeen MLitt, 1985*] If you applied that back over the last century, what happens to notions of Scottish books in accordance to it, which was perfect, really; it made such perfect sense. There's a good Romanticism at base, of course, very attractive to a Catholic, as we were saying earlier, so I wrote that thesis with you, in a year.

IM Less.

AS Less than a year? It was, wasn't it? I just read and read and read and read to do that degree, and I had such a great time. And after that I was applying for something else to do, so there was a choice. You said, why not apply to Cambridge anyway, you've got this scholarship, I remember: I would be able to take it up if I went.

IM What you tried to go to Cambridge to do, which was at the start I think about eight modernist writers from America and England, was a sort of continuation of the Mlitt.

AS It was! It was a continuation of the Transfiguration. It was the idea that ordinariness was the fuel for, the fixture of, the century, from America across to Ireland, and the idea of what ordinariness was, and then it moved from that while I was at Cambridge to reality, how you could convey the notion of what was real, what existed, what was both authentic and tangible in those terms of reality. And it narrowed itself down then to something which was still taboo, which was to talk about America and Ireland together, which you shouldn't do; and to talk about poets and novelists together, which you absolutely shouldn't do. You shouldn't cross those genres. And that's what happened when I got there: I crossed the genres, and was in trouble for it.

IM I seem to recall that you wanted to do about eight writers –

AS I did.

IM And they thought that one was enough.

AS They thought that one was enough, that's right. I should choose one. So I was still in trouble. I was looking at Stevens and Williams and Joyce in the end, as well as lots of other people, around one year, which was 1922, which was a culminative year for Stevens's first book, Williams's early poetry, *Spring and All*, and *Ulysses*, which was great! And the idea that you could put these texts together: you could see something which was happening with the notions of both reality and identity.

IM There's a sense in which I think that all that you've published, all the fiction that you've published, since then, has still been about the Transfiguration of the Commonplace. You've made that as it were almost your theme, the basis of what you do, but I wonder whether you've ever regretted doing all this education, doing all the theory.

AS I didn't do any theory. Hardly any theory: one of the reasons I left academia was I just wasn't interested in it: I wasn't in the least bit interested in it. I've never regretted any of it: again, it was the most extraordinarily lucky time, and I had a life where I could read and read and read and read and read, and write about it, and again it was one of the things that I just happened to be good at. I'm quite a lazy person, and if it gets hard I probably won't want to do it. When it became so power-based, and it really did, suddenly, it was so different; it changed so dramatically. By the time I was teaching it was in comparison to when I was learning – that's a gap of something like five years – it's not very long. . . .

IM I should point out in brackets that Ali went to Strathclyde University to work for some time after submitting her PhD at Cambridge.

AS I worked there for eighteen months; it wasn't even very long, but the seminar groups were huge: there weren't enough seats, and tutorial groups were so large I couldn't remember my second year pupils' names, and that was just absolutely unthinkable: when we learned with you there was just no way you didn't know who we were. It changed drastically, and suddenly you were teaching modules, and you weren't really teaching books any more; you were teaching modules. By the time I came to teaching in academia – actually by the time I got to Cambridge really, it was such a power game anyway there – by the time I went to my job at Strathclyde people were actually asking you, which theoretical criticism do you adhere to? (L) Because I just wasn't interested. I'd rather read one of the novels by Dickens I haven't read, instead of that. So I couldn't be an academic. And apart from anything else, I got less and less interested as I taught.

IM Less and less interested in what?

AS In teaching, as I taught. Yes. What had happened was the workload was huge, it wasn't what I wanted; I wasn't interested; in fact, two things happened, and I'll tell you them both. One week before Christmas I was teaching and I had five lectures that week. I had five lectures: lectures were huge things to write, and I had written two of them before and I had three to write. And I gave them all, and I was absolutely exhausted. And one of the lectures was on Liz Lochhead's *Mary Queen of Scots got Her Head Chopped Off*, and I was lecturing to the class and I had the book open in front of me, and I realised that I'd written numbers in the margins all through the book. And I thought, what's that again? And I remembered that's how I wrote the lecture: number one, the introduction, number two, something I'll say second, number four, the thing I'll say fourth. So first of all I thought, my God, I've numbered this play: why have I done that? And then, very early on in the second semester I was lecturing on Virginia Woolf to a class. Again I had numbered my book all the way through. And I was talking about water imagery, and the class was yawning, and they were writing down everything I said. They were just writing down absolutely everything I said. And I just stood back and thought. (L) I thought, I just don't want to do this; I feel like I'm lying the whole time: I feel like I'm lying. They're writing down everything I say: this is not how to experience this book. (L) It was getting more and more desperate at Strathclyde: that I was teaching five lectures a week was typical. And the classes were huge, and the students just wanted to pass their exams, they just wanted to know the answer. They didn't want to want to think; they wanted to pass their exams. It was getting more and more difficult to teach without pat answers or an –ism to give people, so that people could subscribe to something and pass their exam by saying all the right things, or using all the right vocabulary. I was devastatingly both bored and cul-de-sac-ed by it, and then quite ill, which is not surprising. (L)

IM So the not being well was a direct reaction?

AS Oh, I'm sure it was: it was a real break. It wasn't a bonus at the time: it was horrific; it was horrible. It was ME as far as we know: it was just a time of utter exhaustion and pain. It was a weird thing; pain all the time, in different places: very horrific, – and yet really small, in comparison to other people's experiences of Chronic Fatigue Syndrome or ME. I was lucky again.

IM Not surprisingly, you treat it very understandingly in *Hotel World*.

AS I think she's got Chronic Fatigue, but nobody knows what that girl's got, Lise.

IM Nobody knows what she's got, but –

AS The problem is, there are so many things now. You can go to the doctor and he can say, something seems to be wrong with you, but we don't know what it is. There's a release in knowing what something is. When a doctor finally says to you, I think we can probably call this Chronic Fatigue Syndrome, there's a release in that. But Lise, the person in that book, hasn't got that release, and so many people are undiagnosed; they've got these strange, *fin-de-siecle* illnesses that nobody knows what to call. And there are all sorts of ways that we are poisoned that we don't know yet. Basically, she's poisoned by her work, that girl. She's kind of poisoned by the way she has to work. There's a more or less direct correlation between the kind of thing she has to do at her work, and the way that she is left.

IM There's also the way the narrator keeps pointing out, she doesn't know yet, this is going to happen to her, that what you were saying about it being cyclical, random, and you don't know when it's going to hit you: it really gives a very strong feeling of that. I'm not supposed to be talking about the books just now, but I noticed this time Lise's mother and Amy's mother have something in common.

AS What? What?

IM They're full of themselves. (AS laughs). They act. They think they are wonderful, and they never stop. They project themselves as artists.

AS   But Lise's mother is a love: she's a love when she sits at her bed.
     They're artists – I suppose they are. Lise's mother is the bad artist,
     I think.

IM   She's going to write the epic of the hotel.

AS   She's the artist: she's the scary eyes of *Hotel World*: that's for sure.
     Amy's mother is more – that's an interesting thing, because these are
     the women – we're talking about achievers again – these are the
     women who have embarassingly achieved.

IM   On a kind of popular front.

AS   Yes, and are embarassed themselves, but are not going to give up.
     They are the Julie Andrewses of achievers: they'll march in there with
     their guitar, and they'll sing regardless, whether or not they're
     wanted there; they'll just do it anyway. That's interesting.

IM   Have you ever known any of these characters? (AS cackles again).

AS   I'm not going to tell you. (L) They're nothing like my mother.

IM   I wasn't for a second thinking of your mother. I was actually, I sup-
     pose, with my Scottish prejudices showing, thinking about the kind
     of people you maybe met in Cambridge, very pleased with themselves
     – you almost used a wee bit for Amy as well. There's a side of Amy
     that goes to the Common Room and chats up the older women, and
     has a social success with them, and knows exactly the right things to
     say. She's nothing like as awful as her mother: I don't think she's
     awful at all, but I just thought, maybe poor Ali has known people like
     this.

AS   (L) I'm not telling you.

IM   All right, that's a fair enough answer! Well, the thing that I most
     wanted not to have left out of this first tape is poetry. Are you still
     writing it?

AS   I haven't written poems for years. I think it's because I write stories
     now that I don't write poems any more. I think stories and poems
     are linked. I wrote poetry when I was an adolescent, I wrote a lot of
     poems. I wrote plays and poems, but basically poems. And then when
     I was at university we had *Scratchings*, which was that first creative
     writing magazine, and Willie McIlvanney was there in my first year,
     and Bernard MacLaverty was there in my third, and in my fifth as
     well. And those were great times, and we had *Scratchings*, and we
     had that group with Donald Paterson and Kenny Farquharson, and
     I was in it, and we had such a great time. I wrote awful poems; they
     were absolutely dreadful! When I was back in Edinburgh; when I was

working here, at Strathclyde, I wrote a couple of poems in long lines, in really long lines, and I thought, actually, they don't want to be poems at all: they want to be prose. So I did start to write prose. The thing about a story is, you *can* write a story; you can choose to sit down and write a story: you can think I *am* going to try and write a short story now, but with a poem I never got a choice at all.

IM So you don't miss them particularly?

AS Not at all, I don't miss them at all.

IM And you don't miss the academic world either?

AS Oh, I really don't miss the academic world. It's a relief to be nothing to do with it.

IM But you do like Cambridge, now that you're not academically connected to it directly?

AS It's a very nice city to live in. It's very warm, generally: the weather's much better than it was when I lived in Scotland; and it's quite close to London, which is very handy; but it's not London, so the air is clean; and it's rural, even though it's really close to London. And it's a proper town like Inverness was, a small town and at the same time it's on the edge of being a city. It's very beautiful. It's very snobby, which of course is great, it makes you really angry, which is good. It keeps you on your toes there, as a person who's come from somewhere else, in two ways. Because it's a very rich place, and because it reminds you what it's like not to be. The thing about Cambridge at the moment particularly is that it's very rich and very poor, because recently – I don't know whether the recession finally caught up with Cambridge – but house prices are so crazy that you can only afford to live there if you're very, very rich, so what you see in town all the time is the split between who has something and who doesn't, and it looks very weirdly Dickensian. There's a real crevasse between people, and you can just see it as people walk down the street. That's pretty extraordinary: before, you couldn't see anything of the sort; it was just *Sunday Times*-rich-looking people wandering everywhere: it looked very charismatically rich. Now you can really see the split. Cambridge is quite big for homeless people. Apparently it's quite a good town to beg in, because although the people aren't particularly friendly, they might give you quite a lot of money. But it's really interesting to see that, because you get a real sense of what the rest of England is like: if Cambridge is like this, the rest of England is really bad. Cambridge is the pinnacle of wealth

– it's the show-off place for wealth for England – and it's shocking the gap between money and no money there.

IM   You're obviously very happy in Cambridge?

AS   It's a bit boring, but I'm quite a dull person: I like to do not very much, and it's a small town, and it's an easy place to live because I can cycle everywhere as well. It's a place you live. It's a place where extraordinary people pass through all the time.

IM   But it hasn't got any hills.

AS   No, I know; it's great. And the light in Cambridge is really gorgeous. It's got sea light, even though there's no sea. The flatness is really quite beautiful.

IM   I would have expected, coming from Inverness, you might miss hills?

AS   No: it's this unearthly light. And the skies are huge; the only equivalent are American skies, where there's light coming from quite far away, so the sky stretches really far. In Britain I don't think there's anything else like that. We just ended up living there, we'd both quite like to scoop out our house and put it somewhere else, but we don't know where else yet. It's a funny place, Cambridge: it has a kind of weird reaction that time passes very fast there, as well. I'm not sure where the last ten years went.

IM   You have been doing a bit of travelling. Tell me about that.

AS   Yes, especially in the last couple of years, it's been great to go travelling. I just got back from a Retreat in the States: I was there in September; I just finished my last book there, *The Whole Story*. I had a month there.

IM   Where was that?

AS   It was in New York State, not far from the town of Hudson. A little house called Ledig House, which is three houses, really, two dormitories and a main house. Very lovely and lush in all the right ways. I never thought I would like going on a Retreat, but I really did. I thought I wouldn't like it at all.

IM   In what sense a Retreat?

AS   In that you go, and you're in the place with other writers, and you work. I thought I'd be away from home and I wouldn't be able to work, and it would just be a distraction that there were other people there, and that everyone would be power-building, and hierarchical. It was so unlike that: it was fantastic. People from all over the world; everybody was completely fascinating, and it was really brilliant to talk to people about what they were doing. People really did want to talk about it; the thing they were doing right then. It was quite exciting. And also there was loads of space to work, there was loads of space to walk around. I got there, and within four days I finished that book, and spent the rest of the time editing it. It was a real space; it was really about space.

IM Before that you were at one stage in Canada.

AS Yeah. Someone should tell the Scottish Arts Council to reinstate that fellowship between Scotland and Canada, because that was a fantastic gift of time and space.

IM Can you remember what it was called?

AS It was called the Scottish-Canadian Exchange! With the Canada Council and the Scottish Arts Council. I was there just for eight weeks, or ten weeks or something. I went to Peterborough, which was this little town two hours north of Toronto, where there's a university called Trent University on the outskirts of this quite Gothic town. (L) A Gothic place, but very interesting being there. Sarah got to come too; that was a real gift: we had such a good time in Canada.

IM How did you manage to swing that?

AS Oh, they let your partner go on that, and it was a really, really good thing. This is why it was such a good exchange, because they give you a quite good amount of time, and the Scottish Arts Council paid at that time for your partner to go.

IM I suspect that's one of the reasons why it's stopped.

AS What a shame! Because what a time that was.

IM The Arts Council has been trying to rationalise what is of course not enough money. When Janice Galloway received the Saltire Book of the Year for *Clara* [*November, 2002*], she repeated her oft-made complaint, that most internationally known Scottish writers were on or below the poverty line. Would you think that's true?

AS Yes, I'm sure that's true. It's really, really hard to make a living: you never know where the next money's coming from, and if money does come, you're so grateful that you can't believe it; because it actually gives you breathing space. Again I'm talking about space. It would be a really, really good thing if they took the Irish model in hand, and they didn't charge writers tax here. It would just make such sense. Look at what's coming out of here, and what has come out of here: look at the massive push and renaissance there has been – superb writing, this last while. Look what they could use as a proper asset here, and give people a chance, give people some more space. You know, you don't tax writers. (L)

IM   But is it your impression that she and I for example are right that Scottish writing at the moment is just absolutely flourishing, in a way that English just ain't?

AS   Isobel, I came to Aberdeen and was in your class, and what was the class we all wanted to do? There were two classes, as I remember. We wanted to do American writing of the Nineteen-Twenties, and Modern Scottish literature. That's what we wanted to do. Those classes were phenomenally good. They were so exciting. It was so exciting to be in the Modern Scottish Literature class and to read those books, and that was before we were reading things like Gray or Kelman, and so many people who are writing now. That was the most exciting class, those were the books where books took different shapes: those were the books where different things were possible, and (L) that was what it was like to be alive, actually, to be alive now. It was one of the first chances we had to read books about what it was like to be alive now. Modern Scottish literature is absolutely alive.

IM   And did you think it was an important part of your education that we had writers in residence?

AS   It was crucial for me. Duncan Rice wrote me a letter [*C Duncan Rice, Principal of Aberdeen University*]: he was congratulating me for something, and I wrote back and said, I am absolutely a graduate, because the reason I write at all is because McIlvanney, in the very first year, said, you can do this. He said it to a few people, but he said it. And he wasn't a liar. We trusted him. It wasn't that you were given permission, but you actually could do it. It was all about potential. The same when Bernard was here. It was the idea that potential was reachable, and it was superb; I can't tell you what it meant, how exciting that was.

IM   We had tried very hard, at the students' request, to get a woman writer, but this is before the flowering of the women writing. Liz Lochhead was the only well known woman writer, and the Arts Council wouldn't let us appoint her again, because she'd been to so many of these jobs. Did it matter that Willie and Bernard were male writers?

AS   No, because I was one of the boys, so it was all right for me. I don't know what it was like for other girls (L), but really it was all right for me; it didn't bother me at all. (L) I'm saying I was one of the boys, because it was a bit like that, because there wasn't really a gender question: it wasn't even relevant. They certainly weren't girls: they definitely weren't girls! (L) In a way there's a gender question there; it's implicit, but it was fine. It would have been superb to have had Liz Lochhead: I remember hoping that she would come, but it didn't matter, because Bernard came. I remember being trendy because I had heard of Liz Lochhead – I remember that in 1980 or 1981, I'd read *Memo for Spring*: I remember being the only person in the room who'd heard of a Scottish woman poet. Isn't that extraordinary? It's only twenty years.

IM   Yes. If we move to fiction, to novel and short story, would you say there is a real difference between a novel like *Hotel World* and a book of short stories?

AS   To me of course *Hotel World*'s a novel, and of course the short stories in these books are short stories, and there's an absolute difference. Yes!

IM   Even when the short stories in the books become more integrated and more organic?

AS   Absolutely, because each of the moments in the short stories, each of the stories, are discrete. Each moment is a discrete moment, and in *Hotel World* it's a chronology: and of course chronology might go backwards or forwards or up or down or whatever, but there's still a chronology. There's a chronology with the novel. And also there's a kind of social structure with the novel which is different from the short story collection where you don't have to have that sense of scaffolding or sense of a much larger overall arching structure. Of course you can have an over-arching structure, but you don't have to, and of course at any point in the short story you should be able to enter it and not have that structure: you don't have to have it. But in the novel of course you do, and of course it needs to be the whole thing, and of course it needs to be held as a whole world, a separate world. And short stories can be several little moments of this world. The story is the hardest thing to write. One of the most crafted, craftiest of forms.

IM   The first collection was *Free Love*. Tell me how it got to be published.

AS   Well, it kind of came together by good chance. I had been hopelessly ill, then when I stopped being so ill one of the first things I did was I wrote two stories. It surprised me – I hadn't written a story for ten years. Then as I was getting better, over that next year or so, I wrote more stories, and I sent them all to Xandra Bingley. I'd met her years back when I wrote dreadful poetry, and she was an agent. She'd been a reader at Cape, and then became an agent – she's the reader who picked Bernard's book Lamb off the slushpile and read the first line and knew she'd found something special! [*Bernard MacLaverty's Lamb was published by Cape in 1980*] And when I first met her, back years before, she'd said, 'Poems are fine and everything, but why don't you write a novel?' So when I finally was writing some fiction, I thought of her, and I sent her the stories, and she sent them round lots of publishers. She'd been an agent with quite a lot of writers when I first knew her, but now she only had ten or so: she was scaling down and changing her life. She's one of the best prose-readers I ever met; she's a great, great reader and question-asker, so it was a fine thing, a kind of blessing that she took them on and sent them out.

And after about five or six other rejections, eventually Virago wrote back and said they'd publish them. So I was very pleased. Then Virago, who were at this point still a small independent publisher, promptly went bust! Literally the next week, or the week after, or something. The very day after I'd gone to meet an editor there, that editor was laid off. But then Virago got bought by a conglomerate (and later an even bigger conglomerate), and one of the books they did when they moved was this collection, which amazed me; I thought they'd never see the light of day, the stories.

The other two collections I suppose you could say have a conscious direction, are more than a set of disparate stories. I think *Free Love* is less like this: it's me really trying out what voice will let me do, or what I could do with it, and form and shape. With these stories, if I think about it, I was just seeing what I could do, seeing what would hold water. I remember it as a kind of weak sunlit time, writing them – I was getting better from being ill, and my life was of its own accord changing its shape.

IM   'To the Cinema' is structurally an interesting one, presenting facets of adjacent but unrelated characters?

AS   One of the things I did when I gave up being a lecturer was take a very part-time job tearing tickets in the Cambridge Arts Cinema as was. It's gone now, but it was a brilliant place, an old building that had been a theatre and cinema for years and years – Wittgenstein used to go to films there when he was at Cambridge! I'd left academia, and I was one afternoon standing inside the old doors behind these curtains – the heating system was ancient, and when it got cold you could wrap yourself in these curtains to keep yourself warm. This day I was standing there tearing tickets for Disney's *Beauty and the Beast* (which is a great musical), and I had such a sensation of freedom and joy, thinking what I'd be doing if I was teaching and what I was doing now, that I almost danced for joy! And a woman came in who had been a student when I was one too, and was a Cambridge academic herself, and she looked at me as I took her ticket with pity, and asked me how was I and what was I doing now – like I'd been sacked or lost my job, and I must be miserable. And I was like full of lightness! And this made me think about the way people view other people all the time, and the given narratives of things, the ways stories go and the ways stories are supposed to go, and the freedom in opening stories up, and the danger in stories that close things down. And from that, from there, I think that story from all its different perspectives came.

IM   Okay. Let's move on to *Like*. I've had students who wanted to come and kill you, (AS laughs happily), who were trying to work out the chronology of *Like*, and what happened when, and who weren't sure – and in the end, I'm not sure either – whether there is an absolutely clear structure – even if we're never going to find out – that explains it all.

AS   Good. I think it is a book which is about questions.

IM   Yes, but does it cheat?

AS   I'm not going to tell you. You have to sort that out for yourself. No; absolutely not: that's nothing to do with me. It's absolutely to do with your reading of the novel. I'm going to tell you now that the chronology of *Like* is so closely worked out, and the background to *Like* is so closely worked out and that the answers to *Like* are all in *Like* if you want to find them.

IM   But that's what I just asked and you said you weren't going to tell me!

AS   But I'm not going to tell you what they are.

IM   Oh, I didn't ask you that!

AS   And I'm not going to tell you anything more about it, because that's what people should do when they read the book, and one of the reasons to write *Like* was that it was going to be a book about what things were like, if you like, and there are no easy answers, and you have to find the answers if you look; and you may not find the answers, and there's questions all the time.

IM Well, there's nothing in the book that tells you that the answers are all there.

AS There's nothing in life that tells us that the answers are all there, not really.

IM There's a difference between life and art.

AS It's like. They're like each other.

IM (L) But I found myself spending time, pointless time –

AS How do you know it's pointless?

IM Because they're such silly little questions.

AS Why are they silly? What are the questions?

IM Silly *little* questions – was there a real, particular, bombing? Forty years – [*See* Like, *p 296*]

AS What??? How is that ever a silly little question? How could was there ever a real bombing ever be silly? That's a massive question!

IM Because it's in 1948!

AS What can I tell you?

IM I don't know! It doesn't make sense to me. I expected it to be during the war.

AS Uh-huh. Well, what about the nuclear testings they did after the war?

IM That wasn't *particularly* in 1948. [*Offtape, we argued about this, what particular news story was referred to. Later AS confirmed her sources about 'the US "experimental" atom bombing in the Pacific, which began in 1946 and continued for three years.'*]

AS Well . . . maybe it's not forty years exactly.

IM Ah!! Well then, you see, when do I start trusting the story, and when do I stop?

AS That's a good question! (L)

IM (L) But you said a minute ago I could trust it if I read it carefully enough!

AS No, I never did, I never did indicate you could trust it if you read it carefully enough! No, but everything's in it. In place.

IM But that was one of the questions that –

AS That's not a silly little question: that's a massively important one.

IM The bombing is massively important; whether it's massively important in the book – it all comes together –

AS Maybe the question is whether or not you can trust things which you read or which you hear or which you see as well, a larger question behind that.

IM Yes, but it's a trivial question in itself because – I cannot find any answer to it, and it doesn't make any difference to the story as I read it.

AS Oh no. I disagree. I think the whole of *Like* is about how we put history together, and how we put personal and massive international histories together, and these are massive questions – sometimes there *are* no answers; sometimes there are awful, completely foul grey areas. Sometimes it feels trivial when actually it's major, and sometimes it feels major when really it's very trivial.

IM Like I can't work out – at least I don't think I can – how it happens in the end that Ash has the diaries back. That must mean that that was before –

AS You mean Amy has the diaries back?

IM Wasn't it Ash?

AS No. Ash gets the diaries anyway. She's got them, she keeps them.

IM And she's writing her own diary, and she puts it in. So that happens before her father dies, and she disappears again, and – it just seems unnecessarily complicated.

AS Life is very complicated.

IM I know: but the big question, the biggest single question to me about *Like* is Kate – if Kate is Ash's daughter, why doesn't Ash seem ever to miss her? Or notice that she happened?

AS Ash. Ash's daughter. But Ash's part takes place before Kate is born, in this book.

IM But Ash's actual writing of her own diary takes place –

AS Before Kate is born. It takes place in 1988 (L) Or '87, I can't remember the exact date. It takes place before Kate is born. Ash's diary takes place in the late eighties.

IM When was Ash naked and pregnant?

AS Well, exactly!

IM Her part seems to be written in almost the present.

AS No: her part's being written in the present in the eighties.

IM Does that mean Kate can't be her daughter?

AS You'd have to work that out, but believe me, the chronologies of *Like* are worked out to a hair's breadth.

IM Well I have never had a student who could do it any better than me.

AS Good. I'm glad about that.

IM Well, I'm not sure you ought to be entirely glad about it, because –

AS No I am, Isobel – this is very important to me: it's terribly important that people get so involved with this book, in all its if you like grey areas – I'm glad it's got a grey cover – because it is a book about how things are completely difficult to work out, how things are very difficult to find or easy to lose.

IM   But Kate's so like Ash; her sense of humour, her daft jokes, all the rest of it, and Amy stole her from somebody, after the fire.

AS   I'm not answering these questions.

IM   Well, you're not denying what I'm saying.

AS   I'm not answering the questions. (L) This isn't even relevant. There's the book; you have to read the book. I can't answer these questions for you.

IM   It makes it sound as if the plot was the only thing that's important, and it doesn't seem to me to be so.

AS   But you see, I don't think it is what's important, which is why I find this completely irrelevant.

IM   That's what I'm saying: I get very annoyed with some of the kinds of questions that come up, that don't seem to me to be the right questions.

AS   But this is to do with people's readings: this isn't to do generally with the book itself. This is to do with people's readings of the book, which is also one of the things which I'm very interested about, and glad about. With *Like*. I love it when people come up and have all the questions if I'm doing a reading – I think that's fantastic: here is a book that's made them not be able to stop thinking about what a question might be, and what something might be, or how it might fit.

IM   One of my students said last year that *Like* was a book for people who like crosswords. I suppose there's such a lot of punning in it, and I am ASH-Amed to say, and all that and all that –

AS   It's definitely a book for people who like language. The exception is *Free Love*, which was written in convalescence for me, which was a real experiment for me, whether I could use an arm again, which was sore, and also what would happen if I tried to write stories. But with that exception, each of the reading experiences in some way is about whether or not people will involve themselves with the book, and how far you involve yourself with a book. It is a conscious question, of how far you will put something together, and/or take something apart. And in a way that looks back to what we were saying yesterday when I had retreated from academia. All the split-the-lark questions – if you take the bird apart what is there left, and at the same time what happens if the bird is not taken apart. In a way I think there's always a question with everything, as to how far someone's involvement with a book will go, and what it means, and what it means to be a reader to some extent. How far a book will take you in, and how far your experience of reading it, is very exciting, very interesting.

IM Interesting is not the only way to be exciting.

AS No; it's also a moral question. It's particularly a moral question with a book like *Hotel World*, which is a book about a society which is completely fragmented, and if you are going to make anything of this, then put it together. Can you put it together, question mark? That's the question. It's much the same with *Like*; the questions in *Like* are massive moral questions, and you have to in a way sort them out. Those are the things: it's a larger question of how you involve yourself, what it means to involve yourself, or whether you can, as well, and how far you can.

IM It's very easy to involve yourself with the characters, although they seem so different: I mean Amy seems such a different person in her part of the book from the Amy that is presented in the Ash one –

AS Yes, absolutely.

IM Big things like that one entirely sees the point of, it's whether the little things don't just get in the way of understanding the bigger questions. Do you see what my problem is?

AS Do you see what the problem in life is, which is that the little things always get in the way of the bigger things that we try to solve. They just are, they just do, all the time.

IM That's one of the things we've got art for, so we can get some of the biggest questions out there so we can see them!

AS We can see them but the point is to see what it is that we're doing. In other words, the trivial things get in the way all the time of the big things: they just do. That's what we're both complaining about.

IM (L) This is fascinating!

AS It's uncompromising: I think it's an uncompromising book. And I think that's fair enough.

IM Let's talk about the difference between *Free Love*, which as you've said was a set of free-standing stories, and the development since, in your short stories. There are a couple of stories in *Free Love* where the narrator addresses a 'you', but the 'you' stories in *Other Stories and other stories* are rather different. Is this a conscious development?

AS Yes. One of the 'you' stories in *Free Love* is Grassic-Gibbonish internal second person: in 'The World with Love' I wanted, I think, to send the story out to other people, rather than have it anchored in an 'I'. It's a story about the unexpected shape love takes, so I think that's why. But there *is* the you-me relationship in, what is it? – 'The Touching of Wood' – and I loved the genderlessness of that when I wrote it, and I knew later that there was more I wanted to do with this.

IM In *Other Stories and other stories* and in this forthcoming one, *The Whole Story and other stories*, it's not that all the stories are alike, or built on the same model, but one of the things *Other Stories* is particularly notable for is the stories which involve, not just in that old fashioned Scottish way, the writer saying 'you', as Chris Guthrie might have said, but where the narrator is clearly talking to an individual person, a partner-person, and it seems to me that several of those stories did that, and it was one of the things that people were impressed by and liked. That's six, half the stories. That in itself was very interesting, and gave a kind of intimacy to it. In *The Whole Story* the 'you' has started talking back.

AS Yes, it was deliberate. There are six of those you-me stories in *Other Stories*, and they link the collection together, more or less, – not completely, though, too systematic, I thought, if I did that – alternating throughout the book. I knew there were more to write for *Whole Story*, and I knew they'd be different; they wanted to answer themselves back, as it were, to be multivocal, multilogue. I love more than one voice. I love the coming in of all the voices: there's no such thing as a single voice, not unless you're alone on a desert island and then there's always Friday or your reader! There's never just one voice, one story, one way to tell or see things. This is crucial. I felt with *Whole Story* too that this other new thing could happen in the form – that the character who's more usually the 'you'-half in a story would get to speak back, complete the story – that's why it's a *whole* story, it's the other half at least of a dialogue. I don't know if there's anywhere else it can go – I don't know! – stories and forms for stories endlessly surprise you by appearing out of a mist and going, go on, use me this way, it'll work, go on, try . . .

IM A hilarious one is about the affair with Eric.

AS You like that one? (L) Oh good. That's in 'Believe me'.

IM I have a terrible difficulty with the titles of short stories.

AS Me too; I never remember them either. Because the story is not usually in the title: it's usually somewhere in the story that you remember the moment.

IM I remember that story so well, I found it hilarious, but I couldn't have told you the title, although it's wholly appropriate. But that's a fascinating development, that you're talking in the '*Other Stories*' stories about how a narrator would talk to this very close person who understands and knows them very well, and that gives a special quality to half the stories: it might be too much if it was all of them: I don't know? One would feel too much of an eavesdropper.

AS I think it would. And also it would become predictable. And also there's not that many things you can say to a 'you' who's part-imaginary and part-real! (L)

IM But similar sorts of stories in *The Whole Story* : on one occasion I think the answering 'you' is in italics.

AS Oh, in the last story. The last story is blurred, I think on purpose, because I wanted the italic part at the very end to be possibly from either one. It's also in italics because again it's a chronology thing, it's a reassurance which is put to the centre of the story rather than to the aftermath, so that the story happens around if you like a point which you know is reassuring. But the story itself was quite an anxiety-giving story: it starts 'It was the end and we both knew it'. And then the two parts are equally questionable, and questioning, but the centre is reassurance. It's not straightforward reassurance, but . . .

IM It's not straightforward reassurance, but to me it's almost analogous with *Like*, but it's so different.

AS (L) Thank God for that! We have to move on in our lives!

IM Going back to *Like*, I suppose I should have asked a bit more about the books, again; because books are just *so* important – books and stories in their different ways are just so important in your work. And people keep burning books, in *Like*, in a personal way, not in a Hitlerian way.

AS Yes, nasty. A nasty personal way. And also a self-freeing way, quite selfish ways. In a way the very end of *Like* – of Amy's part of *Like*, which in a way is the end of the chronology of *Like*, is in the future, is less selfish, a kind of giving up of Amy's own selfishness, I hope. *Like*'s a book about the last century; it's a book about war, basically. The war between countries and the war with the border.

IM If you were a reader, what would you think of Amy's career at Cambridge?

AS If I was a reader? I can't say that.

IM   She makes me puke a bit: I think I mentioned this yesterday. Is that
     fair?

AS   Well think about the opposites with *Like*: the Amy character is drop-
     ped into Scotland, in the middle of nowhere. She's this English, posh
     character, and she's dropped into the middle of nowhere in Scotland,
     and that'll serve her right. And then you drop Ash into the middle
     of Cambridge in a way that'll serve her right too. And then Scotland
     deserves to have Amy, and England deserves to have Ash! It's a kind
     of squaring up of opposites that I sensed when I went to Cambridge,
     and Cambridge would sense if it was dropped into the middle of
     Inverness-shire. Imagine! It's a nasty warring book: it's a book of two
     sides. But the sides are mixed; they're squaring up to each other all
     the time, basically.

IM   Amy's lectures?

AS   Amy's lectures are true: those are real lectures, which I either went
     to or heard about when I was in Cambridge. 'The Body of the Text'.
     Again, things we were talking about yesterday, which is that an –ism
     or an answer becomes more than the actual body and more than the
     actual text? (L) What can I say? It'll match up when you write all this
     down (L).

IM   Back to *The Whole Story* . There's several stories – I can't remember
     how many?

AS   There's four 'you-me' stories, one for each season.

IM   Right. So increasingly, I feel, though I felt it quite strongly with *Other
     Stories*, it's not just a book of stories, as you could make a book of
     stories by anthologising. It's far more coherent and organic than that.
     And this is getting even more so.

AS   With *The Whole Story* there's an interesting thing. For me it was a
     book I didn't even expect to write: I was going straight from *Hotel
     World* into another novel, which I had started, and which I stopped,
     because I couldn't concentrate, because all the time with *Hotel World*
     I was having to go and do stuff, and any of that attention makes you
     very self-conscious, and if you're self-conscious you can't write a
     fucking thing. So I stopped writing the novel, and I had a couple of
     stories that I'd written before, and I looked at them and thought,
     maybe there's something here that might work out. And it was a fairly
     logical project: I think I had three stories, 'The Heat of the Story',
     'The Shortlist Season' and 'Gothic'. Those were the three stories I
     had. Each of them was seasonal, and I realised each of them was very

seasonal, and they were each very, very different: two of them were first person and one of them was the third person story 'The Heat of the Story', which is the Christmas story. Someone had phoned up from *The Scotsman* and said would I write a story about Christmas, so that's where that one came from; it's the earliest one here, two and a half or three years old maybe. And I thought, well, there's something seasonal happening here: maybe there's a book in which you could again have those moments which would be separate moments but at the end of the book you'd have come a whole cycle, a full rhythm. And I also realised that each of these stories was in some way about books or stories; obvious. And I have to say it wasn't hard (L) to see there were connections that could make something, and if I was subtle enough about them would not get in the way of a book, and at the same time would provide something which was more organic, which would hold these things into a cycle, and suggest a different kind of progression from chronology again.

IM   Can I ask one of my silly questions? The title of 'Gothic'. In the story, you say that the Gothics were the people who urinated upstairs in the bookshop, and the story is mainly about the man who hangs his wet hanky on the rail and does something else.

AS   Yes: he's Toxic.

IM   I wondered why it was called 'Gothic', or am I just being really stupid?

AS   No. This is a very workaday thing that often happens. Someone writes to you and says, will you write a story for a book I'm doing, full of Gothic stories. I wrote down the word Gothic at the top of a page, and then I looked it up, and it means of course all the things about being barbaric, and its based on barbarism, and I was thinking, what's barbarous here? The question at the back of the story is, what's really barbarous here? What's the Gothic thing which is really happening in the story. Is it that people decide that people are Gothic or that people are toxic, or is it that people are? What's the actual toxin?

IM   Or is it the book that the man was trying to sell?

AS   Exactly. So the larger question . . . So the whole thing is Gothic really, yes.

IM   The apparently throwaway sentence about the urinators is the one that was troubling me.

AS   Well, it should trouble you in a way, because that notion of who they are should with any luck be at the back of everything to do with that story, because there they are, they're urinating on the true crime books; you know, true crime; 'dead by sunset' and the Yorkshire Ripper, and all those things which are tweaky and seductive to people, and at the same time are just the foulest thing in the world: what do you do with history?

IM In an opposite kind of way, I loved 'May'. One character falls in love with a tree; and almost by association the other one ends up also under the tree, having had a choice either to widen the relationship to take in the tree (L) or not. It's wonderful. I wondered about the title of 'Paradise', the one about the three sisters, which is three lovely bits of story connected obviously by the fact that they are sisters, and I love all three stories, but I wasn't sure why it was called 'Paradise'.

AS It's a Dante thing. The first sister is in a kind of trapped hell, the second sister is in a kind of limbo; the third sister is in supposed Paradise. There she is: she's one of the angels. There are a lot of little hints towards the Comedy in the story, very tiny ones, and it's not a deeply dug thing, but that was the probe for me if you like, the impetus behind the story.

IM That's interesting: I shall reread it with another eye.

AS Of course it's based in Inverness, which sounds a bit like Inferno (Laughs merrily)

IM There's quite a Scottishness, which obviously I enjoy.

AS Yes. There's an overtly Scottish story in each season for this book, because the four seasons are each covered by three stories, but all the stories to me are Scottish.

IM 'The Scottish Lovesong', (L) the pipers –

AS That's the least Scottish and the most Scottish – do you see what I mean? The Scottish club in exile. Did you like that story?

IM Hilarious. There's a lot of hilarity really, here.

AS Oh, I'm glad.

IM We shouldn't really be doing a two-person review of a book that hasn't been published yet, (L) but by the time this sees daylight, they'll have been long published.

AS It's reassuring to me, because I just finished this book two months ago, so I have no real sense of how it will read.

IM I have read 'Erosive' before, and I had read 'The Shortlist Season' before, and 'The Heat of the Story', but that's one of the things that impresses me, how you can read them disparately, and then the hidden art, the subtle art of putting them together, enhances the whole thing. Well, let's move to the novel that the Booker people didn't understand.

AS 'A prose poem'!

IM When did James Joyce write *Ulysses*? 1922. When did who write what?

AS Nearly a hundred years ago, it started.

IM No, no no, long before that – *Tristram Shandy!*

AS How many hundreds of years is it going to take for people to think what the novel could be? I was absolutely astonished that people could think that it was experimental in any way, because these are techniques which have been being used openly in fiction for so long. Fielding – Sterne: one in each hand.

IM I have to say I have least sympathy for Penny: you'd expect that.

AS Oh, I got a lot of flak from people about Penny, that she was the least well drawn, and in a way I feel a little guilty about her, because at one point in the book I could almost feel myself, as someone writing it, ready to judge her, in a way which you must never do if you're in a book. At the same time, I think Penny's judging herself. I reread that chapter a lot before I let it go, it was quite hard to do; but I reckon Penny knows, and in a way she's judging herself: she knows herself what's happening, and she's left with this horrendous emptiness all the time. And she knows she is. Her internal life, if you like, is marked by its lack.

IM When I said I didn't like her, I meant she's the least likeable character, not that I didn't like how you'd done her.

AS But she just is. Someone has to take the flak, and at the end of the day, if it's the person whose lifestyling the world, because Penny is responsible, in as much as everybody else in this book is responsible, Penny is responsible for the ways in which meanings are understood. She has power. She's one of the only characters in this book who can wield power, and she wields it badly, and sure, that's a judgment on my part, but it's behind the whole push of the book, that that judgment must be made, and we have to make it quick, because otherwise things are so damaged or lost that we'll never be able to get them back.

IM I was going to ask you questions about Lise, and about Sara, but I ended up needing to ask about Clare, because there's not much tape left! I think Clare is marvellous, and she relates to Kate a wee bit;

you're awfully good at girls, in the (L) old-fashioned sense. Girl children, and their youth.

AS   Well, it's the time, especially adolescence, pre-adolescence and just there, where identity can still be fluid and at the same time for girls, because as we know things close down very fast for girls, they become codified – they do for boys too, but they really do for girls: you have to become a certain kind of girl, otherwise you're not really a girl. At child level, it's not relevant yet, and at adolescent level it's almost relevant; it's really burgeoning, so you're pushing; and so there is this fluidity possible all the time. And there's always a sense it's going to be gone any moment. In a way that's what happens with a progression like through Kate, Ash, Amy. You go child, adolescent, adult, and you've got each of those parts of what it's like to be a girl or a woman, in the way that things do become so closed or codified.

IM   And one of the things recurs in your work is the experience of this child/girl/woman meeting death. 'College' was one of the –

AS   'College' [*Free Love*] was interesting, because after I'd written *Hotel World* I realised that probably 'College' was the start of that, and I don't know why. 'College' came directly out of just seeing a bench with someone's name on it in the middle of one of those posh colleges, and while I was looking at this bench there was behind me a family unit in an archway in this college, looking at the ceiling. And I thought, what if those people . . . There was no connection, but the connection was made visually. It's a funny thing about *Hotel World*, because I started with neither of those characters, neither Sara nor Clare. I started only with the outside stretch of the hotel which had a homeless person outside it, a person working in it, and a guest, which is just a social structure; it's a perfect paradigm for social structure. And then as soon as I started to write it, the first thing that happened was the ghost voice, from nowhere, as far as I could tell, and half way through the book I realised that her sister had to come back and be a book-end for the story in the centre, which is the story of the structure, and I didn't even know she existed as a character, apart from the shady kind of person who moved in and out of the hotel, I didn't realise she had to have her own voice at all: and then of course as soon as I did it was completely clear. They brought themselves, those characters, to this book.

IM   But death: I suppose one should say on the tape, because otherwise it might be confusing, that your mother died when you were how old?

AS   Quite old, actually, as my father said to me in the car as we were coming away from the hospital: you're lucky you had your mother this long. I was twenty-eight.

IM   Where does that happen as regards the writing?

AS   Oh, before it; before any of it. But then you know it's a funny old thing about life, that the worst things that happen are releasing things in a funny way. And for me, after my Mum died, – it just changes your life, and one of the things it changed was that I stopped being on one road and went to another road. And one of the reasons I could do that is because I wasn't answering to what in a way my parents were expecting of me, which was that I would carry on on the one road. It's an interesting thing, because yesterday we were talking about the time after my degree when I went back to Aberdeen and did another degree, because we found money, and there was a real decision at that point, as to whether to take time out and go and write, bum about, which actually I'd have been very bad at, or whether to carry on doing academia, which I did, and I did that because I was a good girl, and also because I was quite good at it, and also because it was an easy choice; and also because actually structurally for me it was much better, really, and they were quite right to pressurise me to do it. But they did pressurise me; good that they did, because I wasn't ready. Life takes its shape.

IM   I lost my mother at twenty-seven, so I know what you mean. But death is still one of the taboos, I find, in an awful lot of contemporary writing. And because you encountered it so closely –

AS   We all encounter death closely.

IM   No! Some people get extraordinarily suspended away from it for such a long time.

AS   I've had hundreds of letters from people about *Hotel World*, saying thank goodness to read something which makes me feel better, because it can't be said. Like you say, it's a terrible taboo. It's just stupid, because what are the certainties of life? You get born, the sun will come up and go down every day, which is a marvellous wonder, which we never even look at, we never notice. This gorgeous, beautiful – you can't look at the sun, actually; it would blind you. Maybe death's the same: you can't actually look at the thing which will definitely happen, because in a way it's kind of blinding. But we have to look (L) and especially now: it seems to me to be absolutely cuspy, and about the finish of a cycle. The book's set on the finish and the start of the millennial time, and if we cannot look at the real things which really matter, which really change things, which really mean, how do we make anything mean?

IM   Yes. But I do think that death is still unsayable. Death heroically, or in a hail of bullets of course, that's fine: and as the centre of a detective story, but in contemporary writing it doesn't occur so often, except in these brave but to me unreadable books with people who know they're dying writing.

AS   (L) As a person who knows what it's like to be on the margins to some extent, because sexuality-wise I'm on the margins, supposedly, I know what happens to gay characters. I know what happens to them in soaps; I know what happened to them in A L Kennedy's *Everything You Need*, I know what happens to them in books; I know what happened to them in Alan Spence's marvellous *Way To Go*, which is that the gay character dies. The gay character dies, the gay character dies, the gay character dies. At the beginning of my book the gay character dies: she does it right at the beginning, but the whole point is that we realise what's lost. The whole point is we realise what happens when you kill someone off, when someone dies, when someone is lost, when someone who's given a sense of massive vulnerability and massive need, and massive potential – gone. To me that was the real push behind this book.

      I think I found out this time when I tried to start the other novel, that probably I should think about writing stories between novels, and novels between stories: it seems to be a natural rhythm for me, so I will try to do that, inasmuch as people will ever pay for them. Because it's much harder, like I said, to get money for stories: I was lucky this time. But with any luck it will keep going, and if it doesn't then it doesn't. You never know: you never even know if there's ever going to be another book.

IM   You mean you might do an Alasdair Gray, who just suddenly said he had nothing else to say?

AS   Basically you never know if there's going to be another book: you hope there will; again it's a thing a bit like the poetry, you don't actually get to choose. You can sit down and try and do it, but it might not work.

IM   But you have to make the same kind of assumption as that the sun will come up tomorrow morning. (L)

AS   Basically that's right.

Books mentioned in the interview

Free Love and other stories, Virago 1995
Like, Virago 1997
Other Stories and other stories, Granta Books 1999
Hotel World, Hamish Hamilton 2001
The Whole Story and other stories, Hamish Hamilton 2003
Mythic Women: Real Women: Plays and Performance Pieces by Women
edited by Lizbeth Goodman, Faber 2000 contains the play *Trace of Arc*.